T0339526

Doing Digital

We have gone through one of the most disruptive societal changes, on a global scale, over the last three years due to COVID-19. Regardless of the personal and professional impact the pandemic had on us, we've all had to adapt to a different reality that continues today. The pandemic has also forced organizations large and small to adjust and rethink their normal business activities – sometimes in abrupt ways – in order to survive a global shutdown.

Organizations that did adjust well applied five major principles that they'll be wise to continue with for the long-term, both when facing extreme events or merely the new normal. First and foremost, successful organizations accelerated digital and the use of digital tools and business models as much as possible. For example, retail operations with modest digital presence suddenly had to sell through digital channels, rather than physical stores. Entertainment content creators had to push everything into streaming services instead of theaters. And healthcare providers moved patient encounters from in-person to telehealth as much as was feasible and safe.

This accelerated the digital transformation movement and is the focus of this book. This thought-provoking book offers fundamental principles and a narrative about the entire journey to doing and ultimately being digital, with the view to help the reader build their own mental model on how to approach digital in their situations and organizations.

The book also draws a story in which concepts and practices are introduced as needed and is based on the author's own experiences at American Express and Disney. Presented in five parts, the author introduces the topics of digital, digitization, and digital transformation; discusses the fundamental concepts and building blocks of digital; describes who makes up the ideal digital team; the principles and processes of execution; and puts it all together in the context of the overall business. The author concludes his narrative with a case study from the healthcare industry – an industry that is still 10-15 years behind in their digital transformation. The book concludes with the author's observations of what AI and ChatGPT means for digital transformations.

Doing Digital

Lessons Learned on How to Do and Be Digital

Tony Ambrozie

Foreword by George Hanna, Chief Technology
and Digital Officer, LA Clippers

Routledge
Taylor & Francis Group

A PRODUCTIVITY PRESS BOOK

First published 2024
by Routledge
605 Third Avenue, New York, NY 10158

and by Routledge
4 Park Square, Milton Park, Abingdon, Oxon, OX14 4RN

Routledge is an imprint of the Taylor & Francis Group, an informa business

© 2024 Tony Ambrozie

ISBN: 978-1-032-644363 (hbk)
ISBN: 978-1-032-644356 (pbk)
ISBN: 978-1-032-644370 (ebk)

DOI: 10.4324/9781032644370

Typeset in Garamond
by Deanta Global Publishing Services, Chennai, India

To my father, "Puiu" Ambrozie, MD, who taught me about leadership with a soul, and whom I terribly miss. I can only hope that I can make him proud, up there in heaven.

To my dear wife, Sue, whose patience and support all these years have made my professional endeavors possible and successful.

To my beloved sons, Michael and David, the souls of my soul. There's no greater joy for a father than passing onto his children some of the lessons learned in a lifetime. May these make your life richer. And please don't forget to pass it forward.

If you think you're strong and powerful, then you might as well use that strength and power to do good.

Do the right thing, whatever the personal cost may turn out to be. And costs may be short-term while benefits are long-term. You owe it to those who came before you – who probably had harder times and bigger challenges to overcome in their times than you – as well as to the ones coming after you – whoever they'll be and whatever they'll look like and choose to do and be.

Then, becoming strong and powerful has a noble purpose and is worth the struggle of achieving.

What else could be more meaningful in one's life?

Tony Ambrozie, 2024

Contents

Illustrations

Foreword

In the dynamic world of digital transformation, where buzzwords often outnumber breakthroughs, there emerges an occasional luminary whose approach is as refreshing as it is effective. My friend and former co-worker, Tony, is one such individual. We shared the trenches and triumphs at Disney, where we undertook a host of daring technology and digital initiatives that left a lasting impact on both the guests and cast (employees) of Disney Parks and Resorts worldwide. Our journey was punctuated with moments of audacity, challenges, and, most importantly, a relentless pursuit of results. It's a journey I fondly remember.

"Doing Digital" is not your run-of-the-mill digital transformation guide. It's a chronicle of Tony's sometimes unconventional yet highly effective approach to navigating the complex world of digital innovation. In these pages, you'll find a treasure trove of insights drawn from our shared experiences at Disney, along with many of his other experiences from his storied career as a founder, technology executive at Amex, and others.

Take, for instance, the whirlwind initiative we embarked upon for Star Wars: Galaxy's Edge. In the blink of an eye, we went from discussing the concept of a reservation system to a fully operational solution in a matter of weeks. It was a project that tested our mettle, pushed the boundaries of what was possible, and, in the end, left both guests and cast members with an unforgettable experience. It wasn't necessarily a typical experience, but many of the concepts and learnings found in this book were applied at a small scale on that effort with great results. Tony and I spent many years putting teams together that focused on uplifting older, legacy systems which laid the foundation for our organizations to then really lean into bigger and better digital experiences. As he mentions in the book, hard to do that without the right foundation and the right people to take advantage of the right foundation – and we had both.

What distinguishes Tony is not just his willingness to embrace the unconventional, but his steadfast commitment to delivering tangible outcomes. In a world often overshadowed by the allure of technology, Tony consistently asked the critical question: "How does this create real value for our guests and employees?" It's this unwavering focus on results that permeates every chapter of this book.

"Doing Digital" is an invitation to accompany Tony on a journey of discovery and innovation. It's a call to action, challenging you to think beyond the ordinary, to question the status quo, and to relentlessly pursue meaningful results. Whether you're a seasoned digital leader or a novice in the realm of transformation, you'll find wisdom, inspiration, and a little humor in Tony's words. Humor, by the way, is an underrated attribute of great leaders and great teams. If you can't laugh, especially at yourself sometimes, this work will feel much more like work. I remember a time Tony and I were walking through one of our theme parks soon after the rollout of ApplePay. We stopped at a retail store, made a small purchase, and asked the Cast member if we can pay with ApplePay to which they politely apologized and said we couldn't, it wasn't a feature available yet. Wondering if that old information was an anomaly we went to the neighboring concession stand, picked up an item and asked the same question and got the same response. We let the Cast member know that actually, that feature should be available and if they'd let us just try we'd be appreciative. We walked outside and couldn't help but laugh at ourselves. For all the planning, negotiating, technical implementation, and testing/validation, we clearly missed the mark when it came to rollout and training. Once we were done laughing a few calls were made and by the end of the week the training gap was closed.

So, as you embark on this journey through "Doing Digital," remember our whirlwind experience with Star Wars: Galaxy's Edge and let it serve as a testament to the remarkable feats achievable in the realm of digital transformation. Tony's experiences, insights, and his unyielding passion for delivering results will undoubtedly leave a mark on your own digital transformation journey.

Enjoy the ride.

George Hanna
– Chief Technology and Digital Officer, LA
Clippers, California, October 2023.

Acknowledgments

Starting to write a whole book is always a very lonely endeavor. For a long time, there are only two players: the author and their creation. While the drive to create may be irresistible, those days and nights of writing and editing can be full of doubts about the final outcome.

But at some point, the creation feels ready to meet its first readers – the reviewers. That's the first unnerving moment for the author: their baby needs to go out in the world, as small as it may be at first. It is unnerving because the readers will not judge you, the author – after all, you're used to being judged – but your creation, your baby, and you always feel the baby is not ready to be judged by the world.

But then, the reviewers help you make your creation better and more ready to face the whole wide world, and you start to feel better about it.

So, I am grateful to those who accepted the co-responsibility for my creation and made it possible. Most, if not all, have been with me in different parts of my technology and digital journey, so they know what they and I are talking about. In no particular order, they are Deepu Kumar, Sha Edathumparampil, Nicole Elvidge, Ravi Raghuram, Justin Detolla, Rebecca Fletcher, Sudhakar Veluru, Divya Parthasarathy and Sue Ambrozie.

I am also very thankful to the team at Taylor & Francis, the exquisite publishers of the manuscript, for their priceless support.

About the Author

Tony Ambrozie is a leader who always seems attracted to where hard digital and technology transformation and change happens, whether in financial services, entertainment and hospitality, or healthcare.

Maybe the attraction to transformative moments is due to the adrenaline rush of starting from a blank slate that could go in unexpected but wonderful places or the desire to be able to look back and see a huge difference having been made. Whatever it is, it seems recurring, so it must be strong.

At the time of writing this book, Tony was Senior Vice President and Chief Digital and Information Officer for the largest not-for-profit healthcare organization in South Florida, responsible for all technologies and evolving the customer and patients' experience to offer seamless digital healthcare opportunities and leading the organization-wide digital efforts.

Before joining healthcare, Tony served as Senior Vice President of Technology and Digital at The Walt Disney Company and before that as Vice President of Digital Platform Technologies at American Express.

Prior to that, in the 1990s, Tony was the IT director and, at the same time, the budget director of a British diversified group.

And it all started with his own startup, *Tony International* Inc., delivering customer software and doing whatever was legally allowed to keep the dream going.

Tony has been the guest of many podcasts, webinars, panels, and keynotes, all talking about digital, technology, AI/ML, leadership, and cloud, as well as the contributor or author of several articles.

Tony holds a dual MBA and Master's degree in Information Management from the W.P. Carey School of Business at Arizona State University, as well as a Bachelor's/Master's in Electrical Engineering from the Polytechnic University Bucharest.

Doing Digital is Tony's first published book.

Introduction

To produce a mighty book, you must choose a mighty theme.

Herman Melville

We have gone through one of the most disruptive societal changes, on a global scale, over the last three years due to COVID-19. Even those of us who were lucky enough to not contract this terrible virus still had to adapt to a different reality in both our professional and personal lives. At the time, we hoped those changes would be temporary, but many turned out to be more permanent in ways we couldn't have imagined in March 2020.

Large and small organizations had to adjust, sometimes in abrupt ways. Who could have possibly imagined that Disney's parks would shut down? Not for days, but for months! In the previous five decades, they had been shut down *in total* for four to five days, mostly due to weather events.

Those organizations that did adjust well all applied five major principles that they would be wise to continue with for the long-term, when facing extreme events or merely the new normal.

First and foremost, they accelerated digital and the use of digital tools and business models as much as possible. It was said that the first five months of the pandemic pushed digital transformation forward by as much as five years. Retail operations with modest digital presence suddenly had to sell through digital channels, rather than physical stores. Entertainment content creators had to push everything into streaming instead of theaters. Healthcare providers moved patient encounters from in-person to telehealth as much as feasible and safe – and going from 2–3% pre-pandemic adoption to 80%[1] during it.

Second, they relentlessly focused on what was truly important to invest money and resources in: in the immediately catastrophic term, but also on what would be important on the other side, when this catastrophe ended. And what turned out to be important in the long-term was building organizational resilience to thrive on change – the firm itself and its supply chains.[2]

Third, they streamlined decision-making[3] and organizational processes and structures, with a special focus on breaking down organizational silos designed for a different world. Those processes had evolved organically – most of the time haphazardly – to optimize a stable status quo that was gone[4] and was being replaced by a new normal that is still not stable and may not be for a very long time, at least not to the level of stability of the past.

Fourth, they accelerated innovation and the introduction of novel solutions, with an unpredictable and unprecedented situation driving the need for a new business environment, where failing fast, learning, and retrying are the norms.[5]

Finally, they became a lot more efficient in terms of execution speed. Stuff needed to happen on the pandemic's time, not the firm's time. And that meant getting rid of non-value-added work.

The first principle about digital is obvious in the context of this book. What is interesting about the others is that they are all principles that, while applicable to any activity, we have been applying in digital for quite some time, almost religiously.

And that is what this book is about.

Why Another Book on Digital

The ability to put something back into the pool of human experience is extremely neat.

Steve Jobs

Too many organizations still struggle with doing digital, years and oceans of ink having been written after digital started taking shape across the world, first of all by the tech companies, then retail,[6] and then banking and finance, with healthcare still dead last, even behind the government.

As such, it is incumbent on some of us with backgrounds in aspects of digital and digital technologies, coming from those industries successful at doing digital, to help explain and guide those who still struggle with the fundamentals. Simply because we can, and should, in the endless spirit of paying forward, we learned ourselves from others as well as from our own experiences.

At the end of 2022, I was speaking at a premier healthcare industry conference. The topic of the session was digital transformation, sorely needed in healthcare, as all of us patients and consumers of care can attest. And yet the questions coming from the audience – healthcare CIOs – showed signs of distress and panic, not enthusiasm for change. Most struggled with what was expected of them and how to do it.

If selflessness may not be sufficient for some evangelizing digital, then self-interest is always around the corner: each of us wants to benefit from improved high-quality digital experiences being offered and available to us in our private lives *as consumers or patients*. As I am growing older, it's in my self-interest for all those Chief Information Officers (CIOs) to provide me with the best digital experiences, making my obtaining care and maintaining health and well-being much better.

The "*what*" goal is simple, the "*how*" is somewhat involved, but the road to get there is not easy. But I and others like me want to help. This book has been inside me, itching to come out in the world for quite some time now. As such, even one person benefiting from reading it is worth my effort of writing it.

While most suggestions in the book can be reused for any digital endeavor, the target audience I have in mind is digital leaders of firms that sell some other service or product, not the digital product itself. The notable differences between the two will probably be around brand versus product and marketing and advertising strategies.

Is this book targeted to early adopters? Absolutely! What about experienced practitioners? Well, they may benefit in part and probably be interested in my own opinions and experiences – at least judging based on what I'm asked on panels, fireside chats, and podcasts. And if the firm has a board member or two, keen on understanding digital, parts of this book may be useful to them as well.

Finally, while most of the book is very applicable to digital supporting all types of users, including internal to the firm, the focus will be on external consumers.

Is This a Step-by-Step How-To or Reference Book?

I started this book as a collection of thoughts on particular topics relevant to anyone's digital journey. Each section was meant to provide thoughts and sometimes offer fundamental (but necessarily high-level) principles, as well as color commentary[7] based on my experience about what has worked and what not.

However, while I think addressing the relevant topics is valuable by itself, it became obvious that a lot of readers will be looking for guidance on how to assemble all the complicated parts and pieces to support their own complicated digital journey. Indeed, some may need a narrative about the entire journey to doing and ultimately being digital, helping them to build a mental model on how to approach digital in their situations and organizations, as well as how to execute on it, bringing all the pieces of the puzzle together in one coherent picture on digital.

As such, I do believe it would be possible for someone doing digital from scratch to use this book as a guide, starting with defining a vision that they can then use to corral the executive committee, board, and the rest of the leaders of the organization, then defining a strategy, building a team, structure and processes, and then following through execution and adoption.

There is an inherent caveat I need to offer here. It is tempting for readers to look for a simple step-by-step recipe to solve any problem or situation. It is equally tempting for authors and experts to try to provide one. But things are not that simple. For example, we have thousands of leadership and management books trying to provide recipes, and yet both of these topics remain elusive in general applicability.

And the reason is simple: there are *no* simple and simplistic rules to guide in *every* single situation. Context, history, readiness, talent, funding, industry, willingness of the organization, maturity of the business model all matter, individually and much more so in aggregate. My own experience as a technology leader taught me the veracity of this lesson, sometimes the hard way. When confronted with seemingly similar situations, simplistically applying recipes for a similar problem that worked in a different context doesn't lead to success. I have used different approaches to the same problem, exactly because the underlying context was different between seemingly similar situations.[8]

As such, the book should be viewed as a light guide toward the light of the tunnel, not a detailed map or checklist to get there.

This book is also not a reference manual or a compendium of sorts on any of the topics discussed here – whether product management, design thinking, cloud, agile, etc. Once high-level familiarity with each topic is achieved, I recommend deeper dives elsewhere. There are plenty of books (some memorable ones listed in the *Reading List* section of this book) on all those topics.

Why Would You Listen to Me?

I came to healthcare towards the end of 2020, during the COVID-19 pandemic, after two successful stints (14 and 7 years, respectively) at two storied, century-plus-old companies, American Express and Disney (parks, resorts, cruises, stores).

I get asked why I would do such a thing and you may ask yourself the same question. The answer is simple: I have been involved all my career in transformative technology and digital initiatives wherever I went. I had nothing but exhilarating experiences in great companies. But when the transformation job was done – and the revolution always must come to an end, gently sliding into a business-as-usual status – time came for the next exhilarating challenge. Blame the adrenaline rush of facing a new challenge, full of unknowns. That time was for me in 2013 and then again in 2020.

By 2020, it was obvious to me that the next frontier to apply all my technology and digital experience could be healthcare. That industry was, and still is, 10–15 years behind all the other industries, even among the best of its practitioners, from digital and technology perspectives. Brutal translation: healthcare digital experience was and is seriously broken and dysfunctional for consumers and patients. Just recollect your last healthcare interaction in full detail – even minus occasional horror stories – and you know what I mean.

It was that desire to help by applying my three-decade career learnings to the healthcare challenges for its betterment that drove me to it. Surely, I could help, I thought. Wanting to help is also why I regularly speak in public speaking engagements about digital, digital transformation, data and AI/ML, cloud, leadership, and more.

However, what I expected healthcare to be and what it really turned out to be are two very different animals. Frankly, nothing prepared me for what I found in healthcare, despite thinking that the very difficult, multi-industry, multi-company, multi-country, and multi-business cultures that I had encountered before would prepare me for this challenge. Healthcare, at least in the US, is one different-than-anything beast.[9]

From the lack of focus on consumers' experience and the excessive focus on internal players, to the archaic technologies that would have been standard no later than the 1990s, to the administrative processes and paradigms coming out of the 1980s, to no development or product management or creative design, to complete lack of awareness of what the world has been doing in the intervening decades or what consumers wanted, cared for, or needed in terms of experiences, to misaligned talent and procurement processes, nothing was quite right about healthcare as an industry.

So, for me this was a massive make-it-or-break-it challenge, building everything from scratch and validating all assumptions and rules in the book. Despite all those against-all-odds challenges, I am extremely proud of what my team has been able to accomplish to date. All of it by applying the rules learned earlier, in less extreme but nevertheless demanding environments.

As they say, what doesn't (almost) kill you makes you stronger (high blood pressure aside). Clearly, there is something for everyone to learn from.

How to Use This Book

I've structured the book in seven main parts, each centered around a big piece of the puzzle, from fundamentals to core to adjacent parts. Each come with a number of chapters focused on discreet topics.[10]

Part I – Let's Talk Digital – introduces the topics of digital, digitization, and digital transformation to the users who have had minimal or only occasional exposure to them. Digital transformation is the word of the day that consultants use (OK, now second to AI). It's important to understand digital transformation as a *business* transformation process more than technology but absolutely based on it.[11] It is the sum of digital efforts, all building up – in iterations and in different places, but coherently nevertheless – to a big and critical transformation of the enterprise.

To use a cooking allegory, Part I is setting up the expectations for your cooking.

Part II – Foundations of Digital – speaks to the fundamental concepts and building blocks of digital, defining a crisp and clear vision, focusing maniacally on the consumer, having a strategy to guide the implementation of the vision, articulating what design thinking is and why it's the core of digital, and then principles of product.

To continue the cooking allegory, Part II describes the ingredients.

Part III – The Digital Team – will make the case for great chefs and cooks. Without them, nothing will happen, short of cold sandwiches and unhappy guests.

Next, it's time to cook!

Part IV – Execution – takes the ingredients and suggests *a* recipe. Product delivery principles and processes, advice on adoption (how to get customers[12] to use the product and other adjacent tools and frameworks to help).

Part V – The Digital Leaders – will discuss digital leaders' outsized influence on digital, what their mindset and qualities need to be, and what they will need to do to drive digital, beyond what's normally required of any leader.

Part VI – The Larger Organization – will put the efforts of the digital product team in the context of the overall business – enterprise players and processes, their role, and the dependencies on them of the overall digital effort success. Those, if not managed properly by the digital product team and leaders can and will break the digital efforts. Or at least make them much more difficult and limited, no matter how well the team does everything else in their power. Your kitchen is as important as your recipe and ingredients.

Part VII – Healthcare Case Study – tells the story of my recent endeavor in healthcare, when all the actors discussed before brought the play to life.

In **Conclusion,** I recap the book and its main lessons to be drawn.

The **Epilogue** is about what I think AI will mean to digital – and to all of us.

An Old Personal Story is the recollection of my own startup, building a software product 30-plus years ago, with very applicable learnings. I did not have a book like this available at that time, so I made all the mistakes I urge you here not to.

And the strongly recommended **Reading List** is where readers should go next after this book. While we learn best from our own mistakes, we also don't live long enough to make all the mistakes ourselves to learn all the lessons needed. So, we learn from smarter people, their books, and their stories.

So, let's see what is important to know about *doing and being digital*.

Notes

1. It has come back down since to less than 15%–20%, but seemingly stable, as we're all understanding telehealth not as an either/or to physical visits, but as an "and". Think follow-ups.
2. For the past two to three decades, the focus on supply chain – how you get your parts and components and products – has been on cost optimization – the cheapest solution from anywhere in the world, the fastest to deliver, and with absolutely minimal, just-in-time inventory. This is a perfect approach for a very well-running global process in a very stable and predictable world, but it is profoundly problematic for a world severely stressed by health crises, wars, inflation, and geopolitical tensions, as well as catastrophic natural or human-made disasters.
3. For some, making decisions while starting on digital can be scary. Naturally, people are concerned about negative outcomes, yet no outcomes due to non-action can be as bad. Others, especially in blame-game organizations, fear they'll be blamed for decisions leading to negative outcomes. But here is the thing: it is the correctness of the decision-making process that must be judged, not a possibly unpredictable outcome. Paths can always be corrected after the initial decision to adjust for new data or situations.
4. In the three years after the COVID-19 onset, we have had to deal with inflation, war, layoffs, geopolitical upheaval influencing supply chain, and, more recently, the launch of almost unimaginably powerful AI.
5. Ask for forgiveness if you fail, not for permission to try. You'll never succeed if you don't try. If you fail, you'll learn something – a child learning to walk never stops until they get it right, no matter how many times they fall. You may not fail immediately (at that job or project) if you don't try but you'll fail later, if nothing else, from lost opportunities.
6. And by the way, don't call Amazon a retail company, even if that is your experience out of all they do.
7. Sometimes that commentary may go against ingrained notions – that would not be the first time in my career – and sometimes it may be inapplicable in some places.

8. That is the art of being a leader and decision-maker. Knowing when and how to reuse past experiences and then changing approach, depending on context.

9. This applies broadly to the entire industry and in no way to the healthcare system that I joined as a Chief Digital and Information Officer (CDIO). Actually, it is one of the good places and clearly wanting to be better in digital, otherwise it wouldn't have brought me over and supported us driving a transformation, with all the costs.

10. I will say that breaking up concepts (that in real life are dimensions of the same reality continuum) in different categories and sections, for the purpose of improved articulation and communication purposes, is not easy nor always cleanly cut. And since they're linked, each piece must relate to others in other parts and chapters.

11. And in truth, too much technology – especially technology for the sake of technology – and incorrectly implemented technology, not factoring in the subjective user experience, is actually detrimental to the digital transformation. It simply becomes yet another pain point.

12. Throughout this book, I will use consumer and customer, sometimes user, interchangeably. They are not technically perfect synonyms – consumer is usually understood as using a service, customer as buying a product, and user performing an action on a piece of software or device. The processes are different, and so is the engagement length and complexity. However, given that services, products, and using a device are all really about the experience, I will take the literary license to use them interchangeably.

Before We Start

I think it is important to level set on a number of critical aspects that will be pervasive throughout the book: clarity, common sense, energy, patience, and perseverance. Without these, nothing will work out.

Clarity at All Levels Is Priceless

Quite a few times in this book, I will talk about clarity and its role, whether in creating the product vision, defining the strategy, or building the product definition. I usually add the "crisp" adjective when talking about clarity just to make it crystal clear.

If leaders are not clear in their own minds or in their communication on where the organization is, on what needs to happen and how, when, and why, then there's no hope for the team to be clear. In the absence of clear direction, the team may try to build their own clarity, but it may be full of conflicts. A bunch of people being clear as mud on what they should do or how can't deliver a coherent product.

Saying to your organization "We will be the best provider of X" has no clarity and means nothing. Best how? Quality, price, speed, all the above? And in what timeframe, three months, or three years? What makes that different from the next company down the street? And how will that be achieved? Etc.

Clarity, thus, is one of those critical leadership qualities that are often missing.[1] It requires the leader to think through deeply about fundamentals, making hard decisions, (over)communicating to their teams, customers, stakeholders, or, frankly, whomever is willing to listen. And when things get offtrack from that clarity, for whatever reason, it is the responsibility of leaders to re-clarify and pull everything back to clarity. Clarity must be developed at all levels and across all decisions and artifacts.

And the place to start with is that the *expected outcome* should always be *crystal clear*. Of course, there will be times when the path to an outcome is not clear and that is where further clarification, research, and experimentation become necessary. That may be quite often the case, and that is OK. But, if you don't know what you want to get out of it, you'll never know what to do.

Employ Common Sense by the Load

There's nothing more uncommon than common sense.

Frank Lloyd Wright

It should be common sense that common sense (pun intended) would be applied to all aspects of digital. Unfortunately, that is often not the case, and that causes severe problems for the success of digital efforts. Common sense is to be understood as being practical, realistic, and reasonable about situations, plans, and goals. Not dogmatic, and not betting on hope as a strategy.

A leader, while necessarily demanding, must also be practical and realistic. That is an underrated skill, yet it is very valuable for the success of any initiative, including digital transformation. That skill operates at multiple levels, from correctly evaluating the effort and timeline required to research, design, and deliver a feature with quality and value, to the effort required to have users adopt it, to the time and effort required for the organization to change its ways to make experiences, digital or physical, better for customers. It does require a pretty good understanding of the situation, the organization, the team's ability to deliver, of human and organizational psychology, etc. It's an art, not a science.

It's also true that a big part of our jobs as digital leaders is to push our teams and organizations to deliver as much as possible and as soon as possible – after all, the consumer wants and needs help today, not at some distant point in the future – and thus be somewhat unreasonable in our expectations. That is the necessary approach to incentivize teams to find imaginative solutions for better and faster outcomes. But we need to be balanced and realistic about how much we can stretch our team before they break. The reality distortion field may have worked for special luminaries such as Steve Jobs, but the rest of us, at some point, must have a commonsense balance.

Energy, Patience, and Perseverance

Any transformation, change moment or introduction of new operational models, requires a lot of energy, patience, and perseverance from leaders to push through and make it successful – and digital transformation is no different. Probably an insane amount is required from both the leader and the team.

That is the case for several reasons. Humans usually don't like and most of the time resist change – it requires effort, it involves risk and potential downsides, the transition period is difficult, and the learning curve may be uncomfortable. If you extrapolate that individual resistance to whole organizations, with their politics, agendas, established cultures, and reassuring feeling of safety from past success and prosperity, then the challenge becomes exponentially more complex. And complexity requires a lot of effort to deal with.

I am not raising this here to discourage anybody from driving change. On the contrary, organizational change is sometimes forced by external events, but most of the time it must be driven by leaders. If the firm's culture naturally drives constant change,[2] then things are good, and therefore the effort must be put into finding the optimal way to execute. But if not, the leader *must* actively and energetically drive change – which, unfortunately, seems not to be the case in a lot of firms. So, expect that you, as a digital leader, must gather the energy, drive the change, stay patient, and persevere.

It is worth it.

Notes

1. And I speak from experience, not arrogance. Whenever I was not clear, first in my own mind, things didn't work well. Without clarity, the boat drifting is the best hope, but its sinking is always a possibility.
2. The way to determine if your culture is change-driving is to look for past change moments versus constant (and I should say natural) change. If a firm finds itself having to do one of these bet-the-company transformations as a firm-wide initiative (digital transformation, Six Sigma, etc.) with the CEO and down driving, then its culture is not change-oriented and most likely the firm waited too long to change.

Part I

Let's Talk Digital

The future has arrived – It's just not evenly distributed yet.

William Gibson

First of all, why do digital? Well, let me describe two hypothetical consumer experiences and I'll let you decide which one you want to use.[1] You have a choice of two merchants.

For the first one, the **non-digital,** you'll have to make in advance a list of products you want to buy, call the merchant's product ordering line, wait on hold until somebody eventually takes your call, spend some time describing what you want, then wait for the product delivery for an extended period,[2] only to find you got the wrong product or quantity (due to a misunderstanding between you and the phone agent). Then rinse and repeat to get your order right, as initially intended.

For the second one, let's call it the **Amazon Prime Experience**, when you need a product, you pick up your mobile phone with their mobile app, select and order in less than a minute (name, shipping address, credit card, other preferences already on file), and then get back to your life. The product arrives as intended, probably in the next day or so.[3]

Not a trick question: Which one would you want to use?

DOI: 10.4324/9781032644370-1

Chapter 1.1 What Is Digital?

What turns me on about the digital age, what excited me personally, is that you have closed the gap between dreaming and doing. You see, it used to be that if you wanted to make a record of a song, you needed a studio and a producer. Now, you need a laptop.

Bono

To put it simply, *digital* is fundamentally about providing user *experiences* using digital technologies, expected to be of high quality and value.

Experiences, thought of as journeys, are all about outcomes: what consumers see and benefit from – purchasing an item, booking a medical appointment or resort stay, paying a bill, etc. When done well, more satisfied customers stay within the company ecosystem.

While digital technologies[4] are what makes those experiences possible, they're by no means the "what",[5] just the "how". We must never forget that difference. If consumers could get the same or better results toward their intended outcomes by talking to fully articulate pigeons, they would.

The goal, then, is to make the technology behind digital experiences as transparent as possible, to the ultimate point of being completely transparent to consumers-.[6] We're not there yet, but that's what we ought to aim for. Until then, we need to make the visible as simple as we can and as close to transparent as possible. Technology exists to support people's needs, not the other way around. Otherwise, pigeons may replace us one day. Or AI.

Is There a Secret "Recipe" for Digital?

There are a few *open* secret ingredients[7] to creating great digital experiences.

First and foremost, an obsessive focus on details. You can't put misfit pieces in front of the consumer and expect good results. The quality of the experience is fundamental to its success: how possible, reliable, intuitive, and easy is it for consumers to engage and accomplish what they want, etc.? Attention to detail in providing that quality of experience makes the difference between bad (or merely mediocre) and great. And we must always strive for great.

Second, coherent, comprehensive, and cohesive end-to-end support throughout the end-to-end consumer journey.[8] Rule #1: don't leave the consumer stranded in a dead end. For example, it's great to have good scheduling of appointments, but if after that the consumer is lost without knowing what they need to do next and digital doesn't help, that is not good at all. The journey must be optimized as a whole, not in pieces. We have learned a long time ago the wisdom of "you need to be where the customer is".[9] What that means is that fundamentally we need to be able to help our consumers in their entire journey exactly where and when they need support.

Third, relentless focus and prioritization. You don't need to deliver everything at once (and you can't do everything at once even if you tried to). Focus first on what is most valuable to most of your consumers (we talk later about deciding on who the target consumers are). *Prioritization* is a 1–*N* list of needs (and thus supporting product features), in order of importance, from most important to least. It's based on the 3 + 1 criteria and answers are discussed in the *Evaluating and Vetting* section. *Focus*, on the other hand, is about the few (2–3 at maximum) that are the scope of your efforts at any one time. It's imperative for the success of the digital effort that the team focuses on very few at any one time. Working on too many things at once leads to delivering nothing any time soon, at least not with quality. Constantly switching context kills concentration and work quality, leading to poor quality products. In both cases, everybody is confused on which end goal to focus on. Most of the time, focus requires hard decisions on what *not* to do at any point.

Fourth, crisp and coherent purpose for your product and experience. Not knowing what you want to offer and to what outcome confuses everybody, your team in building and your consumers in choosing and using.

Fifth, a high-quality product definition and technology implementation. What doesn't work well is not very useful, however shiny. Quality, usability, and reliability are more important than new (but unusable) features.

Finally, the single most important ingredient and best predictor of success for digital transformation is a supportive culture and organization. Without those, digital will be swimming upstream at every turn.

Digital requires strict rigor, discipline, and thus maniacal hard work to get it right.

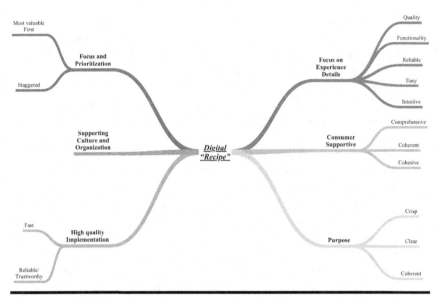

Most valuable
First

Focus and
Prioritization

Staggered

Supporting
Culture and
Organization

*Digital
"Recipe"*

Fast

High quality
Implementation

Reliable/
Trustworthy

Focus on
Experience
Details

Quality

Functionality

Reliable

Easy

Intuitive

Consumer
Supportive

Comprehensive

Coherent

Cohesive

Purpose

Crisp

Clear

Coherent

Figure 1.1 Digital recipe tree.

How Do I Get to That?

The way to get started is to quit talking and begin doing.

Walt Disney

You must start by stopping the debate on whether you need to do digital. It's pointless. You do. Not everywhere and not at the same time, but you need to start with what is most important: the customer needs. If not, someone else will do it. Even if the products and services that their digital solutions support are no better than yours, the consumer will go there. And since poor experiences impact your employees' morale as well, you'll also lose them to firms that do better digital.

The next (big) part is to build the technology and digital product management capabilities. Digital experiences are worth something if they're done very well, and that is not easy – you must be judicious about what to offer that will work well. For that, you need great technologists, designers, and product managers and those are in short supply (more on that later). Respect them and give them what they need and remove barriers, politics, and agendas.

To create truly great experiences, you'll have to enact changes in business, organizational, and operational processes. Those, however, take time to implement. If you're a retailer, you may have the greatest digital platform, but if your product supply chain and warehouse are inefficient and it takes you three weeks to deliver what Amazon can deliver in two hours, you're going to be history before you finish this book.

Who Should Be the Focus of Your Digital Efforts?

There are three major focus areas: external users (customers, those paying your bills), internal users (employees), and third parties (vendors, partners).

The customers must be the *primary* focus for two major reasons. **One**, because they pay the bills and if digital helps them and they're happy, they'll keep coming back to your firm and pay more bills. **Two**, because, except for the Apple's, Amazon's, American Express', and Disney's of this world, most companies provide appalling experiences to their consumers, digitally or otherwise. So, unless you work for those firms, you will very likely have a lot of work to do.

Other (internal business) stakeholders and leaders in the organization will insist on you spending efforts and money on their experience *instead* of the consumer's – but they would be wrong about that. Some of them have clout, some money, and some both and they're making the argument in the room where the consumer is not present. That is why the digital team needs to be the proxy for the consumer in those meetings, so the consumers don't unknowingly lose out to the firm's priorities.

Just because you focus first on the consumer, it doesn't mean you should not address the needs of other stakeholders, especially your staff. It's fair (for retention and efficiency reasons) and beneficial to the firm that they benefit from digital, plus they'll be in a difficult position to support customers without proper digital tools.[10]

Digital and Digitization Are *Not* the Same Thing

The first rule of any technology used in a business is that automation applied to an efficient operation will magnify the efficiency. The second is that automation applied to an inefficient operation will magnify the inefficiency.

Bill Gates

So let's be clear here and now: digitizing existing inefficient processes is not the same as being digital.[11]

This is not just semantics. Unless the legacy processes – usually historically developed to fit existing business models and operations – are effective at meeting consumer digital expectations – most of all full self-service – digitizing them would not lead to evolution nor new opportunities to provide value.

Being digital through digital transformation means changing or creating an opportunity or process that did not exist or was not otherwise viable – for example, e-commerce versus bricks-and-mortar, mobile food ordering, and all non-procedure medical telepresence.

Don't forfeit a historical opportunity of being digital just to have some web forms replicate some paper forms.

Chapter 1.2 What Is Digital Transformation[12]?

There's no alternative to digital transformation. Visionary companies will carve out new strategic options for themselves – those that don't adapt will fail.

Jeff Bezos

There are many books, seminars, and conferences that explain digital transformation extensively, but the simplest way to define this vague concept is **coherently transforming, evolving, and changing a firm's business models, processes, and tools to continuously enhance its success with customers, employees, and shareholders, based on and made possible only by digital (and data) technologies**.

It is emphatically **not** about technology. It's **not** a technology transformation. It's a **business transformation and evolution**.[13] The technology transformation – cloud, agile, etc., – is indeed necessary to support the digital transformation, but it's not the same. The former is just the *how* to do digital.

So how does *doing digital* and executing *digital transformation* relate? Digital transformation is about changing the company in a variety of ways to enable digital experiences for consumers. But it works both ways: digital needs the company to change as much as the company needs digital to change it.

Digital in the lingo of professionals is about the digital product and the digital experiences that they enable. Doing digital is about execution towards that product and experience. It is what some working solely on digital work would say if asked "what are you doing for the company you work for?". They would never answer "we're doing digital transformation". It's true that my job description as a CDIO said "driving digital transformation", but it also said "responsible for consumer and patient digital experience". Two different things.

Using a cooking allegory I use elsewhere in the book: doing digital is about the sausage making of the digital product and experience sausage. That humble sausage is what a whole restaurant is built upon, and that's what the customers come to consume, but how the restaurant owners go from that sausage to building a successful operation is only marginally discussed in this book (get the sausage good first!). Transformation would be the focus of a next book that I may get to write, maybe called Transforming (Businesses) Through Digital, and it would deal solely with changing/building processes and business models. That book would say "here is how you take that less-than-functional process or business model of yours and transform it using digital products and experiences (and a lot of AI) to make it more beneficial to your users and make more profit out of it".

We will discuss later about what processes and models need to be transformed, when, for whom, and how to go about executing it. Fair to say that it's going to be a constant *balancing act* (guided by the vision and directed by the strategy) between how much you can change (for example, what capabilities to deliver to consumers even if the business processes are shaky) versus what you'll have to accept as not changing at that time – as you can't change everything at once.

All those elements are important, but not as important as the fact that you should absolutely do digital and digital transformation.[14]

If you find yourself in the dire need of a company-wide do-or-die transformation, instead of a multitude of across-the-board natural changes and evolution, then you're already in deep trouble: you waited too long not doing digital and now you have to catch up in a massive way through a formal transformation effort. I worked in technology and digital at American Express and Disney Parks and Resorts, but neither were doing "digital *transformation*" – instead, everybody understood the power of digital and proceeded to *continuously* do digital.

Today, no other industry is more in desperate need of a digital transformation than healthcare, simply because healthcare has been so insular to what else was going on in the world, focused on expansion and little on consumers and their experiences or even business efficiency. And now everybody in healthcare wants to do digital transformation, but because of the long inaction, it has become a bet-the-company exercise. Not a good place to find oneself.[15]

Transformation Strategy: Don't Try to Swallow the Elephant

There are two major philosophies when it comes to transformation, including digital transformation.

The **first** approach, taken by some organizations, based on their business culture, is to start the transformation through an enterprise-wide, top-down-driven initiative. That process would start by defining everything that could possibly transform an organization under the overarching umbrella of one grand initiative, sometimes defined in great detail,[16] attempting to map all nooks and crannies of the organization and their expected digital future, in an exercise involving tens or hundreds of people.[17] That phase is followed by an equally grand planning phase where every step and action is defined in detail (but only later followed up by execution[18]). Each of the two phases usually takes 6–12 months or more, depending on the size of the organization and leadership's focus and commitment. Implicit for this size of an effort would be a vast number of unproven assumptions. How long the subsequent execution phase can take (if it even happens) is anybody's guess, but the guesses are usually all wrong for reasons of *unknowability* that we will discuss later.

This approach creates a sense of order and predictability that most people and organizations crave, especially the top executives.[19] Many times, the process is executed with the "reassuring involvement" of a leading consulting firm that is supposed to know how to transform. Sometimes, the consulting firm runs the entire effort, with partner-level involvement.

What is wrong with this picture? This approach won't work for several reasons. For one, it is not customer needs driven, but organization driven. I will talk later why that is problematic. For another, consumers and the business will not see any material improvement during the process (1–3 years). End to end including full implementation could be 5 years or more, during which the business environment (and organizational priorities) will absolutely change, plus discussions and alignments from the initial phases will be forgotten. Newer people in the organization would not have been part of the process so whatever initial alignment – possibly token agreements – was reached, will vaporize. When the implementation starts, it will invariably encounter challenges not originally anticipated. As to everyone's feelings being important, this process cannot serve as organizational therapy. Not to mention that this approach allows individuals and groups involved in the definition to introduce self-serving bias – usually avoiding change and pushing it away from their teams.[20] This is the path to the graveyard of transformations that never happened.

The **second** approach, which should be abundantly clear I solely support, based on what I have seen working, is an incremental and iterative process, starting first with areas of critical customer and firm needs[21] and continuing with the rest, in time. While an overall strategy with a 2 to 3-year time horizon can be directionally defined, it's just a guidance framework for constituents to understand, at a high level, what the effort is about and how it will be executed. You can start with high priority areas or low hanging fruit to reduce risk, depending on the time criticality of the need, the maturity of the team and technologies – and then work up from there. For that defined set of needs, you go from detailed definition to planning to execution, including operational models and process changes, as needed and feasible. Then rinse and repeat to the next set of priorities. Opportunities outside the area of focus are to be surgically avoided, even if it means that those areas are transformed at a later stage. Changes to the capabilities implemented and processes transformed can be incremental and iterative to prevent destabilizing impacts to operations.

The positives here are, first and foremost, that it increases accuracy and feasibility through deep yet narrow focus, coupled with experimentation that weeds out any dead ends early. Second, but equally important, value to consumers and the firm, even if fractional, can be delivered much sooner. It's also easier to agree and execute on smaller (and thus less risky) changes to business models and processes. Not to mention that with an incremental approach, it's easier to change direction or just adjust when the reality on the ground turns out to be different than anticipated.

The negatives that must be managed are that the organization at large may feel that the direction is not as grandiose and/or progress is marginal (at least at the beginning). Communicating constantly the broad strategy as well as the incremental improvement and progress can adequately mitigate this challenge.[22] Another, yet marginal, risk is that of scope creep when folks feel unconstrained by rigid plans. The digital team leadership, leaning on the vision and strategy and always keeping an eye on the big picture, will need to keep the effort on track and away from distractions.

Does the second approach mean the focus is tactical on steps and tasks as opposed to strategic on full journeys and flows?[23] No, those journeys and flows should still be mapped at a reasonably high level but executed in iterations. Do iterations, as they are executed, focus mainly on steps and tasks due to the practicality of delivering technology and business changes? Probably, but that doesn't mean the end goal is not the full journey and steps and tasks don't build up to that journey – they absolutely do. I will talk a lot more on journeys throughout the book.

As to how to go about doing it, it's very much down to the same fundamental steps as with any organizational change and transformation. We will talk more later, but you start with the vision – where do we and our customers want to be at some point in the future - define a strategy to get there, build the assets – people, structures, funding, supporters, alignments, communications, protocols – and then relentlessly execute.

Digital Transformation Timing and Breadth

Digital transformation, done as a big bang event in the name of "comprehensiveness", even if possible, would be a very big shock to the system, akin to the replacement of all the parts of the bus while the bus is still running at some speed. That would be extremely disruptive for people and still functional (albeit with gaps) processes, and thus, unlikely to succeed.

The amount of organizational and business model changes any company, outside of startups or bankruptcy, can successfully absorb and manage in any one finite period – while also running day-to-day operations – is ultimately limited by bandwidth, adoption capability, other priorities,[24] internal expertise, and talent. Usually, technology and digital progress can be faster than the change an organization can absorb at scale.[25] Frankly, it's improbable that you'll be able to marshal the resources and the bandwidth to do it all at the same time, plus coordinate, plan, and execute. A transformation requires a lot of thoughtful planning and execution. So why try to boil the whole organizational ocean when, even if successful, you couldn't use all that hot water at once?

Thus, deciding carefully on the timing and breadth of the effort is critical, involving evaluating what digital experiences are most valuable and what processes need to evolve and when and thus be addressed in what order. You must make hard decisions on what is value-added today versus tomorrow (or next year). Changing too soon and too fast may impact current operations, but waiting too long will damage long-term organizational survival.

So, as a first step, you'll need to assess what needs to become digital in the short to medium term. The focus must be driven solely by what will be most impactful in that timeframe – customers' digital experience benefits and satis-faction[26] leading to financial benefits.[27]

I don't believe every process or business model in a company needs to become digital immediately and certainly not all at the same time. In that timeframe, a lot of the less critical processes probably still work fine and should be lower on the prioritization list. And that is OK. That will change over time, as once you start somewhere and get done there, probably the pressure – whether from your own changes or the marketplace – will move your efforts to what has not changed and now needs to.

Should Every Company Do Digital and Digital Transformation?

> *The enterprise that does not innovate ages and declines, and in a period of rapid change such as the present, the decline will be fast.*

> **Peter Drucker**

Every company should do digital and digitally transform. I can't see how they would survive long-term in a world of digital experiences. Why? I hope more will become evident from the rest of the book, so I will just summarize it here, focusing on two aspects.

First, customers today expect and value the quality of a digital experience almost as much as the quality of the service or product being supported by digital – let alone if the digital experience is *the* product (for fully digital firms). Unless your actual product or service is unique or massively better than the competition, consumers will prefer your competitors' offering more than yours, as it will simply be easier to access through digital.

Second, when applying digital to internal operations, there will (eventually) be efficiencies and operational capabilities that will be superior to the competi-tors who chose not to do digital. Simply put, digital organizations will be able to do and offer things others can't and the rest will be done more cost-effectively – i.e., they will have competitive advantages. Over time that disparity, ever increasing, will eliminate weak competitors simply based on economics. Do you want to be that company that customers must interact with by fax (yep, still used in healthcare between medical practices and hospitals) versus your competitors having advanced digital, AI, and automation enabled? I don't think so.

Maybe unglamorous, but both arguments point to digital less as a competi-tive advantage and more as a future cost-of-doing-business consideration.[28]

You must not, however, underestimate several difficulties that will need to be addressed head-on if the transformation is to lead to positive outcomes. Among these, the need to (ultimately) transform the business; the inevitable process, system, and business model disruption; the learning curve and figuring out along the way, especially with new consumers and products; finally, the natural resistance to change by those who may fear losing their current power base or may not fit in the digital ecosystem, whether by lack of interest or skill sets.

The Architecture of Digital

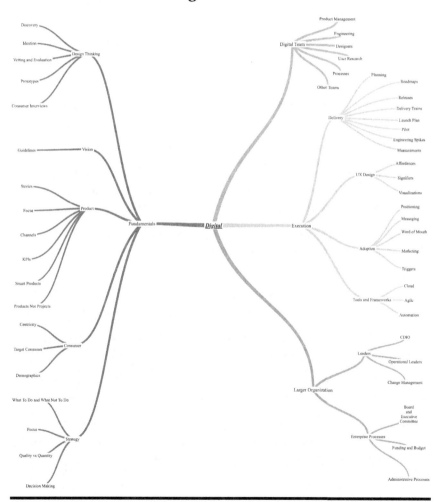

Figure 1.2   The architecture of digital tree.

Notes

1. This is for exemplification purposes. In this day and age, most merchants have a digital experience they offer customers, *but not all*. And in healthcare, the first option is still prevalent in most places.
2. At this point, you may say: wait, what does getting the delivery in an extended period have to do with how you ordered (by phone or digital)? Simple: if that merchant did not put the effort into providing a great consumer experience for ordering, do you really believe they invested in the supply chain digital systems to get your order right?
3. Same argumentation as in the previous footnote: just replace right with fast.
4. Web, mobile, internet, cloud, AI/ML, etc. Maybe the metaverse.
5. I'm using throughout this book the "who", "what", "why", and "how" symbolism to signify the difference in concepts.
6. That doesn't mean they don't exist, but rather that they can't be obtrusive. Think automation or machine learning filtering out unnecessary steps or options behind the scenes. Consumers would never know what challenges they could have had to wrestle with but didn't have to.
7. I am being sarcastic here, of course. The "ingredients" should long be known by now; I am just trying in this book to put them together in a coherent story.
8. Consumer journeys or flows can be at different levels. The series of steps required to make a dinner reservation at Walt Disney World is a flow, but if you stay on the property that is one part of a larger journey that includes hotels, parks, and attractions. The goal would be to wrap each story in the next higher level in ways that you can discover them by navigating up and down that hierarchy.
9. That is a variant of retail's "it's about location, location, location".
10. In a previous role, after years of investing in digital consumer capabilities, we found ourselves with staff needing to support customers who had better tools and superior information.
11. To be honest, in this day and age, when we can do so much more both from a technological and product management viewpoint, just digitizing forms (that is, replacing paper with a digital interface) is disrespectful to consumers. While maybe temporarily unavoidable, in the long-term it is lazy and unforgivable.
12. I speak here of digital transformation because it's important and constantly talked about, but I very much prefer the term *doing digital* (although the two are not technically exactly the same), hence the title of the book.
13. I remember reading somewhere that a digital transformation is not a business transformation, the reason being that while business transformations have a beginning and an end, digital transformations must be continuous. While I totally agree with the latter assertion (that's why I use words like evolution and continuous when describing digital transformations and that is also why I speak mostly of digital, as a continuous process, not digital transformation), I strongly disagree with the former: you have to continuously and organically (that is, not through top-down one-time initiatives) transform your business to adjust to evolving consumer needs and preferences, economic and competitive environment changes, new regulation, new markets, etc.

14. And preferably do it in increments, before you're absolutely forced to. As they say, the best time to plant a tree for shade was 20 years ago.
15. Jeff Bezos: "What matters is companies that don't continue to experiment or embrace failure eventually get in the position where the only thing they can do is make a Hail Mary bet at the end of their corporate existence. I don't believe in bet-the-company bets".
16. I have seen consultants' decks covering this stuff extending to over 200 slides. I will talk more about management consultants later.
17. At that scale, the participants are rarely dedicated, so this exercise is perceived as not much more than a distraction from day-to-day work demands.
18. Not surprisingly, this is the part most strategy consulting firms prefer as it provides them ample opportunity for "analysis and planning" work.
19. Too bad that sense is misdirected, because, you guessed right, of unknowability. Wonderful word.
20. The "everybody must change but not my team" syndrome.
21. For example, I started in healthcare focusing on consumer access to care and records. Then I moved the focus to in-patient experiences. Then providers, etc.
22. (Over)communicating should be done in any case, irrespective of the approach.
23. The consulting firm McKinsey uses the term *domains* to signify entire journeys.
24. If there are more than three to five priorities, then there are too many and they need to be ruthlessly scaled down to that number. That is really the maximum number the organization and its leaders can focus on. When too many things are a priority, nothing is really a priority and there's no realistic chance of focus.
25. This fact is either unknown or missed by most organizations introducing change. In many cases, it's the reason for "technology" projects failing. Change management, describing the change (why and what), and how processes and people need to adapt (how) is crucial.
26. Consumers and their needs must be at the top of the list because for most organizations the consumer digital experience is not great and sometimes it sucks, especially in most areas of healthcare.
27. Consumer satisfaction, delight, and loyalty are what create financial success, but without a positive business case, you're doing all for naught. But financial success will probably only be seen in the medium to longer term.
28. Any technology competitive advantage is temporary and must be continuously maintained, otherwise others will catch up. The only enduring competitive advantage a firm has is its culture – if it's great – that is difficult to replicate by competitors. But that's a topic for another book.

Part II

Foundations of Digital

> *The product vision describes the future you want to create, and the product strategy describes your path to achieving that vision.*

Marty Cagan

The foundations of any product and experience creation are, in this order:

- **Vision** – It's about defining an image of the future. It must start ahead of everything else as it will guide everything else. Vision will be necessarily high-level, to guide people and teams.
- **Consumer** – Knowing who the target consumer is and what their needs are. It follows directly from the vision and it's ahead of strategy.
- **Strategy** – How are you getting to where the vision is pointing? It will be constantly tweaked, so no point in being stuck trying to find the ultimate strategic perfection in the beginning.
- **Product** – What are you doing to get there? What products will support the experience vision?

Vision and strategy are critical,[43] as they are the guardrails for making decisions along the digital journey. They must be incredibly crisp and clear, as they must direct what you're *not* going to be and do.[44] Defining the right vision and strategy is hard, but it can't degenerate into a never-ending analysis paralysis. And to be clear, the digital vision and strategy must support and be supported by the firm's own business vision and strategy.

 DOI: 10.4324/9781032644370-2

Chapter 2.1 Digital Product Vision

Be stubborn on vision but flexible on details.

Jeff Bezos

The vision will articulate, in a meaningful but crisp way, what the consumer will be able to experience at some point in the future.[45] It's about ambitiously imagining what that point in time will feel and be like. It's the True North and the guiding light to getting there.

The vision needs to articulate the expected needs of the consumer in that timeframe and be ambitious enough compared to what is being offered when the vision is defined.

The meaningful and crisp part is very important, because everybody needs to understand it almost intuitively and validate all subsequent actions against it (if next year the focus is on partners and employees and not consumers, that should be a warning sign the vision is muddy).

It can't be a long and meandering statement, either so vague as to be unusable (stay away from statements like *"we'll be the world leading provider of X"*) or too full of disclaimers that readers get lost and confused.

What is *not* referred to explicitly in the vision is either not going to be done or is subservient to the main concept. For example, cloud and agile are not mentioned in a consumer digital experience vision, but they'll be key ingredients and tools for the success of it.

The vision also gives the engineering team an early indication of what they need to be prepared to deliver against and to the product management and design teams what to research and design for.

The point in the future that the vision speaks of usually is something like three to five years away.[46] Shorter and it is too narrow, longer it would probably be unrealistic due to the many unknowns in terms of customer and markets. The vision can be "modernized" over time. As such, one question often arises: How firm (fixed) should a vision stay over its declared lifetime? The answer is *pretty* firm. That is because the vision for digital follows both what the consumers want to experience and what the organization wants to do. Both are usually stable over three to five years.

Having said that, when the point of arrival described by a vision is achieved or close to being achieved, a new vision for the future, hopefully building on top of the previous one, needs to be built. And so, the cycle continues.

The vision must be shared, adopted, and supported by the entire organization, or at least the relevant leaders in it. Aligning everybody, however difficult of a job that may be, is part of a CDIO role. If individual business leaders and units have their own narrow agendas – and they do – digital efforts will be only modestly successful, if at all. And that would be a tragedy for the enterprise – but not necessarily the consumers, who will go to someone else who can get their collective digital act together.

Chapter 2.2 Consumer

You have got to start with the customer experience and work back toward the technology – not the other way around.

Steve Jobs

Simply put, the customer is the one buying your products and consuming your services[47] and they are your consumers as long as they perceive that you're providing value but also convenience and control. They are the reason the enterprise exists and implicitly why the enterprise is doing digital in the first place. The happier the customers your product serves, the more of them coming through the door and the more staying inside.

When I talk about the consumer from a digital viewpoint, I have in mind the following hierarchy of concepts:

Consumer – a human with needs and wants to interact with your organization in the process of reaching an outcome (buying a product, getting care, consuming services, etc.). Yes, employees are consumers from a digital perspective, although the focus of this book is mostly on external consumers. Yet employees are critical for helping you help external consumers pay your (and your employees') bills.

(Digital) **Experiences** – what the consumer experiences and encounters (and how well that satisfies them) in their interactions. Experiences must lead to successful outcomes for the consumer.

(Digital) **Product** – a piece of technology that supports the experience and leads the consumer to obtaining their desired outcomes in a satisfying way.

When doing digital, sometimes we use the terms consumer and experiences interchangeably, because a consumer is a consumer only through their experience. And one bad experience and the consumer stops being your consumer and becomes someone else's. However, neither is interchangeable to the product. Product serves the experience and not the other way around.

Consumer Centricity Is All about the Consumer Experience

Customer service should not be a department. It should be the entire company.

Tony Hsieh - Zappos

Three words define consumer centricity: **Relentless. Consumer. Focus.** Consumers are above all other stakeholders' groups, with digital experiences supporting their needs and wants.

Consumers are looking at the quality of your experience, including the digital experience, as a critical factor in choosing your product or service. And that is so because they extrapolate their other day-to-day digital experiences – with Amazon, Apple, Disney, their banks, travel companies – onto your business and thus their expectations of your digital product will be high.[48] And frankly, there's no reason for expectations not to be high. It is hard, but most companies can and should do consumer digital experiences well.

Besides, in certain industries such as healthcare, a poor consumer or patient experience is the last thing consumers need when they have a critical problem. If all the mechanics and logistics are simple, convenient, useful and supportive, then they can focus on their problems versus fighting the dysfunctions of your system. Why would they go to a company that is hard to deal with when other firms are very easy, all other aspects being equal?[49] They'll come to you if your experience is great (at least better than alternatives) but will go somewhere else if not.

What the target consumers (more on who the target consumers are later) mostly want is usually pretty basic: Know where and how to find the product or service, book or buy it, check in (as in hotel or medical appointment), pay for it (with or without insurance coverage), check out, view transactions, medical records, or accounts statements, etc., or variants. Yes, there is a lot more, but these are the basics you need to do very well.

However, there is usually a difference between what customers *say* they want and what they really need. That will become evident through elements of design thinking – Empathize, Define (the problem), Ideate (on solution), Prototype, Engineer, Test – and then after launch through what large numbers of them actually do.

You must consider the entire customer journey and not just some disconnected parts or episodes. Otherwise, it's like a cellular mobile service with lots of no coverage spots – pretty useless. It's true that when you start from scratch very likely you'll only be able to build the support for the journey incrementally in iterations. You'll have to figure out how to compensate for the gaps in the short term. Explaining the current, incomplete state and future plans to consumers may keep them interested.

Without trying to be overly prescriptive, there are a few key points to what *consumers* consider good or great digital experience.

They really want **full self-service, 24/7 experiences**, so they can be in control of the experience and at the center of it. Constantly switching from self-service to agent-assisted (i.e., calls with agents) in one flow is confusing and frustrating.

They want **digital to guide and support as a personal assistant would**, wherever they go and whatever their needs may be.

They expect **familiar experiences** for which they already have mental models[50] for how to operate. That means standard, simple and intuitive experiences – digital is not like the user manuals of VCRs in the 1980s – not that anybody read them anyway.

Did I mention **convenience and availability** of digital capabilities, at the place and moment that they're needed?

And yes, **high availability and low response time** for the digital product is table stakes. Consumers don't have patience with slow or unavailable digital, so you need to make sure the experience works very well, it's fast, and apps or websites don't crash (please, no stack dumps on a web page, as they're as bad as they're insecure). Nobody cares for Ford Pintos.

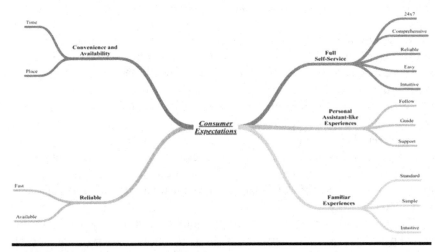

Figure 2.1   Consumer expectations tree.

But beware. You can't build a set of successful and comprehensive customer-centric digital experiences in a firm that, whether because of hubris or ignorance, short-term profit obsession, geographic or product monopolist position, or internal agendas, thinks it doesn't need to be focused first on consumers. No amount of super-brilliant digital design experience and delivery can compensate for an organization that doesn't want to change for the benefit of the customer. Yes, those firms still exist.

If that is the predominant culture in your firm, you, as a digital leader and practitioner, are better off looking for alternative employment in a culture that cares for customer experience – that is, one that cares about getting *and keeping* customers.[51]

Who Is Your Target Consumer?

One of the most remarkable things about consumer focus is how many organizations don't know who those consumers they most need to please and gain their loyalty because they're important in some way to the organization are – aka the target consumer. That fact is easy to spot when one consumer, in the off-target category, complains about the digital functionality and its perceived shortcomings and the entire firm goes on a frenzy to address that when, in truth, it shouldn't.

Wait, you shouldn't worry about the feedback of one customer? That sounds antithetical to the credo of consumer focus! Well, nope and nope.

Ok, so here it comes. The fact of life is that not all consumers and customer segments are born equal. One is more important to the firm than another and therefore one's needs are more important or better fitting to the firms' offering than another's. You can't serve everybody, everywhere, every time with the same (high and comprehensive) focus, otherwise you will serve no one particularly well. Serving *the* consumer doesn't mean trying to serve *every* consumer, as that would make your product a mishmash of multiple niche features, each targeted to "special" consumer groups.[52] You must decide who your most important customers are because you must prioritize your digital efforts to serve those consumers *first and best*. Your product can't be all things to all people.

Who is the most important customer category is driven by who: a) you can serve the best with your current assets and brand, b) are the best fit to your product or offering, and c) produces the best returns to your organization. The last criterion doesn't necessarily mean you need to go only after the most profitable customers.[53]

But the focus of your digital efforts must be your regular consumers[54] and, among them, those that can effectively use digital technologies in ways that provide enough *value* to justify their investment in using your product (at least by creating and maintaining a digital profile). Hard choices must be made on who to focus on first and foremost and then carefully adjust over time based on metrics. You ought to probably be focusing on the top 60–75% of your consumers and not 100%.[55]

There will probably be 2.5 target categories that you should absolutely focus the majority of your digital efforts on.

The main target category (on to whom most focus and effort must be applied) is the very **engaged** consumer, who is actively interacting with your organization (or industry), whether on their behalf or others'.[56]

Next, with a slightly lower level of engagement, is the **connected** consumer, who is already engaged at a somewhat episodic but regular level with your company, but is open to being convinced to increase that involvement, based on long-term need and strategic interest.

Both are also likely to be technology-literate enough to be capable of using digital.

The last half category is what I would call *spill-over target*, those who are **engaged only very occasionally** with your organization (and industry). They are in the camp of digital engagement and thus capable of using your digital products, but only when forced to by critical and special life events. What differentiates these consumers from the next category is that they're likely to become engaged sometime in the future.

The final category is those who are either averse to digital – whether because they're not digitally literate or don't care for a digital experience or attribute no value to a good or great experience.[57] They are *not* your target digital consumer and therefore your digital efforts will provide either marginal or no value to them. While, as an enterprise, you still need to serve them, they ought to be out of focus for your efforts.[58]

Each of the target categories are, however, different and because their needs are different, you may need to adjust your product in different yet *consistent* ways. We will talk later in the *Product* section what to do if you have multiple subcategories of users among your target consumers.

Once you reached a decision on your target consumer(s), it's a great idea to talk to them again to validate they indeed are who you think they are vis-a-vis your product.

Having said all that, you will have to decide how to prioritize the cadence of your work. For example, you can choose, at least at the beginning, to serve the full needs of only a subsection of your target consumer population to the detriment of others or provide broad but not as comprehensive support to your entire target consumer population. That choice is a matter of *strategic prioritization*.[59]

Segment Your Demographic – By What They Do, Not Who They Are

It's natural for marketers and product managers to try to segment their potential user base. It's critical for both to try to understand their customers well enough in order to target different products or features of the product to different segments or your target demographic.[60]

Different segments have different preferences, some stronger than others, and that has to be considered for product definition. For example, older generations are *generally, all other things being equal,* less digital savvy and require bigger user interfaces (i.e., desktop screens or large tablets).

With all things considered, it's dangerous to simplistically apply stereotypes to understanding your consumers. That applies to whatever technology channel and preferences, social, ethnic, or economic inclinations, etc. Humans are very complex creatures, and they may claim some things but apply opposite judgments in actions or put some things – fashion, cost, peer-pressure, etc. – above others, such as environmental good. If you care to look, you'll be surprised by what you'll find.

I have seen 75-year-olds latching enthusiastically onto the latest version of the mobile app and using the latest features of iOS. You know why? Because it provided them with value to solve their health problem and as such the investment of figuring out how to use the increasingly complex digital interfaces was worth it. When you have cancer[61] and you're in a treatment facility several times a week, you'll use whatever technology you can to make that life experience a little bit better.

I have also seen youngsters not wanting to use any technology for their needs – whether retail or healthcare – because they did not care, did not think it was useful to them, they did not want to be distracted from Instagram or TikTok, or because they knew their parents will deal with everything else, digital or not. Even if they were in their 20s and their parents – who had come of age pre-internet – in their 50s.

So, the advice here is simple. Don't rely on simplistic segmenting stereotypes and instead get to know your consumer[62] through observation, feedback and systems tracking. Segment by *what* they do, need, or want, not by *who* they are.

What Comes First – The Consumer or the Firm? Both Need to Win in the Long-term

> *A risk-taking creative environment on the product side requires a fiscally conservative environment on the business side.*

Steve Jobs

Before we go into further details, let's back out for a second and talk about the two approaches that companies take in their business philosophy vis-a-vis customers.

The **first** one puts operations and their functional processes and financials above everything else and hopes that consumers will accept the fact and the business will just make money somehow.

The **second** one puts the consumer (of services) and customer (of products) first and foremost and then expends all efforts in making the organizational processes efficient enough – through process reengineering, automation, simplification, etc. – to extract economic value to continue the economic cycle.

Short of monopolies and governmental organizations, I know of no organization being successful over a long period without focusing *first* on consumers. Focusing on the consumer is the only financially successful business philosophy. Throughout this book I constantly emphasize a maniacal focus on consumers, based on the simple principle that happy customers eventually make a happy business.

Of course, the business must do a lot of things right – internal operational efficiency being critical. But achieving operational efficiency has a lot of other ways to achieve, none of which should force a degrading compromise of customer experience.

However, the constraint on any enterprise – including non-profits – is to make at least enough money to cover its costs, however high its customer satisfaction may be. As such, digital and digital transformation must eventually lead to some positive outcome for the business. And I say eventually as in sooner and not (too) later. Yes, acquiring customer satisfaction and product adoption can happen at a loss for a while, but not forever – the world is full of bankrupt organizations which failed to understand and/or accomplish that.[63]

Digital and the digital transformation efforts will need to (again, eventually) support the business goals, stakeholders, and commercial success. However, digital leaders and teams should not start with the business financial needs and wants and be driven by them[64] but instead be intensely focused on the consumer.

Whose Data Is It, Anyway?

For a very long time,[65] I have never been one to care much for regulations, at least not the arbitrary type (which government-imposed ones tend to be). I always preferred market and social mechanisms to be allowed to adjust and influence what happens in the economy and in the social sphere – usually by what most people settle on, whether through voting at the booth or with their wallets.

But as I have grown older (wiser?), I also understood that free markets have imperfections that at times happen to negatively impact *too* many people. And although I find the EU regulations on data, namely GDPR, too restrictive and prescriptive, data ownership is one aspect where regulation is necessary to prevent abuse on individuals and disruption to the healthy operating of a democratic society.

So, here I say it: I resolutely think that consumers absolutely own their data generated while interacting with a corporate entity, be that a for-profit, not-for-profit, or healthcare organization. All those entities are only *custodians* of the consumer data – that is, they're *entrusted by consumers* to manipulate data for the purposes *defined* by the consumer. The consumer must be able to decide what happens to that data, how it's used (or not) and who it's shared with (or not) beyond the strict confines of the explicit encounter that generated or collected that data in the first place.[66]

I find it disgraceful when consumers pay for a service and then their data, collected in the process of delivering that service, is monetized independently from their explicit wishes, all for corporate benefits. That is, to me, the equivalent of first selling the product to a consumer and then asking for a rental arrangement for that same purchased product.

Sure, sometimes consumers freely and explicitly – and free is the operative word here – choose to trade their data for some "free service" (think Google search or Gmail). But it has to be *freely and explicitly*, and the consumer must *get something in return*.

At times, for legal or compliance reasons, governments, commercial entities, healthcare systems or heavily regulated industries like financials must retain that data. But the data cannot and should not be monetized for corporate interests.

Digital interactions – whether what is provided by consumers or collected directly (forms) or indirectly (sensors, AI/ML[67] models inferences, etc.) all involve massive amounts of data, most of it sensitive and private (because it records what people do in private). For all the reasons above, I think consumers own this data and they ultimately need to *freely* decide what happens to it.

US legislation[68] doesn't yet take the same view of data ownership – although it's starting to provide strong protections in certain areas – but it will, sooner or later. As digital practitioners, technology owners and custodians of data, we should prepare ourselves for that time. If for no other reason, but because it's the right thing for us to do, out of respect for our consumers.

That is why I think that rules such as the one instituted by Apple in 2022 forcing app owners to provide their users the ability to delete their accounts and profiles[69] is, on balance, valuable.

Some may hate Apple's ability to enforce policies through their app store, yet they're proven right in many cases.[70] But as a user that is still trying to get some sites to delete my old accounts (and stop charging me for it!), I welcome those protections. As well as the convenience to be able to view all my subscriptions in one place and be able to cancel them with ease.

Chapter 2.3 Strategy

The essence of strategy is choosing what not to do.

Michael Porter

Strategy is about the principles and guidelines on how[71] to reach the declared vision endpoint,[72] as well as the process, articulated as clearly and crisply as possible.

For example, simplistically summarized, a strategy supporting the vision would state "*We will fully control and build our own digital experiences*". Or "*We will selectively partner with third parties, integrating them into our products*". Etc.

As many illustrious others have said before, it is important to choose some things and reject others (the importance of saying *no* is discussed at some length later). Continuing the prior example would be: "*We will not allow vendors to control our experiences*". This aspect is so critically important that we will address it in the first section of this chapter.

Do not confuse strategy with roadmaps or plans (we will talk about those and their importance later), as those, important as they are, talk about *what* and *when*, not *how*. Strategy is less about goals or metrics (yet those are important to evaluate progress of your activities), although it is possible and sometimes necessary to introduce milestones into strategy. For example, a variant of the above examples may be "*While we build our internal capabilities in the first year, we will have to rely extensively on third parties, but we will replace those products when we are ready to do so*".

Strategy needs to be more precise in the short term – since more is known in the short term – but more high-level in the medium and long-term as, over time, consumer needs, markets, competition, regulations, people, and technologies change.

Often, a new technology or vendor coming into the market changes how and when you could implement the vision.[73] For example, if the metaverse really becomes a thing in a couple of years, one that consumers want to use to interact with you as described by the vision, you will need to make the decision whether to add the metaverse to your digital channels. And AI will allow you to provide more personalized experiences in intelligent (pun intended) ways.

Strategy will necessarily need to stay flexible (to allow for catastrophic events, like COVID 19), as a rigid strategy not considering changes in the environment will gradually get disconnected from reality and thus become useless.

You'll need to make sure the entire organization is aware of the product strategy. This avoids endless and fruitless debates while executing it. So, take the time to communicate (really, to evangelize) your strategy to the executive committee, the board, other stakeholders, and anybody else interested – it will pay off later and will save you unnecessary grief.

Several directions for the strategy have been set once you have defined the vision – you're providing *digital* experiences to *consumers* – and then who the target consumer is and what their needs are. At this point, the strategy focus is obvious: defining what **choices and decisions** you're going to make to provide target consumers with digital experiences.

Realism and practical experience in delivering digital capabilities will drive several fundamental decisions.

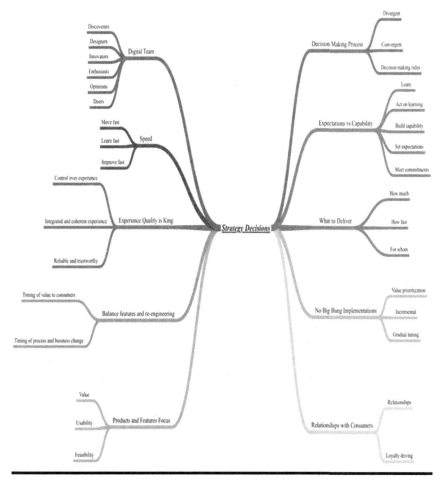

Figure 2.2   Strategic decisions tree

Deciding What You'll Deliver on (and What *Not*)

You've got to choose what you put your love into really carefully.

Steve Jobs

The **first** decision is that you need to expect to deliver only a percentage[74] of consumer needs (not 100%) in the timeframe described by the vision.

Limiting to most but not all needs may sound strange, but a) realistically you can't deliver on everything that the consumer needs, b) not all the needs are born equal, c) the individual needs will change, and d) you don't really know what all their needs are when you start, so why set an illusionary target anyway?

Now, this doesn't mean you'll arbitrarily cut the list down to that number, just that realistically that is what you will end up with anyway.

No Big Bang Implementations

Great things are done by a series of small things brought together.

Vincent Van Gogh

A **second** bit of realism is driven by the fact that rarely have big bang implementations ever been successful (or valuable enough to wait for extended periods of time), so you'll need to choose to deliver, say, 50%[75] soon versus 100% later. Comprehensive digital experiences can't be built immediately.

Necessarily, they are built *incrementally* and that means some consumers get *some* valuable capabilities sooner rather than wait longer for everything, which is a good thing from their perspective. It also means you can validate your assumptions sooner and adjust as needed, through Try-Test-Learn-Tweak-Try again cycles.

It is unrealistic for anyone to demand immediate operational benefits – more customers, more revenue, more profit – from digital in the early stages of product build up. I'll talk about financials later in the book.

With that said, however, there is a minimum, core functionality that must be provided by the product for it to be useful and valuable, and thus adopted.[76]

The Business' Relationship with Consumers

The **third** major decision is what kind of relationship do you want, or can your business model support, with your consumers. If you're just selling undifferentiated widgets, then probably *transactions* are what you're most interested in. Warning: This book is probably not going to be very interesting to you, as I put a very high-level of importance on customer *relationships*.

However, most firms are looking for long-term *relationships*[77] with their consumers,[78] so building consumer loyalty through consistency is a critical goal.[79]

This is an important decision, as it influences how much effort you dedicate to user satisfaction (which leads to *intent-to-return*[80]), how to design journeys (none needed if you shoot for transactions) or how important it is to differentiate your experience.

Quality of Design and Implementation Is King

Digital experiences need to be designed to provide value, be user-friendly and create long-term loyalty by consumers. It is the digital team's job to create that experience. This leads to the **fourth** big decision to be made: how important[81] the experience quality is to the organization (it's *always* important to the consumer).

Realistically, to create a great user experience, you must control the entire digital user experience. Digital is what the consumer sees first of your firm. An uncoordinated experience delivered by different and non-integrated products will signify to consumers an uncoordinated firm's offering – and that impression will probably be accurate.

Control of the experience will likely mean in-house development, or at least defining it and integrating in cohesive ways with third-party products (I will talk later about build versus buy decisions) but ensuring coherent experiences by integrating at an API[82] level versus UI.

For the digital products I delivered in all my assignments, experience always had to be top notch and only full control – definition and build – delivered to that expectation. But it's not easy to pull off and requires assets that many don't have or know how to build – yet.

Speed – The Faster You Go, the Better

The **fifth** major decision point is how fast you want or need to progress in your digital journey. Remember, you're not just competing with your firm's competitors, but also with consumer's expectations of what your experience *should* be. They may be willing to give you a pass on an incomplete experience for some time as you get started, but not forever, so the sooner you provide what they want, the better.

On that, my philosophy is to move *fast*, learn *fast*, and then improve *fast*[83] with emphasis on learning all the time what works and what doesn't. You ought to be heavily biased towards action, never stuck in analysis-paralysis. Start with a hypothesis, analyze it internally, tweak and tune, internally test, and then release it and learn.[84] The digital team and the organization must therefore be ready to move fast. Speed is a factor of mindset and ability that needs to be built up.[85]

The digital experience is about more than individual interactions; instead, it has to include all the consumers' experiences over time, both digital and physical,[86] under the premise of a firm-to-consumer relationship, defined by simplicity and loyalty through consistent delight. That hefty goal requires driving changes in operations, and it is the digital team that has the responsibility to not just deliver digital products. but be that driver for change by being the consumer advocate on how well the physical services or products that your firm sells work behind the digital experience.

But changing business processes is always a lot slower than the speed of delivering digital products. How to balance both is the focus of the next section.

Digital Speed Versus Process Reengineering – Keep at Your Main Thing

> *The main thing is to keep the main thing, the main thing.*

Jim Barksdale

And that is the **sixth** strategic decision you'll have to make: how to balance delivering some value to the consumer at the soonest possible time – which should be your reflexive bias – versus being absorbed in re-engineering a particular firm's operational activity for extended periods of time.

My philosophy is: Change enough of business processes immediately in order to get as much of a good digital experience out, and then come back and change more later. For that, you'll need a maniacal focus on executing on what can be done now versus later. This may mean that in the short term you must rely on technical "hacks" – aka technical debt that you'll absolutely need to deal with later – or process workarounds.

Sometimes digital on the front end but manual on the back end may be required for a while. It's not ideal but unless the back end was digitized first or you're willing to wait an extended period for that to happen, this is quite a common case in practice.

Know Your Delivery Focus

> *People think focus means saying yes to the thing you've got to focus on. But that's not what it means at all. It means saying no to the hundred other good ideas that there are. You must pick carefully.*

Steve Jobs

The **seventh** strategic decision to make is about what functionality you are going to focus on to deliver to consumers.[87] There are three intersecting criteria to use here.

The first is about value to consumers: What delivers the most value the soonest to most consumers. The second is about usability[88] – how usable can you make a capability in the timeframe. The third one is about feasibility – technical and process-wise. Can we build it into the timeframe to make it a priority above others and can we get the operations changed or at least supporting it?

Balancing Expectations with Capacity to Deliver

Anywhere you are, you will have to deal with a mismatch between unrealistic expectations on digital – and thus your team – and what your team can realistically deliver in any given timeframe.

Either the consumers, the firm, or both will want more and faster than what you can do.[89] That's true for all companies but is especially true if you start digital from scratch and have a gigantic need to fill. Yet you are just starting to build the team and its processes to build the product. Both take time that you may not have very much of.

This mismatch, if not addressed, will create problematic tensions between the firm and your team. The team will feel attacked unfairly for not delivering as fast as expected (and they will eventually leave the team out of frustration) while the firm will think they're not doing their job well (and thus probably should not be funded and staffed as needed) and consumers will think either that you don't care or you you're not capable – or both – and they'll give up on you.

And this leads to the **eighth** decision and approach. Both sides of the equation must be worked on at the same time: You'll have to build *both* the reasonable expectation *and* the delivery capacity.

Building the delivery capacity has to start immediately. There will be legitimate reasons for being slow at the beginning – lack of talent or funding, processes and practices, infrastructure, etc. – but that justification can only go for so long before it is seen as just an excuse and the whole enterprise perceives you as not serious about digital and its consumers. Where there's a will there will be a way, so you must act.

But even when you have built the capability, however much your heart bleeds for your consumer's unmet needs today,[90] you probably will not have the bandwidth, money, process, tools, or technology to deliver for them as expected by some in the firm. Maybe next month or next year, but not today. Yes, it's your job as a digital leader to make things happen somehow, but there are still limits. Limits for you to push as far as possible – and to solve for *tomorrow*.

In either case, you'll need to establish the right expectations, possibly both with your consumers as well as with internal interested stakeholders, by communicating broadly and constantly what the plan of delivery is and why it is that way. In firms without historic awareness of technology delivery processes and their rules and constraints, references to what other firms and teams do and how fast can help establish some initial understanding.

But once you set the expectations – in truth, commitments – you absolutely need to deliver (see meeting commitments elsewhere in the book). Don't disappoint – at least not in a material way.[91]

Ground Rules on Strategic Decision Making

The best ideas must win.

Steve Jobs

The **ninth** decision you'll need to make, from the beginning, is about defining the rules on how strategic decisions (and they will be many, some big, some small, some easy, and some very hard) are being made, communicated and executed on, mostly inside the team but also relative to other stakeholders.

First, the digital team,[92] the extended teams involved with digital (I will talk later about them and their importance) and the operations team, ought to work as collaboratively as possible. Vibrant discussions and disagreements based on facts and data are the best way to create a better product. However, that collaborative model doesn't mean getting bogged down in seeking consensus[93] every time before you act, as that would be a recipe for lack of delivery.

Second, you must agree about what criteria or principles will guide decisions. What data, what insights, what testimony, what thresholds, who, and how? For example, decide that you'll decide on a design if A/B testing shows solution A being at least 60% of consumer choice (A/B testing and its caveats are discussed elsewhere). Do you always wait for data to have a confidence interval of 20%, 40%, or 60% (it will never be higher than that, unfortunately) before you decide? Will you wait for any data before deciding based on educated intuition? Etc.

Without having criteria clarity, decisions may be made inconsistently or out of a rash impulse. And by being clear on the criteria means that when a decision needs to be made, you don't have to debate what the process will be every time you make one. The vision will provide powerful criteria to make decisions: "*Is this decision aligned with the vision?*" Of course, there may be exceptions, but having the criteria for the normal keeps exceptions to a minimum and also casts a bright light on why exceptions are needed.

Decision making is usually based on either intuition – or, at its worst, executive fiat – or data, or both. But there's a certain method to the apparent madness. If you have little data or it's not trustworthy, especially for decisions on new things, you'll have to rely on your vision and (educated) creative instincts.[94] If, however, you have data, you should use it to *inform and validate* your decisions and that method should be followed. However, data, or its absence, is not a panacea for making – or not making – hard decisions. You can't hide behind data or external consultants' *opinions*.

Along this process, you'll evaluate, reevaluate (when new data becomes available before a release), and tune features and products constantly. As Jeff Bezos says, be stubborn on the vision but flexible on how to get there, as there will be many paths to get you there. What you can't do, though, is stop after every single step of the journey and renegotiate whether the *entire* journey is worth continuing or be abandoned. A step can be debated, but not the journey described by the vision.

The Digital Team

We have a chance to make these things beautiful, and we have a chance to communicate something through the design of the objects themselves.

Steve Jobs

To keep the experience usable for consumers, there absolutely has to be a maniacal focus on simplification and convenience, including on operational processes.[95] You ought to consistently innovate[96] for better, simpler, and more convenient digital experiences, even outside the limited norm of what your industry currently offers. Innovation must accept trial-error-learning cycles if consumers are not materially impacted. If it's aligned with the vision, you'll learn from a variety of perspectives in meaningful ways.

And that leads to the **tenth** and final strategy guideline: You, as a digital leader, will need to assemble a digital team, a great one,[97] that is able to discover the consumer needs, design for them, innovate and improve constantly, and implement and release products. A team that is not only capable of doing, but is enthusiastic and optimistic about the mission at hand.

What makes a team great? Its *spirit*. A lot more on this later, but for now here is a simple example of that spirit: what others see as showstoppers, your team simply should see as challenges to be solved through *both* creativity and proven methods.[98] They will not be discouraged by an improbable future problem that may not come to pass. They prepare for future challenges and address them when the time comes.[99]

Assembling the right team is the number one activity that will best predict the success of digital in your organization and your number one job, as a leader.

Evolving Strategy and Product: Experimentation Is Fundamental

It's not the strongest species that survive, nor the most intelligent, but the most responsive to change.

Charles Darwin

A question that comes up quite often (and if it doesn't, it needs to be asked and answered by the digital team): *How much of digital is grand strategy and how much is figuring it out tactically?* That this question is even asked usually freaks out those, especially CFOs, who want a precise and predictable process with assured success to justify the investment in time, money, and focus.

Well, those folks will not like the answer but there is a silver lining for them.

You must have a high-level digital strategy to guide you on the path to the point described by the vision. With that said, you shouldn't try to produce strategies to the lowest levels of details, and never in the form of roadmaps and plans, for two fundamental reasons.

First, there will be a fair amount of figuring out and learning that only happens through trying in small and iterative increments, followed by learning from watching what customers do.

And **second**, the world changes in ways you can't anticipate and that may change how you'll need to execute. The learning will come from constant, early, fast, and iterative experimentations that will reveal what works and what doesn't.

And the *silver lining* I was talking about earlier? Experimenting and learning fast, constantly and in small increments saves a lot of money in the end by avoiding falling off seemingly unexpected cliffs in a big way.

Digital Product and Business Strategies Alignment

A digital team ought to be maniacally focused on consumers and user needs. That is the main purpose of the team. I use the term *"maniacal"* consistently in relation to consumers,[100] obviously in a good way: We're here to make our users' lives better and that takes effort, dedication, empathy, and understanding.

That being said, your business (and I use that term loosely to cover any entity, including non-profit organizations) must have a strategy for its success that aligns with the needs of your consumers.

Your consumer may look for products and services that your business is not prepared, willing, or in its core competency to offer. If your business is a hospital – high acuity care – its strategy may not be to offer primary care – low acuity – services,[101] irrespective of what your patients may need or want. Similarly, if your business' core competency is the consumer market versus the enterprise market.

Long story short: Your digital offering may be able to offer a product, but that product must be supported by the enterprise strategy and should make sense to that strategy – i.e., make money for the business.

Just because you're good at offering a particular digital product, it doesn't mean your company wants to or should provide it. Sounds obvious, but some teams can get distracted by a feature or product just because they can deliver it.

Chapter 2.4 Design Thinking

If you define the problem correctly, you almost have the solution.

Steve Jobs

I started this book with the intention of having this section inside the *Product* chapter, and that would have made sense as design thinking is how you create the product (that, when used and done right, delivers the great experience).

But then, as I was writing it, it became obvious to me that design thinking is too important to not merit its own separate discussion. If nothing else other than to raise the awareness about the importance of design thinking concepts for all starting out digital leaders.

The concept has a long history, over several decades, with a lot of great thinkers adding to the practice until it stabilized as a powerful concept-turned-discipline under the current terminology and shape in the last couple of decades.

Some of the books in the *Reading List* section at the end of the book develop at length the subject in ways way more competent and eloquent than I could possibly do. I strongly recommend you read more about this discipline.

In this chapter, I will add some personal color commentary based on experience in order to provide some strong arguments for design thinking and against some anti-patterns used by some companies (consumer panels, operational leaders, consultants as designers, as well as blindly following data to make decisions).

What Is Design Thinking and Why Is Everyone Talking about It?

Highly simplified, design thinking[102] is an iterative process that starts with carefully understanding the consumer needs, questioning, challenging and creating hypotheses and (testing) assumptions,[103] generating ideas about the problems and possible solutions, designing solution and then prototyping and testing, followed by release followed by another cycle of learning, designing and solutioning. All centered around *consumers and their needs* and done in iterations and increments.[104]

Design thinking is not just for designers, but anybody attempting to solve a problem. It's also not just for products or digital, but it can be applied to processes or even businesses. It's a mindset, as well as a method, to solve a problem.

Let's dive into details.

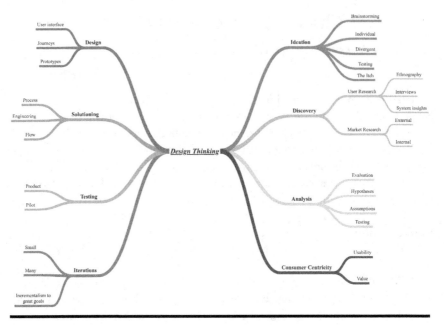

Figure 2.3   Design thinking tree.

The First "Itch"

In the open source software[105] (OSS) world, there's this saying that all good OSS starts with someone – usually a developer – trying to "scratch an itch" (i.e., a nagging need or inconvenience) for themselves and then deciding that others have the same problem and therefore could benefit from the solution (and possibly participate in the solving it, in an open form). With more users and creators, momentum towards bigger and better products builds.

The same principle applies to uncovering unmet digital product needs.[106] Someone, a startup founder, or a corporate digital product manager, has a vexing problem themselves, that is otherwise not addressed in the marketplace and, if it turns out from user research[107] that (many) others have the same problem, they decide to solve it and have others benefit from it – usually in the form of a product.

This primordial "itch" is an extraordinary force for innovation and product creation, in my experience orders of magnitude more powerful than corporate committee-based design.[108] That is true not just for startup founders and entrepreneurs, but also corporate folks who have a problem and decide to make it into a solution for customers. CDIOs should take notice.

However, while the original itch scratcher is the one who probably promotes (hard) the idea or product to become reality, it must not only be based on the need, experience, or intuition[109] of that one person alone.[110] They may be having a niche need not shared by many others. Their tastes, experiences, digital literacy skills and expectations may be different than most other folks.[111] So, if most of the other users prefer something else, however deep one's "personal gut" feeling may be, the other users ought to win the product focus.

To avoid a misguided product focus, one that would have most consumers not interested in the product and its value, the right approach is design thinking. Whereas the idea[112] can come from anybody's itch, it must be validated through evaluation of target consumer needs and uses, designed by the team, prototyped,[113] validated, and then relentlessly tweaked.

Sometimes, even at the end of all that design process, an idea and its implementation may turn out not to be very useful and, as such, it ought to be discarded, as, if released, it would clutter the experience unnecessarily.

Existing Product Versus New Product

Creating a new product – new to your company and your consumer or the marketplace – from scratch obviously introduces a vast amount of uncertainty, risk, and complexity.

Why obviously? You don't know your customer and market as well as with an existing product, you have probably not exercised and refined your team and processes well, you'll have to convince a lot more people the product is worth the investment and the risk, etc., and you may start your product based solely on the itch.

Maybe scary to start from a green field, but certainly full of opportunities to do something better than what was done before. The only redeeming factor when you start from little, I guess, is that when you only have a small user population, well, there are fewer users to disappoint by any early missteps. Still not great.

With an established product – that is, regularly used by consumers and with well-functioning features – the consumer profile and needs are relatively well-known and thus the results of introducing new experiences are more predictable. That doesn't mean necessarily that there are no unknowns or risks to watch out for, it just means they may be fewer and lesser. On the other hand, making an uninspired change to an established experience that lots of customers use or love can have damaging effects on their loyalty to the product. Big changes affecting many users must be researched and evaluated carefully.

However, the design technique and process are largely similar wherever you are in your product maturity journey.

Iterative Process

The next few sections may provide the impression of linearity – discover, then ideate the design, then build, then test, etc. It is linear, but *per iteration*.

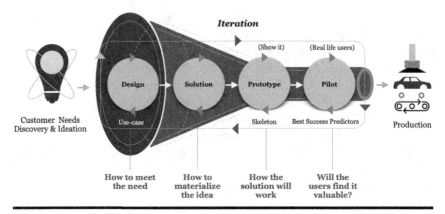

Figure 2.4 The design process.

The real flow is usually an iterative, back-and-forth, process, where learning from later stages (for example, testing) could send the product back to earlier stages activities (redesign, re-solutioning, rebuilding). But this only works well if the releases are small[114] and many.

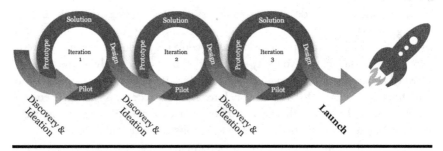

Figure 2.5 Iterative design.

Product evolves by incorporating feedback from previous releases and new ones.

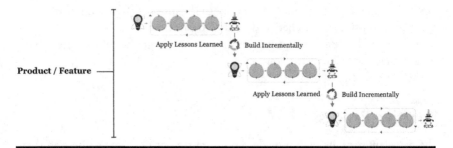

Figure 2.6 Sequential iterations.

For a healthy digital effort, these activities should happen in parallel in multiple streams or multiple products, features, or versions.

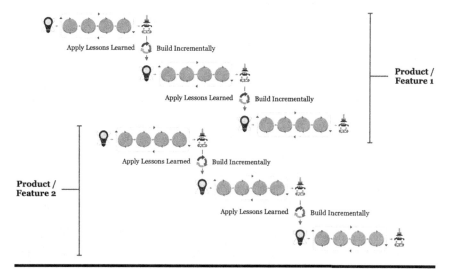

Figure 2.7   **Multiple parallel streams.**

Ideation – How You Get Your Ideas

The creative process is fabulously unpredictable. A great idea cannot be predicted.

Jony Ive

Ideation must be understood as the team's process of coming up with a variety of artifacts and ideas: prioritized areas where the team should focus its ethnography and user research, analysis and discussions on insights coming out of research, design options or solutions. As such, it has to happen at every stage.

The process has two distinct phases. First, the *divergent* phase, in which the focus is on collecting as much data, ideas, options and solutions as possible. Here, no idea is too outlandish to dismiss outright, as it may be either improved upon and developed or be later incorporated into bigger and better ideas and decisions. This phase, then, is followed by the *convergent* phase, in which options are weeded out to lead to the final two or three options that should be evaluated *comparatively* for best value/usability/feasibility.[115]

It's usually a combination of individual reflection, collection of data and impressions (yep, you can call them informed opinions at this stage), and joint team discussion and debate. With my team, I tend to use a brainstorming technique, but that works well only when the team is more mature and well gelled, in a way that *everybody* feels free[116] to bring up their thoughts and *all* want to influence the process for better outcomes since they all feel they *own* it. Brainstorming is great but it's not a replacement for individual reflection. The team can then debate, filter or adopt, and mesh together individual viewpoints.

It's expected (and actually a sign of a robust team understanding the consumer and marketplace) that the team members, preferably as consumers themselves and definitely as consumer proxies, come up with the product ideas (for both the needs and the solution).[117]

The most surprisingly successful ideas (that is, proven after implementation), come either from the original entrepreneur or, in the enterprise realm, from the digital product teams,[118] both seeking to address an "itch".[119] Rarely from customers[120] or consultants who provide ideas that your digital team should already know about.[121] The digital team producing ideas, however, is by no means a substitute to talking to consumers.[122] A product manager with special product talents coming up with great ideas can get you started but then you still need to talk it over with your consumers and observe them using your prototypes or products.[123]

It's quite common that additional ideas or needs are raised by other well-intentioned folks, such as extended team digital stakeholders. They should be evaluated on their own merits, but never influenced by who the idea comes from, even the CEO. Let's face it, there are few CEOs with product sensibilities like Steve Jobs'.

The best predictor for ending up with quality ideas is having lots of them generated or collected by the team, simply because more ideas lead to more to choose from and thus, statistically speaking, more chances to get better ideas.

All ideas must be taken through the digital team evaluation and vetting process.

Discovery – Finding the Stuff Customers Need

Everyday people are not very good designers.

Don Norman

Product discovery, led by the product management team, will find opportunities that the product ought to support, subject to further evaluation of *value to consumers versus effort to deliver*. The process starts with ethnography and user research[124] that are key to understanding what consumers' needs and journeys are, and observing what the consumers actually do. The focus of product discovery should be looking for points of friction,[125] challenges, or unmet needs.

It would be incorrect to see this process, just like the other processes we talk about here, as a one-and-done. You discover new things about your customers all the time, some that you can ignore, others that are too important to miss for the ultimate success of the product.

It's important that all your digital team members, to various levels of involvement, are part of discovery, if not the fact-finding part, then at least the evaluation phase. I always have the engineering folks, as well as the designers and of course the product managers, talking to consumers or shadowing them to see what they do and how. While they may all observe the same picture and hear the same stories, through different lenses, based on their backgrounds, they'll come up with different and always interesting insights. So, have all groups participate.

Discovery is pretty hard to do well, for two related reasons. **First**, because you can get overwhelmed by what you hear. The **second** and more important reason is because the universe of needs that you'll discover has many opportunities and solutions. Both are difficult, in the absence of a method to always prioritize and focus on what is more important to the most people the most time, at any one time.[126]

The most important tool in the discovery process is consumer research and interviews, i.e., talking to your users and observing what they do.[127] That should be among the first things you do when you start on an opportunity, and you should continue to do so throughout the lifecycle of the product.

Consumer Interviews and Research – Watch What Customers Do

> *Ethnographic research is no more than the starting point for a new frame. Ultimately, you have to chart out what it could be and get people on board with that vision. To do that, you need to create a new narrative that displaces the old frame that confined people.*
>
> **Roger L Martin**

This book is full of references, that should be clear by now, to getting user feedback, whether by talking to them, observing them using your product, or even monitoring what they do through system logs.[128] That is what I define as consumer feedback. There are a few rules to make these effective and useful to you, as a product manager and designer.

The **first** among all is that the interviews are focused on the end outcome. You want to learn – facts finding – in order to make the experience you provide better. Never to prove your pre-conceptions.

The **second** is that the consumer interviews must be focused on, well, the consumer. They're not polls about the image of your product or company (that may be useful but in a different context).

If the product is new, then you need to spend extensive time doing ethnography and user research, prototyping and showing them what you think you learned, to make sure you understand their needs sufficiently well before you can consider yourself a proxy for them and start making design decisions. What do you usually ask the consumers at this stage? Just ask them to show you what actions they take and how they perform them in their current lives, *without* your product ("*Describe a time when you tried to book this service*"). That represents their story of their need. The insights will validate *what* to build. While you should ask them what they need, don't ask them what *you think* the experiences *should* be.

As the product becomes more mature and established and you have something to put in their hands, ask them to use your prototype or product and then *watch* how they use it, noting how well that works (or not, but remember that negative feedback, especially at the prototype stage, like any learning, is very valuable). At this stage, you would ask them to show you *how* they would use it. If they have feedback, especially the frustrated kind, they'll absolutely communicate it – you don't even need to ask too hard. Avoid leading questions and any judgmental comments (like "*Did you consider using that CTA*[129] *instead of this one?*"). That will validate *how well* the product definition works.

It is always important to remember, when doing interviews, two things. **First**, what customers say may not be what they do. They may start with a concept – say buy product based on quality – but they may end up repeatedly actioning based on brand, advertising, fashion, peer influence, or cost. That is why the interview must focus on what they did, not what they feel like doing or thought they'll be doing. Accurate recollection and self-awareness are not always strong points for humans. **Second**, when people are being watched, they tend to be conscious of not looking stupid when using a product and technology – whereas without the observation they would easily figure out on their own what they need to do – and thus they are unnecessarily defensive and negative. That is why it's important that the observing is as un-intrusive and nonjudgmental as possible.

Without coming across as not helpful as an observer, avoid providing suggestions – after all, in the wild, the users will not have somebody to handhold them. This is a feedback interview session, not a user training session.[130] You'll have to decide how passive or active your observation needs to be at each stage of the product lifecycle – earlier versions and prototypes that are incomplete require more active involvement.

You ought to record everything in detail, including who they are, their comfort with technology, app versus web, where they are in a particular journey, their level of familiarity with your product or similar products, what they need to do, why they did what they did, and how they did it.

It is to be expected that most of the insights coming from interviews will be qualitative versus quantitative,[131] especially when it's about what customers felt while using the prototype or product. And that is fine, consumer emotions are part of what your experience provided by your product is supposed to factor in.

How often should you talk to your consumers? All the time. But in different ways and at different times in your process, as described above.

In any case, while serendipitous conversations with consumers can provide useful insights, it's important to have some structure and goalposts on when and how you engage with them. For one, so you don't "forget" to do it.

Unexpected Consumer Feedback and Why It's Valuable

> *I no longer listen to what people say, I just watch what they do. Behavior never lies.*

> **Winston Churchill**

We have all heard stories, usually accompanied by rolled eyes, from consumer feedback evaluations, about the crazy ways users are "mis-using" a product.

However, seemingly out of place actions – i.e., not fitting with what you would normally expect, with your product being used for different purposes than what was created for – is a great place to look for interesting insights into consumer needs, problems, or opportunities, some that neither your prior user research nor their explicit feedback may have provided. For that, you must be ready to notice unexpected ways and purposes for which they use your product.[132]

These unexpected consumer actions could be due to faults or systemic gaps in the product but could also be completely uncontemplated avenues of usage and signs of unmet yet unarticulated needs that can provide potentially valuable opportunities and directions to develop the product. And if you discover those needs this way and your competitors don't, maybe because they're not listening, then your product has an edge and your customers will be happier than they would otherwise be, with a feature they did not know they could have and use.

What if you're not getting any surprising feedback or requests? That could mean two things: one bad, that you may not be listening and asking questions well enough for consumers to volunteer feedback; the other, very good, meaning that your user research, combined with the team's creative ideation, are discovering users' needs.

Assumptions or How Not to Fool Yourself That You're Right

As you get to know your domain space – what your customers need and want and do – you'll make assumptions of what or why[133] they do it, whether they want and will use a feature or that the feature can be delivered in a usable and technology-feasible way.

What you must then do is find ways to clarify and validate your assumptions before you build the product. There are many methodologies for uncovering your assumptions, but they all basically get down to answering one fundamental question: *Why do you think this assumption is true?* A companion question, usually about the outer ecosystem, is: *What pre-condition needs to be in place for this assumption to be true?*[134]

For customer-related assumptions, you'll have to proceed by doing more pointed interviews (focused on those assumptions areas) and/or use prototypes of various levels of acuity. For technology assumptions, you may need to run technical spikes.[135] You'll need to make sure that however you attempt to get clarification and validation actually does the job and you're ready to measure it.

It's important not to go deliberately into a feature release with incorrect assumptions.[136] Now, if there really is no way to validate those decisions – because, despite the best efforts, the data you collected is not complete or accurate[137] – you'll just have to take the plunge and go in but be prepared to learn from what you'll see customers do and be ready to adjust fast.

Testing important assumptions on a production release with real customers is not great because of the potential blowback if the assumptions were very wrong and very impactful. Doing it just because you did not bother to do your homework properly at the right time is no way to go about building and releasing features and products.

Evaluating and Vetting or How to Weed Out the Unimportant Stuff

The opportunity – ideas, needs, requests – must be vetted by answering 3 + 1 questions. Each of these questions may return a *"no"* answer, or a *"not now but later after more work"*.

Value to users is really the answer to: *"Will they derive enough value to use it?"* Frankly, a lot of apps and web sites out there make the user scratch their heads in befuddlement at their purpose as they don't seem to do anything useful to be worth keeping or visiting.[138] Unless you can pivot the product to provide some value or at least the future promise of that, this would be the first showstopper.

Usability ("*Is it easy enough to use to be worth the effort for the end goal?*") is a tricky one sometimes, as the experience may be too awkward and complicated for anybody to operate it.[139] That problem is usually a reflection of confusing or too complicated business rules behind the experience. Work on simplifying those and very likely the experience will get simplified to the point of good, if not great, usability. If not, this is the second showstopper.

The engineering team must assess its capabilities, processes, and technologies for **feasibility** ("*Can we build it, production quality?*"). If the answer is no at that point, but value and usability are positive, then really the answer is "*not yet*" and the team must invest in building up to the ability to provide (build, buy, integrate) it, with production quality.

A **business value/risk assessment** really evaluates how beneficial the product is to the business ("*Will it (eventually) make money for us?*"), balanced by any risks to the company or its customers ("*Will consumers be harmed? Is this product ethical or used only for ethical purposes?*"[140]). That assessment may involve members of the extended team (legal, finance, etc.). At times the risk aspect may be a matter of judgement on legal liability and of risk acceptance. If the business value is negative or the risk is unacceptable, this would be the fourth possible showstopper. If the business value is minimal but consumers may still benefit in a way the business value may come later (harder to assess with hard numbers, but intent-to-return can be useful) then I would argue that the answer should still be yes.

Without the first three answers being a yes, consumers will not use or buy your product. Without the fourth, the organization will not stand behind you and you'll not be able to build much to provide any value.

With that being said, a word of caution. Even with all these criteria well analyzed, it doesn't mean that the final success or the desired outcome is assured in any way. Realistically, you have limited and sometimes conflicting insights, yet you also can't devolve into analysis-paralysis in order to design the perfect solution for the need.

And, for someone to start using your product, they probably need to stop using something else, even if that is paper forms or calls to your call center. Digital must provide a better value – although knowing the pains of paper forms and phone, it should be a low bar to beat.[141]

Especially in an opportunity-rich environment – lots of customer needs not yet met – evaluating ideas through the 3+1 prism is not to be done one idea at time in isolation. The question to answer is not whether we should pursue a particular idea, but whether we should pursue it in the timeframe and with priority *over another idea*. Or over another ten.

This is where the value is the biggest predictor of what to take on, all other things (feasibility, usability, etc.) being equal – which idea will provide the biggest benefit to consumers in the time frame.[142] And yes, in target-rich environments, that is a hard balancing act because you have so many needs to tackle.

Feedback from production users should be vetted through the same process.

Most ideas will not make it through the vetting process and that's OK – better to eliminate bad ideas early, before efforts are spent to make them production-ready.

Designing Products Is the Ultimate Joy – Or Hell

Once the need is identified, designing the optimal experience starts with the digital team: product managers, creatives, and technologists.[143]

Design is the ultimate creative process. It's about imaginatively combining pieces of a puzzle, but with a big catch: You must come up with both the pieces *and* the ultimate puzzle of your creation – as nobody creates them for you in advance. So, both the pieces and the ultimate puzzle are *fluid* and can change constantly. And there are no right answers, from an outcome perspective: only better than less good, or downright bad answers – if customers can't or won't use the product you designed.

That may be scary for some, but being free to come up with creations that solve problems and create opportunities for people is the ultimate joy for everyone, once they let themselves explore and try – that is, *if* they allow themselves to be creative.[144]

Now, joy doesn't mean simple and easy. Depending on the problem – its magnitude and complexity, timing of events, available resources, moving parts, or conflicting constraints – it can be extremely complicated, slow, and frustrating most of the time.

Design may sound like a straightforward process to come up with the solution, starting with the idea. It's not. It is a constant back and forth between needs, goals, and implementation constraints or limitations. You need to constantly add new pieces, remove some, or alter some until all pieces fit well, always remembering that the end outcome is what's important.

Having imaginative, ingenious, non-conformist,[145] and creative teams and team members – patiently assembled for their creative and technical competence and acumen – will make the ultimate difference.

You should not underestimate the amount of effort the digital team will be putting in coming up with a good design. It's time, effort and focus intensive: needing to clearly understand the need, requiring making hard choices and redoing work if the outcome is not of the right quality. That is why a lot of companies don't do it – but then they and their customers end up with poorly thought through products.

It could very well be that a need and the feature to support it may turn out to lead either to a very cumbersome and awkward experience or an impossibility to implement technically. Sometimes a small but stubborn obstacle can derail the process. At that point there are two paths to take. On one hand, you can either abandon the product or feature or put it on hold until you can figure out how to solve for the obstacle. Or, alternatively, you can go back to the need and its scope and try to adjust there – maybe you can support some of the need but not fully, yet provide value.

Where do you start with the design? First, as individual team members but then as a team, start with the customer and their experience – what do they need to do? Then start drawing – always have a whiteboard and pens in your office – or using Post-it notes to imagine what the processes, flow,[146] or interfaces (wireframes) *could* be.

Figure 2.8   Designs teams at work (author's collection).

The first drawing or arrangement of Post-it's – or the next 10 or 100 – will most definitely be wrong. But that's the beauty of boards or notes – they can be erased, re-arranged, or discarded easily. For remote teams and team members, there are plenty of interactive tools that can serve as the equivalent of the free-form white board.

What if the interface is not visual but text-based (chat) or audio (the likes of Alexa)? Well, the process and the tools – sticky notes and all – are still valid, but the wireframes may be heavily simplified or not necessary altogether.

And iterate, iterate, iterate. You may want to keep your board or wall intact until you release in production just so you can go back and adjust, if needed.

Assuming the design comes out well – and the team must be its own fiercest critic – that designed experience is then refined with consumers, as a prototype or pre-release testing and evaluation.[147]

Prototypes and Proof-of-concepts – Nothing Like Trying Designs Out

Good design costs no more than bad design.

Richard Koch and Greg Lockwood

Both of these concepts refer to testing a concept or product in various stages of completion.[148] Sometimes it's a very basic design – paper or design tool based. Sometimes it's a product that reached almost full implementation.

Prototypes and Proof-of-concepts (POCs) either try to assess the consumer reactions or, respectively, the feasibility of the implementation. The goal is the same: to help validate your design choices and how they meet your consumers goals by putting something in their hands or their close proxies.

Prototypes help answer the question *"What design and implementation options do I have and should use?"* You should always do prototyping, even if on paper and definitely if a tool is available.[149] Unless you see and feel how the product may look *and* work, imperfect visuals as it may be, you can't understand how good it will be.

A Proof-of-concept (POC) tries to answer a different question: *"Does this product or feature make sense and will it be used by users?"* Sometimes, as disappointing as it may be, the answer is a resounding *no*. If so, then try to figure out why not and whether it can be changed into a *yes*, after another round of proving the concept. They are (almost) baked products that you deploy for a subsection of the user population or for a limited period, in order to get a feel for what users think about it – experience above everything else – and possibly how well the implementation works. I use POCs for new, yet unproven, products to assess the usability and value in ways that maybe early user research can't reveal. I always do that for version 1.0 of an unproven product or experience. Sometimes, depending on the culture of your organization, a POC is a strange and novel concept. Sell it if you must, but do it, nevertheless.

Depending on what you're trying to solve for, you may need to use both of these concepts. They're very useful and can answer questions early in the process with yet unknown answers that could become big problems later in the process.[150] For simple product features, you may get away without a POC – a sketched prototyping in a tool is so simple and yet powerful that is hard to see why you wouldn't do it.

For smaller or less risky features, where the build effort is not significant,[151] you may decide to get the same learnings by putting them out straight into production – that is a great benefit of being agile and using fast delivery and deployment tooling, like the cloud. But they need to be production quality, otherwise you lose more in credibility than you gain in lessons learned.

Try by testing, then learn and adjust.

Demo Your Product Effectively

Some of us, old enough, remember the embarrassment of Bill Gates giving a product demo and getting the (in)famous blue screen of death (the operating system reaches an unrecoverable error condition, serious enough to stop its entire execution). It may be that even Steve Jobs may have experienced one or two in his public demo career. It happens to most of us.

This section is not about famous embarrassments of that nature. It's also not about giving public demos of your product to the public at large – the nature of digital product diffusion these days means most product launches to the general public are limited to the likes of Apple.

However, as a digital leader you'll need to be able to do effective and attractive product demos. Slide decks just won't have the same impact as people seeing a product, at least not without adequate narrative behind it. There are two different internal audiences for those demos.[152]

The **first** will be either the executive committee of the company or the board (or both) for the explicit purpose of obtaining organizational support and funding. The main focus with that audience is articulating the benefits to the organization. But this is not talking just about organizational dollars and cents – the audience is made of people (and probably customers themselves) so the demo must also appeal to their emotions, as users, not just as hard-core executives.[153]

The **second** type of demo, equally important, will be done, most likely by your product team, to your business partners, to elicit support for the business and process changes that will be required to enable your product and its features. This type of demo will focus not on the benefits to consumers – not that this audience doesn't necessarily care about consumers – but rather the benefits to their groups[154] and then on the changes they'll be required to make to their operations to make the full end-to-end experience work.

For both types of demos, though, there's one requirement towering above all others to make them successful. If you and your team can't convey your *genuine* enthusiasm and conviction for the mission and product at large, and the respective feature in particular, then you might as well not do them as they won't convince anybody of anything – actually, you may inadvertently convince them *against* your product. Besides, if you don't have genuine enthusiasm for your own product, you're not going to be really successful, and you might as well look for another job.

But demos must always be honest and never fudged, as well as clear and concise.

The First Design Solution Is Not the Best One

You're starting to design for a particular need. Lots of opinions are offered by the team on how best to meet that need – functionality, UI/UX, technology.

The thing to know is that whatever that first solution the team proposes, it's very likely not the best and should not be the final one. As everyone will be fine-tuning their thinking and understanding of the problem and potential solutions, whatever they come up with first is very likely to be too unnecessarily complicated to implement and awkward for consumers to use.[155]

What you'll then need to do[156] with that first design is ruthlessly simplify and improve it, through as many iterations as needed to get to a good experience. Challenge assumptions and ideas and ask why[157] as many times as required to understand the need and the domain and then evaluate solutions, repeating the process with the goal to simplify at each iteration. Sometimes it is about challenging the need for users to input too much data – especially in healthcare, where asking for excessive information "just in case it's needed" is endemic. Other times it's about business rules, that may not require such a complex implementation as you thought or were unnecessarily required by your operational partners. Or it's about a technology component that must work differently than anticipated. Simplify and improve until there's nothing to simplify and improve in the realistic timeframe you can afford.

Have Users Tell You How Your Product Works for Them

User testing, usually performed by internal staff, is very useful but should be used only for what it literally says: internal users testing the mechanics of your product to make sure it works as designed, from your *firm's* perspective.[158]

What I am referring to here is enrolling real users in a validation process with a view to improve a design through real-life experiences,[159] from *their* perspective.

User testing must validate your answers to the questions of **value** and **usability**. *Do users find your product valuable for their needs? Can they actually use it?*

You'll have to watch users closely for both, making sure you understand why and why not (and how to recover from "*no*" answers).

Consumers come up with interesting suggestions about the experience that your digital team may not have thought about. Some are frustratingly simple interface misses[160] or are profound feedback on confusing or awkward experience design and implementation. Often, the feedback will only apply to one person, thus unlikely to be material to the product.

The rule is to test as much as you can, review all feedback and decide, as a product design team, what to do (or not do) about it. Once you decide, execute on the decision.

What about the famous A/B testing? This refers to offering two (or more) alternatives of an experience to different users and then see how many prefer one over the other, by using it more[161] (or providing feedback, usually negative).[162] It's relatively easy to do, especially for web, moderately less so for native apps, but only if your application is designed accordingly. Most companies that I know of use this method, to some degree. I've heard that some companies make A/B testing into a religion and maybe it works great for them.

One caveat is important (and that is true for all user feedback, however it is collected): You need to design your tests and then analyze the results correctly in ways that will tell you *why* one option was better than the other. If it's just a matter of a color scheme, things may be evident,[163] but for more complex interactions it may be harder to tell. In those cases, after understanding what people liked and why, you may be better off designing a third option combining the best parts of A *and* B. And for those more complicated interactions, you may want to use proof-of concept and prototypes discussed earlier.

Slide Decks Are Not for Defining a Product

Slide[164] decks are used across the corporate world as if they're as inevitable as the law of gravity. It seems these days, in enterprise environments, we can only think and communicate in slides.[165] Sometimes they're the easiest medium to present tabular and graphs updates. While you can fit more words (and graphs) in a deck slide than in a tweet, it's pretty much the same paradigm but with more real estate.

But for things that need thoughtful reading and should not be subject to the tyranny of sectioning ideas into slides (pages), their use really is detrimental. Amazon is famous for requiring business or product proposals to be presented in a text editor format. I wholeheartedly agree with that. Other companies have similar policies, at least for internal documents.

When I defined the consumer digital vision and strategy document for healthcare, written as a prescriptive document for the organization rather than descriptive for external readers, I started it in a slide format because of the expectations of internal staff. It quickly became counterproductive for information articulation, absorption, and processing – the paradigm of a slide was oppressive in properly discussing topics – so I quickly switched to a text editor.

Slide decks are not the right format to discuss materials supporting customer user research and ethnography, brainstorming session, design, user flows, etc. Expansive Figma and Lucid charts and text documents or, if the team is located in an office, even an old fashion hand-written white board or Post-it notes boards are much better, collectively. Many times, a slide deck-free conversation does miracles. This is a medium, not a product preference. All to get the best results.

But whatever the medium, the rules of telling the story are the same: Articulate what the problem or opportunity is, present the facts, situation, and circumstances, present the solution and its pros and cons and then move onto implementation details, plus the mechanics of status tracking and updating the audience.

So, don't use slide decks to *define* a product. Fine for status updates or marketing.

You'd Better Learn and Act on the Lessons

Across this book we consistently talk about learning. Whether what you hear from consumers ("*What they say*"), or what we learn from product instrumentation ("*What they do*") or from external experiences and analyses, constant learning is critical.[166]

Continuously collecting and reviewing data, metrics, and feedback on digital experiences is the only way to know where and how to improve. Even the most brilliant digital team and the most rigorous discovery and design process can't build perfect experiences, especially not for the first few releases of a feature or product.

There's a constant learning process[167] for everybody – the team, the organization, even the consumers – and that is perfectly normal. Digital done well is a marathon, not a sprint. Organizational leaders and stakeholders need to understand that and be patient and supportive.

Learning is not merely receiving feedback or signals. It's analyzing what you're hearing and getting and converting it into actionable and actioned insights. That may be harder than it sounds sometimes – most of the time it's not an *a-ha!* moment, but a head-scratcher and for those times you'll have to think long and hard (and get more data). Learning and acting requires a very structured and rigorous process.

Insights and learnings must absolutely be acted upon and not ignored, otherwise collecting insights is an enormously wasted opportunity. Learning – from measuring and getting feedback, to testing assumptions and potential solutions – is useful and not mere entertainment only if actively applied to some positive outcome. This includes changing the strategy and possibly the product, what you choose to do and how, avoiding the same or similar pitfalls and making things better in the future.

For the learning to be valuable and not isolated and therefore lost, it must be shared widely, discussed, and analyzed with the entire team. What you learned, why and how, internal or external stats and data, what it means to your team and product, applicability and limitations, and what are you doing about implementing learnings in solutions. So, everybody is crystal clear. And for future team members or when your memory lapses, these learnings must be documented in some knowledge database or wiki of sorts, so everybody, well trained and versed in the process, can find what they need to know for the next product, feature, or release.

Unfortunately, a lot of enterprises (probably) collect data and most definitely receive feedback (just check the app stores consumers comments) but don't seem to act on it, at least judging by how little and slowly they improve.

Listen and measure. Learn and act.

The next four sections are what you would consider design thinking antipatterns: asking consumers what you should build, looking for consultants or creative agencies to tell you what to do or them doing it for you, taking direction on product from business stakeholders, or blindly follow any data you may have.

All have two things in common: lack of product management expertise and the desire to have a cover if outcomes with the product don't go as planned.

Anti-pattern #1 – Consumer Panels Deciding on Products

> *Our job is to figure out what they're going to want before they do. [...] It's really hard to design products by focus groups. A lot of times, people don't know what they want until you show it to them.*

> **Steve Jobs**

In organizations with weak or non-existent digital product management, there is a common practice of relying on customer panels or focus groups to actually decide *what* products and features the digital team should build and deploy – *not* just feedback on a prototype or pilot. And then, once the survey process is complete, it is summarized and then the build begins.

I guess in the absence of nothing else – because the firm has not developed its own product management practice, or it does not trust it – this is the nearest best thing that creates a sense of comfort that the firm is informed on where to invest in digital. But that is a false sense of comfort that will not lead to good, let alone great, outcomes. It, however, provides the cover up for when things turn out not as expected – executives will point to the output of these panels and focus groups and say: *"But we have done exactly what the customers told us to do, it's not our fault things didn't turn out well!"* Well, it is your fault if you allowed this to happen and that is for several reasons.

First, for practical reasons, focus groups will, well, focus on a particular piece of functionality. It is very hard to get a group of customers to be presented with a whole product and understand what to make of its overall value.[168] Could you enroll customer groups to basically start from vision, strategy (about which they cannot speak as it is driven by a variety of factors they don't understand or that you cannot share with them for competitive reasons in any case) then all the design and all the implementation decisions and features – aka the product management role? Theoretically possible but improbable to get a large group of people to dedicate a lot of time to do all this work – these groups usually are assembled for part of a day, not weeks. If you use multiple groups for different pieces to get around the time commitment constraint for any one group, they will invariably contradict each other.[169] And then you're back to square one, not clear what to do next.

Back to single functionality focus groups, they will see only slivers of the product and they will ask for functionality for the sliver put in front of them and not the entire product. The direction on different slivers will be counterproductive for the entire product, which will come out incoherent. And yes, sometimes individual features, viewed independently, may have constraints that are necessary to make the overall product valuable.

For example, if you only ask them about booking a hotel room or medical appointment, they will try to optimize that in ways – like wanting non-authenticated standalone booking experience triggered by a text message that avoids creating a digital profile and accessing the full product – that will make accessing other parts of the journey difficult, as without a profile and access to the full product using the rest of post-booking experience, such as cancelations or changes, is much more problematic.[170] If you only ask the consumer about one feature, they may optimize that standalone approach not knowing they're missing a variety of useful features in the larger product.

Second, customers – unless they are a bunch of digital team members – don't understand what the product or feature *could* be, simply because they don't know the available technologies, firm's assets, and capabilities, let alone the vision. They will suggest common features they use with other vendors' products,[171] but the digital team will already be aware of these through their own research[172] and thus nothing new is learned.[173] And if you are trying to build something that is better yet different than whatever else is in the marketplace, you'll get nothing other than me-too suggestions.

Third, some of the feedback will either be based on a) the consumers' perception of what they *think* they do and need, not what they actually do or need, when faced with a real world product and consumer situation, b) biased by a recent experience – positive or negative – that will overshadow a cold-headed evaluation of what they are asked for feedback for, or c) theoretical opinions about a need they never had and they cannot imagine, at least not in the absence of a prototype to evaluate.

The advice is obvious by now, given what I have talked about so far in this book: Let the digital team (that you should build up so you don't have to rely on others) do their job – user research and ethnography, ideation, design, technical research, and feasibility assessment, etc. – come up with the best design they can, develop the product or even a (very realistic) prototype.[174] *Only after* all this work is done, put that prototype in the hands of consumers and collect insights and feedback by observing and learning from what they do.[175]

Anti-pattern #2 – Management Consultants Advising on Products

> *You do get a broad cut at companies but it's very thin. It's like a picture of a banana: you might get a very accurate picture but it's only two dimensions and without the experience of actually doing it you never get three dimensional. So, you might have a lot of pictures on your walls, you can show it off to your friends I've worked in bananas, I've worked in peaches, I've worked in grapes, but you never really tasted it.*
>
> **Steve Jobs on consultants**

A variant to the previous anti-pattern replaces the consumer focus groups with external consultants to decide what product and features to implement. Some of the same challenges are present in this case as well, but new ones are added.

First, despite all the artifacts and materials that consultants are able to produce (and they are usually reused from other accounts), management consultants cost a lot of money and provide very little added value – unless they are solely engaged for market research and not to advise on what the team should do.

Second, unless they are very entrenched in the firm, very broadly and over a long period, they don't know the business, the technology, and the assets, let alone the vision and strategy, at least not enough to be able to provide useful recommendations. They are rarely committed to your long-term success.[176] They are, well, mercenaries.

Third, while they may have done work for many other client firms, they didn't actually execute on all the activities, and they were rarely still engaged after the end of a project or product launch to allow them to understand (and learn from) the quality and outcomes of their work. More than once in my career I have gotten strikingly different feedback from them compared to their clients. I am not saying in any way they were misconstruing the results; they just didn't stay engaged long enough to see the inevitable faults of their recommendations. Studying a Harvard Business Review business case in MBA school is *not* the same as actually doing it more than once. This is what Steve Jobs was referring to in the quote above.

Finally, let's also be honest about something else: Consultants have an inherent agency problem, that is when their own interests – mostly billing hours – conflict with the client's. You can use them for point expertise, market research, evaluating technologies based on your specification, but they are not a long-term solution.

If I haven't convinced you so far of talking to consumers instead of consultants and you may still be inclined to ask "experts", here is an interesting nugget. In 2020, we were hearing from "retail consultants" that we should offer curbside pick-up for store's online sales. And indeed, some stores were seeing great uptake, given the panic of Covid-19. And yet, in our company, we weren't experiencing it. After our own research, it turned out that was because not all stores' sales conditions were equal and not all geographical topologies were equal – mall setting versus stand-alone store setting, critical-goods versus nice-to-have goods. "Experts" may have been right in very general terms (*"a majority of shoppers will prefer curbside pick-up"*), but they didn't necessarily speak in an informed way for *our* customers. We had to validate for *our* case by talking to *our* customers.

The solution is clear: Build up your internal talent to give you what you need instead of relying on consultants.[177]

Anti-pattern #3 – Operational Stakeholders Deciding on Products

Doing everything business units want I call a servile strategy.

Roger Martin, A New Way To Think

Operational leaders are responsible for business units and have P&L (revenue and expenditure/investments) responsibilities *for those units*. And because they may control funding[178] (possibly in coordination with the Finance department), in traditional organizations, they will want to decide on what happens in digital,[179] dictating to the digital product team what products and features to implement.[180] Out of old habits, those organizations still look at the technology and digital group as order-takers, with the digital team being just an implementation team, not a product-defining team. And their product definition process is not one of design thinking, but one of organizational influence thinking.

If the product team doesn't have the clout or courage to push back, the process will continue to happen the old-fashioned way – operational leaders issuing "requirements" to the "IT" team. This would be fine if it led to great outcomes, but it usually doesn't simply because it leads to misalignments between product and consumer needs, for a few reasons.

First, very few operational leaders are good proxies for consumers. They don't understand or have had no exposure to the not-so-secret sauce of imagining, discovering, designing, implementing, launching, and constantly improving digital products – aka design thinking. Do some operational leaders understand design thinking in their own right? A few indeed do and they deserve kudos. Can they have their own product managers since they understand what it takes? And engineering? And creative? Of course, they can, and, in very few organizations, they do and in some it's even somewhat successful. With one very big caveat that we talk about next.

Second, unless they're the CEO responsible for the entire organization, operational leaders, even when personally committed to consumer satisfaction and even delight (think American Express, Disney, etc.), have a strict focus and are measured by the financial metrics on their *own* business unit. That makes it difficult for them to be able to see the larger picture of consumers' needs – who need to experience *all* the firm's services,[181] not just that operations executive's slice of it.[182] The "business requirements" they want to provide to digital teams to work on are exactly what they sound like: what their organization wants, not what the product team may discover consumers need.

Third, business stakeholders, not familiar with the potential or limitations of the technology delivery and solutions, will not be able to accurately design the product and the experience. Under- or over-estimating what can be delivered, while imposing a decision, is not a good predictor of timely solution delivery.

It is an incredible waste of talent, dedication, focus, knowledge, and method (as in the design thinking) to disempower the digital team from making product decisions. When that happens, it eventually shows in the product in a big way – for example, when you see one company with multiple websites and mobile apps, usually each with its own consumer digital identity and login/password, sometimes with overlapping features. Ugly![183] And that is why the CDIO or Chief Product Officer, as owner of the product and the roadmap (what to do and how to implement), is a critical role for digital's success.

So, my advice here is three-pronged.

First, involve those stakeholders in your sausage-making process, where they can see for themselves the consumer needs, the evaluation process, limitations, and constraints but also opportunities and the value provided by the process. This close involvement of business stakeholders leads to them seeing themselves as *co-creators*.

Second, you as a digital team must build credibility with operational leaders over time. Credibility is two-fold: first, that you know what you're doing and, second, that you care for the operational stakeholders' outcomes. When you have none yet, find other areas where you can carve out for yourself the freedom to do things the best way that they can be done and thus gain credibility through independent success. Do your user research properly and then have numbers and insights to help you have an informed debate over facts and not executive opinions and emotions.[184]

Third, when what operations executives want is narrowly tailored to their individual business unit needs, a strong counterargument is the disfunction that local requirements or optimization introduces[185] for the larger firm. If you're an integrated value delivery firm (providing multiple different services, trying to retain your customer within your ecosystem), coherence across units, in order to ensure a value proposition for the whole firm, is a very strong argument. Then you can point to the value of your method and work as being superior (you need to be able to prove that in some undisputed manner).

At that point, the conversation becomes a lot clearer: Do you want to do things this way with good results for the firm or your way with going-nowhere results? Either way, though, you need to honestly build the facts and arguments to strongly prove your points. Measure the results of the method and then have the argument.[186] In the end the results should speak, not relative influence and control over the budget.

So, what is the role of operational leaders in the digital efforts?

Operations folks are legitimate stakeholders and subject matter experts (SMEs) on business processes[187] and strategies. Them being active as *equal* partners to the digital team is critical. Both parties must partner well for a great outcome, understanding each other's goals and constraints.

It's up to the digital product team to evangelize the concepts of digital design, build business expertise, acumen, and credibility to the point of pushing back to centrifugal tendencies and put the consumer at the center of all the company's experiences.

Anti-pattern #4 – Data-driven Product Decisions – Well, Sometimes, Maybe

The data wasn't a guide. At best, it was a crutch. At worst, cement shoes. It was analysis paralysis.

Tony Fadell

The lazy answer to the question of how to choose what to do would be to follow what the data tells you.

And indeed, collecting data on how users use products and features is paramount to validating the digital team's choices and making products better, sometimes a lot better, over time. Observing and measuring (through instrumentation) followed by careful analysis and calibration is priceless.

Gathering data on why certain users (but not others) use or stop using certain features or abandon a flow (*Not enough options? Confusing experience? Flow too long?*) can be the difference between a successful tweak or letting a feature die.

Nevertheless, sometimes the data you collect, through whatever means, tells you nothing of any value. Lack of data can't be the excuse for inaction, which is much worse in a fast-moving environment like digital than trying, failing, learning, and then adjusting. Trying and adjusting is the best way to get better and not waiting for more data that may never come.

The data you collect can't be the ultimate arbiter of your actions. Data is supposed to enhance your decisions, not supplement them, especially when it makes no sense to your informed selves, and you can't dig deeper into what it really means.

The worst of all (and that is a version of hiding behind consultants or focus groups results) is to use the data to run away from your responsibilities as digital product team – which is doing the hard design thinking work in order to eventually produce positive outcomes for your customers.

Chapter 2.5 Product

If you're going to make something, it doesn't take any more energy—and rarely does it take more money—to make it really great. All it takes is a little more time. Not that much more. And a willingness to do so, a willingness to persevere until it's really great.

Steve Jobs

A digital product is the technical implementation – mobile, web, etc., and the backend processes supporting them – that enables a consumer experience – i.e., what they can do and how well.

In the process of defining and building that product, digital teams are maniacally focused on all the pieces that must come together for it to work well. Yet the team should never forget that what the consumer cares for is their experience, not your product and certainly not your effort to create it.

Products are judged solely by how (well) they enable or improve the experience. A car gets you to your desired destination. A phone keeps you in touch with those important to you. A mobile map app directs you to wherever you need to go. If these products can't deliver the expected outcomes, they would have failed.

What the consumer cares for is determined by what they need and when, not what is technically or organizationally preferred. Organizations will provide great consumer loyalty only thorough consistent and prolonged positive experiences.

The product goal must be aligned with the product vision and strategy. Otherwise, you're just clocking hours, not delivering outcomes for the consumer.

The Product Is about Life Stories, Not Transactions

People don't want quarter-inch drills. They want quarter-inch holes.

Theodore Levitt

Stories and their importance is, quite probably, the ultimate lesson I learned at Disney. Disney is fundamentally about telling and living stories. And I don't mean just in their movies – that is obvious – but in all the journeys their customers (aka guests in parks, resorts, cruises, etc.) engage in with the company. For Disney, it's not about selling tickets for a movie or a park entry but providing living stories.

If you think that is just brilliant brainwashing of customers, well, it's not. Here are two major arguments, one coming from psychology and the other from economics.

Studies in psychology and neuroscience[188] over the last 40 years have found that humans don't merely record facts to be simply retrieved later. They learn and compose mental *stories* to which they associate memories of facts – or the perception of facts – from experiences. The brain constantly builds a narrative and constantly fills in the perception gaps. When dealing with experiences, the brain builds mental models – templates, if you wish – to make sense of them for future encounters. It is those mental models, stored in the memory as *stories*, that get recollected when encountering a new experience or a new instance of a previously encountered experience.[189]

Clayton Christensen[190] of Harvard wrote about consumers not looking for products or services, but rather looking to "hire" solutions to their lives' problems and needs. And usually, those problems and needs are never transactional but in the context of a larger story. He described the role that a humble shake – the one with milk, fruit and ice in a plastic cup with a plastic straw, sold at fast food locations – plays in the context of the larger life story of the need for nutrition between home and work and between home, school, and kids sports.

All this means one fundamental thing: Products must take the customer story and context into consideration and *ultimately become part of* the story. You and your team must be able to articulate that story to your consumers because that is what they're going to consume and that is what will make them use your product or service.

Story (and its context) here is used in two different ways but always happening together and at the same time. **First,** the product must fit the story of customers' lives, needs, struggles, and wants. Consumers don't need a particular product or service in isolation and out of the blue, they need to fill a gap or need in their lives, both before the firm's offering comes into the picture and after.

The digital experience must take the context into consideration and fit the product and service as a flow within the larger flow of people's lives the best it can. Your design for your digital experience needs to be as simple as possible in convenience and choice.[191] But if you offer a broken flow for your product and service, you'll break the rest of your consumer's life flow.

Think about someone who, in the midst of a busy life, precariously balancing a challenging occupation and career, family and children, mortgage and other bills to pay, gets suddenly sick (let's hope from a relatively minor affliction, nevertheless impacting their life). How are they going to fit in finding a physician or urgent care location, booking an appointment, checking-in, and obtaining and filling a prescription, let alone follow up appointments and remembering all these steps in the right order or at the right time, and all while navigating obscure rules your business has for them? Remember the "precariously balancing" part? Well, your experience is just a part of that balancing act and it needs to help not hinder and make things even worse.[192]

All good stories start from the very beginning, when a customer has a need in their life, then they get a glimpse of your product or service, and they decide to use it to solve their need. The story ends well after they used or experienced it, (preferably) with positive memories and reminders. And what their story is decides what you'll provide to the consumer. *Not* the other way around.

Second, the experience *itself* must be designed as a story or journey. Which means, when designing your digital experience, you must design the digital experience as a journey (consumer view) or flow (organization view), not just a point transaction.

The digital experience must be explicit in showing that journey, flow, or process that the customer will follow and not force them to guess what else they need to do. Just providing for the booking of a transaction (purchasing a product or making a healthcare appointment) is neither the beginning nor the end of the flow.

Furthermore, if the consumer buys a product, can you offer (even through a partner) the installation of that product? If the consumer visits a doctor, can you help with transportation to and from the medical facility (offering tele-health, when possible, would be a great start, but also integration with ride share companies), even if transportation or tele-health is not immediately your business?[193] And when I say help, I mean right then and there in the digital experience you're offering. And *that* needs to be your digital product.

Map the flows/journeys visually. For example, the following is the journey a hotel guest follows for a stay:

Figure 2.9   Consumer journey flow.

Subsequently, you need to track the coverage of your product features to flow steps, probably in a table format, for everybody to be clear on product-to-need coverage. For example, for a resorts'[194] product, that journey and the supporting features' availability would be (empty cells suggest still incompletely implemented journeys; over time, as the product becomes more sophisticated, new cells can be added, for example, for booking you would add making, rescheduling or canceling it):

Product Features	Finding	Booking	Checkin	Checkout	Payments	Account Management
Rooms	✓	✓	✓	✓	✓	✓
Tickets	✓	✓			✓	
Rooms & Ticket Packages	✓				✓	

Figure 2.10   Product to features matrix.

A product always evolves and is never "completed"[195] because the story evolves over time and with different people. Walt Disney once said: *"Disneyland will never be completed. It will continue to grow as long as there's imagination left in the world"*.

Product-Enabled Experience Guidelines[196] – Getting It Right

Consumer digital capabilities will target what most consumers need on a consistent basis. Neither internal operational agendas or efficiency drives, nor vendor offerings and not even what the competitors are doing[197] should drive what the consumers get to experience.

The goal of your digital efforts is to provide experiences that, through simplicity,[198] comprehensiveness, convenience, and user-friendliness will create "wow" emotional moments in a consistent manner. That in turn builds loyalty and differentiation – between your digital experiences and the quality of the physical service and product, you will be above others in your industry – thus in long-term relationships that are good not just for the firm, through repeat business, but for consumers through reassurance of quality.

Think in Logical Layers and Tiers

It is important to talk about thinking in layers and tiers. I realize this term may be remnants of my technology background, where we think in terms of abstraction layers constantly when designing technical products.

But the reality is that the digital team operates across multiple layers, levels, and tiers all the time, whether logical or physical, product or experience. It is common for them to navigate up and down across the hierarchy of layers in one conversation. Sometimes the conversation is full of precision statements on where something belongs. For different issues and discussions, the layers may be different, but they are all part of that logical hierarchy and layering.

So, what do I mean by layers and tiers, with all the implied hierarchy?

At the very top of that hierarchy, if we can imagine something vertical, sits the user and their needs and wants. Next down is the experiences, digital or physical, that could meet those needs. Then next level down is the tool or digital product that provides that experience – in digital's case, very likely a product like a mobile app or web site. At the bottom (no disrespect), is the underlying back-end technology – code, infrastructure, integrations *as well as* the underlying operational processes powering the business and providing products and services to customers.

Just because one day we talk about cloud infrastructure or an API (bottom of the layer hierarchy), it doesn't mean we don't care about customer needs (top of the layer hierarchy). And just because we keep talking about experience, it doesn't mean we're ignoring the fact that somewhere, someone, or something must write a piece of Java or Flutter code. One doesn't work without the other. And security controls must coexist with easy access to data across the hierarchy – or stack, in technical parlance.

How complete and how well all these layers are put, and work together determines how happy those customers are with what you provide. Nice house curtains can't hang on unfinished walls. You can't drive anywhere with a car without wheels.

It's true that if one team, at one layer, focuses exclusively on their layer at the cost of the other teams, the whole hierarchy will suffer. But we need to manage the focus, not negate the existence of hierarchy.

It's all a continuum of layers and it's their quality that delivers the final experience.

Output *and* Outcomes

> *Rather than being measured on the output of their design work, the product designer is measured on the success of the product.*
>
> **Marty Cagan**

We manage work through features or roadmaps but that doesn't mean we only care for output and not outcomes. Focusing on output – easy to measure and easy to achieve – is only detrimental when it's done for its own sake and not as the way to achieve outcomes, which is the end goal. But outcomes don't happen without timely and speedy output, as described elsewhere.

Output and adherence to self-declared committed dates should absolutely be measured because they reflect the team's efficiency and effectiveness and give information on what improvements need to be made to the team's processes, structure, and technologies. Here is an example: If releases are very slow (low output) and the culprit is manual testing, including regression testing, well, you need to invest in automated testing (which you should do anyway for quality, not just speed, reasons). Voilà! No outcome was harmed in the making of this output movie.

Outcomes are measured from a consumer viewpoint, output from a team's operational pace perspective. Outcomes and digital capabilities output are related in another way. The way I look at it, every month that a digital feature (*output*) is not out in the hands of consumers to provide value (*outcome*) is another month that the consumers lives are not as good as they could be.

And that is not, by any means, limited to digital. It's the same with building houses or cars: Consumers want to live happy lives and they need houses and cars for accomplishing that, but at the other end someone needs to lay down a brick or assemble a metal part to make it happen. And fast.

Focusing only on output is bad leadership. Talking only about outcomes is disconnected-from-reality leadership.

Product Ground Guidelines

Your digital channels ought to be the first place consumers should think about when they have a *need for a life problem solution*. Notice that I am not saying "*when your consumers think of you*"! They want solutions, not you. A product is only a product if it provides a solution to a need for someone. You ought to build digital experiences such that your consumers' minds connect them to solutions to problems – like getting better when they feel ill. *Not* as a prop to navigate a bad process.

The difference between the former and the latter is the difference between consumer delight – that is rewarded with loyalty – and mere consumer acceptance.

You absolutely must evaluate product features based on **value to consumers**, **usability**, **viability**, and **feasibility** – each and all together evaluated in a balanced way.[199] Particular capabilities must receive focus based on what target consumers want and need and how their needs can be best satisfied with the most significant positive impact, factoring in technical and business feasibility. End value being equal, prefer prioritizing features that can be used as soon as possible versus features depending on delayed operational or technical readiness.

Stay away from features designed just for niche categories of users (by definition *not* your target consumer profile), as while useful for those individuals, they will be a mismatch and downright clutter for most others. Design must be focused on outcomes[200] not spurious features, so to be usable by most in the *target* group.

Thou shalt never put features and functionality above security and privacy considerations. That should obvious, but in a lot of cases it is not happening effectively, whether because of lack of priority or technical ability. Protecting the digital footprint – whether securing communication over the open internet or preventing account takeover – is critical to consumer adoption and is directly proportional to their trust in your product. Don't fail digital adoption by not putting adequate focus on securing apps and data.

You can't expect that any "killer" feature will singularly drive product adoption. Only aggregate useful features build up to useful products. Other features will need evolution and sustained effort and patience in order to become valuable.

Some features may not live up to your value expectations and you should be ready to retire them, so they don't clog your product. The product can't be burdened by useless features – clutter is not conducive to efficient use.

Focus – Keep Your Product Eye on the Ball

While it's quite common (and useful) for digital products to be(come) broad and comprehensive, they also can't become encyclopedias for every possible piece of information that you think your consumer may find helpful. That is what we have Google and Bing for or the old style (ca. 2000) "internet portals".

For example, if you're a hospital, unless you have original medical research and information, you're better off relying on other places on the internet to talk about hypertension and cholesterol. It may be tempting to fill up screens and pages to show a "rich" digital experience, but that is to be avoided. "Rich" comes from a few things that are very valuable and, when done well, satisfying to users. Prefer value and quality over spurious quantity or successful outcome over empty output. That is especially true for your mobile experience, which should focus[201] on the mobility paradigm – providing services in any time and place, but mostly not at home.

Too much – screens, items, content – to navigate through distracts from both of these goals. Every time you put one feature in front of consumers, once there are too many features, their attention is distracted from the important things.

Often, while using a web site or a mobile app, it's not clear what the focus of that experience is – that is, what does the digital team behind that experience want the consumer to solve first (and maybe second). In these cases, the experience feels chaotic and not very usable.[202]

If your company provides lots of products and services (marketplace, video, music, cloud, like Amazon; parks and resorts, cruises, streaming, stores for Disney; mail, storage, office productivity tool, etc. for Google and Microsoft), you may need to break down your digital products in some way. Maybe by type of product, or market, or customer segment – internal customers versus external and individual consumers (B2C) versus corporate customers (B2B) – etc. That is of course driven by your firm's business model (you are a B2C business or a B2B one[203]) but also the mechanics of providing the appropriate product experience – through user interface, backend systems, resources, and product management team focus.

Thinking you can serve multiple types of consumers equally well in one product is naive and unrealistic. The consumer who's going to pay you with a credit card for a one-time, few-hundred-dollar transaction is colossally different than the corporate purchasing manager who's going to pay you multi-million-dollar annual bills. And then you must ensure that the result has a clear focus, and the experience is optimized for that focus.

The main counterargument to breaking up products would be that, unlike in the one-app/web-to-rule-them-all product strategy, consumers may not know about all your digital products (did you know that Disney Parks offers a Play app?) and that is a valid argument. There are two ways to expose consumers to all your products in some fashion: app bundles and links (or deep links for mobile apps) between products.

The other concern is the proliferation of UI/UX styles, logins and profiles between these products that confuse or annoy a user of multiple products. Here, depending on how the digital efforts are structured, it's either a matter of governance (between different business units' digital teams) or coherence (inside the one digital team).[204]

Continuous Touch Points – Stay as Close to Your Customers as You Can

> *The true purpose of a business is to create and keep a customer, not to make you money.*

Theodore Levitt

It is intuitive that in the absence of an enduring and constant relationship with the consumers, you, as a service or product provider, may slip from their minds. In the absence of a memorable digital experience that has the loyalty of users, they may go somewhere else, especially for simple, transactional services.

The good news is that consumers really want close relationships, verging on mutual loyalty, with a small number of organizations, for simplicity reasons.[205] There are two ways to create *both* product usage (understood to provide most capabilities commonly needed to customers) *and* enduring loyalty and high-level of commitment.

First, there's no better way to create customer loyalty than by providing moments of gratification through *unexpectedly simple*,[206] *fast*, and *convenient* experiences *on a consistent basis*. Companies evolving from basic user satisfaction to user loyalty – and evangelism – put intense focus into carefully designing and implementing products and experiences. It's hard and it's expensive – probably 80% of the effort delivering the top 20% benefit (see also *How Good Is Good Enough* section). Deciding to go the extra 20% is a business strategy choice, rarely a digital product choice.[207] You can either chose to be Apple or Dell[208] – not both.

Second, your product must *follow and support* the consumer, in the qualitative ways described earlier, at *all stages of their journey* with your firm – from early adoption to maturity, from small interactions to big ones, from single step to extended interactions, etc. If you're present for your customer on some occasions but not others, they'll forget about when you can help and when not (too complicated to have inclusion and exclusion sets for an app or site) and they'll go somewhere else where they get the full and constant support.

That is why this section is called *Stay as Close to Your Customers as You Can* and not *Sometimes, Maybe, or Maybe Not*.

What does that mean in practice?

Start your users accessing your digital experiences by encouraging them to register for a digital account[209] in advance of a need, allowing them to interact in all future cases as a *known user*. That allows them to access their information and interactions in a timely fashion. From there, users may use your digital product in the morning to book an appointment, purchase a product or a ticket to an attraction, in the afternoon to check-in to the event, in the evening to check their status, and at night for any activities for the next day. These are all moments in the user journey that the product will need to support.[210]

New customers will only have awareness of their upcoming events (hotel stays, medical appointments, products being delivered, etc.) and marginal awareness of the larger product and as such must be kept interested by new and exciting upcoming capabilities as well as being introduced to features that they yet have to use. Established customers will have used more features through past engagements, but they still benefit from regular reminders of what is available but not yet used.

Delivery Channels or the Places You Go to Get Your Experience Out

You'll need to decide what technical channels you'll be offering your digital experience through. That is web-based (mostly for desktops but also mobile) or mobile apps or both. They could be on user-owned devices or company provided devices – think kiosks or iPads that you're offered in lobbies accessing a business or in a hotel or hospital room (including using the room TV and remote control).[211]

It may very well be the case that you'll have to offer all the above – if meaningful to your consumers – with users having the ability to switch between channels at different points of the journey through *continuity features* (booking an appointment or travel at home on desktop web and checking in the car on the way on mobile). Some users prefer mobile apps, some desktop web, some both at different times and places. Some have mobile phones, others don't, so some company-provided channel is needed.

And yes, some consumers can't effectively use technology because of unrelated limitations and others will adamantly want nothing to do technology (possibly due to previous frustrations with poorly designed and implemented digital experiences[212]) so you'll probably need to decide to offer in-person, paper/mail, or phone[213] support. And yes, those who prefer in person but aren't located in your geographical area may not become your consumers.

Defining a consumers/experiences-to-channels matrix could help you think through the decisions[214] of what you *should* do. Clearly the next step from that is to decide what you *could do, when and in what order.*[215] While multichannel and multi-platform parity is eventually important, the focus needs to be first on where the most important needs are or how the important customers prefer to interact with the firm.

Mobile First – For When Your Customer Is on the Go

As of the time of the writing of this book, I strongly recommend a mobile-first strategy.[216] I strongly believe mobile, as the tool and medium to accompany the consumers in all their locations, must receive special focus.

Consumers are mobile – not just in a physical mobility sense but platform preference – and so your digital offering must also be mobile. Of course, depending on your user's needs, mobile may not always be the best.[217]

Mobile needs to be understood not merely as a different form factor than desktop but one that is, well, mobile and location specific, where geo-location and interaction with the physical world[218] is fundamentally determining the function.[219]

Desktops may be more convenient to some, given screen sizes, but the power of digital will come through the ability to interact – sometimes physically, as in a tap or Bluetooth or NFC – and be interacted with at the time and place of need.

We did say that the goal is for consumers to be supported and helped by digital experiences and features at every step of their journey, including in-person steps. And since nobody is going to bring their desktop to your front door to use your web experience, mobile is the only way to go. Thus, mobile is that unifying focal point for all digital interactions.[220]

So, what makes for a good mobile experience?

Top of the list: real time integration with backend sources of data, especially Enterprise Medical Records systems (EMRs) and Enterprise Resource Planning packages (ERPs). That is true of all digital products, but it's kind of ridiculous to have a mobile app basically the equivalent of an off-line web form when consumers usually expect real time data and function on the phones.

Almost on par with #1 is the rule of *"Better search*[221] *and finding, not scroll or browse"*. Do you really think that consumers like scrolling among thousands of products on a 5-inch screen? At a hospital, or in the middle of an entertainment park in sunny, hot, and humid Florida, a user, looking for what they need with urgency, doesn't want to get vertigo scrolling through endless lists, menus, screens and taps when they are trying to execute a simple activity.

A mobile app experience is driven by a time/place/need context, guiding users through a small number of logical entry-points on the Home Screen, with a sticky bar[222] as the entry to larger self-contained stories. Navigation must be optimized for both the form factor and for finding and executing a transaction in the fastest way,[223] while you are on the go, at times and locations that don't lend themselves to time-extensive discovery. Mobile has location awareness and sensors to make the experience intelligent and context-dependent through end-to-end integration and very likely machine learning (ML) (see section on *Smart Digital Products*) to push relevant information and provide contextual functionality to users versus them pulling.

I am not a fan of mobile web simply because it doesn't provide a flawless user experience. Having to re-authenticate in the middle of an app because it's really a web view into another site and the experience doesn't provide SSO integration through Security Assertion Markup Language (SAML) between the two sites/apps is really *unnecessary*, in this day and age, and a bad experience. It is true that some users prefer mobile web to downloading apps, but that is less prevalent when they are looking for constant interactions versus one-offs – i.e., a relationship – making the investment of downloading an app worth the effort.

The user flows should not require back and forth between multiple screens, and it should be free of dead-end steps. If a flow is interrupted for whatever reason, the state of the flow needs to be saved for the consumer to be able to resume from where they stopped (technically, that should be the case in any channel, but even more important for mobile given higher level of attention interruptions). And if the consumer gets somehow stuck in a flow, a bot or rep texting feature should be available – at the point of the obstacle – as backup.

You, as the digital team, and your company must maintain control over your digital experience. Digital is your face to consumers who are not physically in front of your staff.[224] That pretty much makes mobile apps provided by vendors very problematic simply because there's little feature control nor the ability to augment well with your other data and functionality.[225]

But mobile-first doesn't mean mobile-only, so you likely must design for a multi-channel experience, including one in which different parts of the same journey may be executed in different channels.[226]

What about This *Metaverse* Thing – Whatever That Is?

Finally, with all the current hype around metaverse, it's fair to ask: What about the metaverse and Web 3.0? Where will it fit among all the other channels? Is it even a channel or something else altogether?

The reason this section is phrased as a question is simply because the metaverse, at this point in time, doesn't even have a coherent definition, let alone a clear and crisp implementation to describe a path forward.

It's conceivable that our current web and mobile interfaces will give way to richer experiences, based on A/R[227] interfaces, maybe controlled by voice[228] and powered by AI, with the hope those will more closely resemble our experiences in the real world.

So, instead of scrolling through a list of products on a screen, we will have the ability of seeing different pictures of the product (or service?) from different angles and maybe some videos to give us a more natural feeling of what the products are like, akin to walking into a store and picking up products for 3D examination.

Whether that experience would feel natural over extended periods of time is to be seen and probably subject to a lot of technology and experience evolution over time. And although the speed and direction of evolution of technology may very well surprise us, for now we should just wait and see[229] what makes sense not from a technology perspective, but from an experience viewpoint.

If a metaverse experience becomes superior to what we have today, it should be adopted in due course.[230]

The "Digital Product" and the "Consumer Experience" *Are* One

The consumer perceives the product as the path to what they want to get, buy, consume, or experience.

As such, what they evaluate is not only the digital tool (hopefully that is done well and serves the purposes of the consumer), but what they experience – *both* digital and physical – in their consumption journey. The digital tool and the physical product or service are faces of the same coin from a consumer's viewpoint. If the firm's operations providing the service or product fail – for example no product is available to purchase, or no medical appointments are available in the desired timeframe or with the preferred physician – then the brilliant self-servicing or self-scheduling app in front of those transactions is worthless.

App reviews in app stores (Apple's or Google's) often have ratings and comments that are *not* about the app itself but the underlying physical service. Some of those reviews about the physical part of the experience – the not-ready-at-arrival hotel room, the damaged state of a delivered product or a delayed delivery, the grumpy overworked medical staff – are bad and digital teams sometimes find that their app getting this feedback is unfair, with their day-to-day maniacal focus on digital.

However, the digital teams need to remember that in reality they, as the entry point into the journey, are responsible for the full experience, the one that is both digital *and* physical, all in one box. Congratulations to the digital team, you're also responsible for the customer experiences in the physical world. This sober realization leads to an important responsibility for the digital team: As the consumer advocate and the face of the organization to the consumer, digital teams must pursue the quality of the whole product, both digital *and* physical. While delivering digital is (mostly) within your control, the underlying service usually is not, but you, the digital team, are responsible for making *both* great. As such, you must actively work with operations – through influence – to maintain a good quality physical service.

It's *your job* to make the entire consumer experience great. Or be blamed if it's not. Accept that.

KPIs, if Chosen Correctly, Are Important

When talking about Key Performance Indicators (KPIs),[231] let us make sure we understand the fundamentals so we don't put the cart before the horse.

So, you have a vision, a strategy, and a number of milestones you set for yourselves to make sure you get to that El Dorado described by the vision. Then understandably, you need to see how you're progressing in your journey towards that point and against those milestones – in order to course correct and adjust along the way. For that you're needing to gather various metrics. Having metrics and goals is important.

The problem with metrics measuring your progress towards your vision, is two-fold. **First**, it is very easy to fall into the trap of measuring output and not outcomes. **Second**, metrics are necessarily going to be an imperfect measurement – a proxy, really – of your progress towards your customer-oriented goals. That is because your vision has to be bold but necessarily high-level. Yes, well defined milestones along the way help, but since you're shooting for complex customer outcomes, tracking quantifiable metrics, even in aggregate, is both a relative imperfect proxy and difficult -to-asses gage for how well it works out. Only asking every one of your consumers how they felt using your product personally would provide you the full measurement, but that's not feasible.[232]

So, when defining KPIs, you need to start with what your outcomes need to be by milestones. For example, you want your customers to benefit from using your product – that is why you built it in the first place! So, you measure app downloads and web and app logins, right? But just because the consumers downloaded the app and they logged in doesn't mean they're benefiting from it,[233] so you should measure next what features they're utilizing. Very likely you are going to be surprised about what they're actually using versus what they told you they're interested in.[234]

But when monitoring features, you must be granular. Just because they start a flow to obtain a service doesn't mean they'll finish that flow. Why? It could be that they're not interested in that feature after all, or it may be the experience is poor and they gave up in despair (that's bad, second only to the product "losing" customer transactions). Or maybe they can't get what they want because the business process doesn't give them what or when or in the quantity they need.[235] How detailed your KPIs and your measurements need to be, will be dependent of what is important to measure to assess progress towards your particular milestones.

However, there's a big danger that unrealistic KPI are set too soon in the lifecycle of a product, especially for a brand-new product and/or a new market. Organizations want to ensure they're getting their money's worth and that is OK – but that is only predictable for *established* products. When the product or market is new, or driving a significant strategic innovation, standard KPIs must be adjusted realistically, factoring in the maturity of the product and of the business strategy. Too unrealistically ambitious too early and it may kill your organization support for digital as the evolution will be slower than unreasonable expectations placed on it.[236] I talk elsewhere about managing unrealistic expectations.

These caveats aside, it's valuable for realistic KPIs to be set, simply to guide the product team towards the right actions and outcomes. Digital, like every other activity, once at a certain level of implementation, must be managed through metrics and KPIs.

There are two, somewhat overlapping, dimensions to track KPIs for. The **first** one is from the viewpoint of the consumer. That is very important, as convenience and satisfaction (measured in multiple ways) directly drive intent-to-return and, longer term, loyalty.[237] It's somewhat hard to measure, usually through proxy and as such imperfect metrics.[238]

Some common high-level examples[239] would be:[240]

Adoption:
- Mobile app downloads
- New users
- Number of visits per period and trends over time - such as monthly average users (MAU)

Engagement:
- Percentage/total number of customers active on the platform on a monthly basis executing a meaningful flow
- Time on app/feature continuous utilization
- Conversion rate
- Flow completion rate
- Basket size
- Friction – number of steps to accomplish a standard function
- Total minutes on product
- Mobile versus app usage
- Percentage of consumer interactions performed through digital versus phone
- Repeat users
- Ratio of new users/repeat users over time
- Churn – new users versus ghost users (previous users who stopped using the product)

Satisfaction:
- Net Promoter Score and app/mobile experience rating and feedback
- Moments of gratification testimonials
- Customer referrals (outside NPS)
- CSAT (customer satisfaction score)
- CES (customer effort score)
- Cart/flow abandonment rates
- Personalized offers

The **second** dimension is measuring from the organization's viewpoint.[241] Simplistically put: How is the digital offering benefiting the firm, especially from a financial perspective? Depending on the business and the nature of the digital experience – whether it's supporting a physical product or offering or, on the contrary, it *is* the product – there could be different metrics, but they usually fall into two categories of benefits. Either (mostly) labor savings: reallocate agents and front desk staff to other activities or eliminate through natural attrition. Or digital driving the increase of consumption of services or sales of the product.[242]

Of course, measurements are relevant only if compared to some meaningful goal, whether absolute (*e.g., X% of customers use digital channels versus in person*) or relative (*e.g., increase of Y% digital usage over previous reporting period*). The goal must help the firm achieve both the digital vision and the organization's.

Both dimensions and the exercise itself are important. They require focus, structure, measurement, data, and a *dedicated team* to collect and analyze.

What is also required is that the team is prepared to *actively* use the metrics – both consumer and operational – to drive improvements in digital or operations or both. For example, if you're a primary care provider and your digital channel tells you that most of your patients are looking for types of appointments (Medicare, new patient, regular checkup) that you don't have available, you should change the mix of appointments in the scheduling grid. If you do that, both your customer satisfaction and product and business metrics will go up, through higher usage.

"Smart" Digital Products

Digital in 2023 is not your grandpa's (as the expression goes) digital of 2010 (and neither is Buick, where the expression first started) where raw information and options were dumped onto the consumer, who then had to figure out how to find what they needed.

That means that digital must become intensely personalized, smart, and intelligent for the activity-on-hand, time, and place of the user. That leads to the need to combine with two adjacent technologies to enhance the experience: data/AI/ML[243] and sensors.

A simplistic example here would be your digital product "learning": what consumers are most likely to be interested in, depending on timing, location, past actions, etc., and showing that first or on the home screen/page. If the consumers check their transaction history first thing on Monday morning,[244] then that's what you should put in front of the them first, and so on.

To be clear, I am not saying that these two technologies have just supporting roles for digital experience. On the contrary, each has ample roles to play that need to be expanded, but making digital experiences better should be a priority area.

Revolutionary Versus Disruptive Versus Evolutionary

When you're about to make a new product that neither the marketplace nor your customers have encountered yet, you ought to shoot to make it revolutionary. That is, changing the existing paradigm in a way that makes sense and is highly needed.

There are two reasons for that, both simple. **First**, you must get your customer's attention somehow and the best way to do that is by providing something no one else has managed to do or at least not in the way you're trying to. **Second**, you have smaller risks if you fail when few know of you, compared to transforming an existing and possibly beloved product in ways consumers will hate.

Now, with that being said, you should try to not shock your customers just for marketing gimmicky reasons – they're not going to respond well to shocks. What you do is all about what will benefit the consumer the most.

Disruptive products are rare, in that they need to not only be revolutionary, but they need to completely upend the existing order of things in the marketplace. You don't attempt disruption just to promote your product, but because what the marketplace currently offers is really inadequate at meeting consumer needs and someone or something really needs to shake things up.

But let's be realistic here. Building a revolutionary product is very, very hard to do. You basically know next to nothing, have little else to learn from, try to create a brand-new story and narrative that consumers may not understand, at least initially, and your product marketing will struggle with positioning and messaging. Despite all the preparation work that you absolutely must do in any case, everything will be a gamble, with more failures than successes.

You will have to be ready to deliver very well – product vision-wise, not just technology – if you attempt a revolutionary or disruptive product, even if your consumers are ready for it (whether they know it or not). History is full of references to those who bit off more than they were able to chew. The iPhone was a success not only because of its revolutionary and disruptive nature, but because Apple, with years of successful product design and build, was able to deliver. As is often quoted: under-promise and over-deliver.

Not for the faint of heart. Not trying to discourage you, just setting expectations.

Evolutionary product releases are what you'll do most of the time. This is about adding new features – for your consumers to be able to do more things that add value to them – and improving existing ones – so the consumers can do those things better. This may not sound as glamorous as revolutionary or disruptive – who of us would not want to bring to the market an earth-shattering product such as the iPhone? – but it's nevertheless highly valuable.

What you can bring to the market is purely a matter of what is needed and valuable, matched with what you can deliver on *really well*.

Use Advanced Press Releases

Amazon has pioneered an approach that many have since adopted. The idea is to write a mock press release *before* the product is designed, describing the market to consumers, and to observers, what the product is about, what is it going to do, and why it will be good to have it.[245]

Now, that may sound counterintuitive to most people, as traditionally press releases have been written once the product is about to be launched, as part of its marketing campaign.

I think it's a brilliant idea. And the reason is equally brilliant.

Simply put, released at the beginning of the build but after the user research phase (that is always a requirement, that should be clear by now) and, possibly, after some high-level early design is done (for feasibility purposes), this advanced press release articulates in a crisp, newsworthy-like way, what the product/feature is about – and, by deliberate omission, what it's not – and focuses the digital team and keeps the detail design and implementation manically focused on what was articulated.

If a feature is in that simulated press release, once approved and aligned with user research by the team, it must be delivered. If it's not, it's probably an unneeded distraction not worth the effort and delay and shouldn't be done.

Products Not Projects – You Drive Products or You Don't Drive

Where we are seeking to bring something into existence, there is no data to analyze, which means that you have to create data through experimenting with prototypes. You have to create the data by prototyping-giving users something they haven't seen before and observing and recording their reactions.

Roger L. Martin

In the old days of the traditional "IT", the business stakeholders asked for and funded product implementation work to be done through individual "IT" projects, formed to execute on a request. This could be as simple as adding functionality to an existing product or, at the other extreme, implementing an ERP or EHR package. All so those stakeholders can run their operations. In this arrangement, "IT" was simply contract labor. Projects were about product stages.

At some point, even before digital came along, a big drawback of this approach became evident. With everyone focused on implementing new projects and (barely) keeping the lights on, nobody was really focused, at a tactical level, on other issues: proper maintenance, patching (including security),upgrades (unless there were new features in the package or application that again the stakeholders wanted and that would turn into another project), small enhancements, and bug fixes – which, although not glorious, enhance the functionality, or at a strategic level, on the lifecycle product management (from implementation, to retiring and replacement).

In some companies, nobody really knew who was responsible for these applications, as their original project team had long moved onto other projects, with the unfortunate consequence that underlying application knowledge was lost.

To compound the problem, software products have infrastructure dependencies – like servers and operating systems – so when these came out of vendor support there was no team to help with migrating the application onto new servers (and newer product versions). That's as close to data center as a zombie-land as you can get.

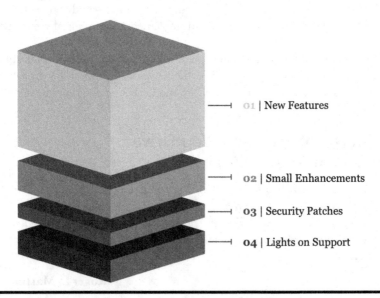

01 | New Features

02 | Small Enhancements

03 | Security Patches

04 | Lights on Support

Figure 2.11   Project driven, new features focused lifecycle.

Unfortunately, because of the problems highlighted above, this approach led to very "sick" products, where most of the effort had to be switched to keeping them running, with barely any bandwidth and funding for new growth, maintenance, etc.

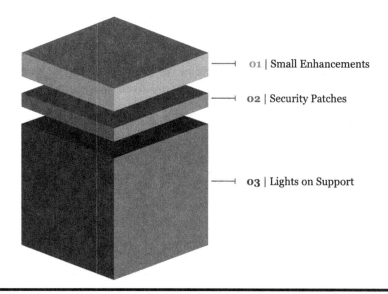

01 | Small Enhancements

02 | Security Patches

03 | Lights on Support

Figure 2.12   Lights-on driven, mostly reactive-focused lifecycle.

When it came to digital, with its fundamental focus on customer experiences and the products that support them, there are two additional, very big problems with projects driving digital products, especially in companies where the business-driven, project-based methodology was (and still is) very ingrained.

First, if projects are still the driver to deliver features, instead of consumer needs leading to product decisions, there is a danger of a mis-prioritized and fragmented product evolution because features (that should be what the customer needs) are still driven too much in terms of projects (what the organization wants). Not to mention that product maintenance and constant improvements are problematic to support.[246]

Second, if, every time there is a need for a feature, the digital team needs to navigate the project funding allocation process, even just to evaluate a need or do early stages of design thinking (aka project seed funding), then delivering anything in any stable and consistent way becomes very difficult. In addition, while parts of the digital team are invariably busy with constantly asking for chunks of money, the other parts are either waiting for the money (assuming you can pay their salaries while waiting for money) or stressed out about whether money will come and in sufficient amounts to support the product they know they need to deliver for customers.

That is a mercenary consultant model and talented product team members will not accept it for long. And when they leave, *both* product knowledge *and* consumer knowledge would be lost. Then you'll have to spend more money just to rebuild both.

What would be a sustainable, win-win solution, then? To address the first challenge, products and features should be the driver, evaluated for benefits to consumers, *followed* by an evaluation of the investment needed to deliver, looking from a firm's perspective at value and affordability.

To address the second challenge, the digital team ought to be allocated a lump sum to cover the *probable* cost of a product or major features *estimated* to be delivered over long enough periods of time – say a year (to coincide with the firm's accounting cycle) or, even better, as a program over the time horizon of the vision.[247]

But wait, you would say, how do you know what you will deliver over that time, especially if you don't yet know all the customer needs and how you are going to deliver if you don't manage it through the formal specifications of a project? Well, you don't, it's a best guess estimate, usually larger than what it will end up being, if you run your team's efforts well and you focus on outcomes, with no spurious output.

But wait, your nervous CFO or even CEO will say, if there is variability in terms of what will be done and how much it will cost, how do we know that what we are getting will be worth the money, that is, if we're getting anything, without the formal controls of a project? The cynical response– that I don't recommend giving, so keep it to yourself a validation of this approach – to that is that they don't know in the alternative project-driven approach either: They may get what (output) they paid for, but in the absence of all the unquantifiable fine tuning towards value that happens in the design thinking and other processes described in this book, it will unlikely deliver enough value to consumers for them to flock to the firm and give it their business. Not to mention that projects have their own delays and budget overages.

The answer comes from agile concepts, as well as the enlightened approaches to evaluate innovation ROI. As you go along through your iterations and features, there ought to be reviews of what was delivered (output), compared against the value delivered, *first* to consumers and *then* to the firm (both outcomes, factoring in the delay between the two). If they're *roughly* in line with what the *reasonable* expectation was, then you should continue. If not, you should adjust. Rinse and repeat with the next iteration or feature. In other words, prefer to evaluate after the implementation and user feedback versus trying to predict before in the absence of data.

If for accounting or other enterprise process reasons, this approach must be structured to work as projects (don't ask!) then so be it, as long the project is really a program with a broad mission and the project mindset doesn't once again take over the approach trying to control features. This distinction may be semantics in some places but could become a problem in others if the fundamental principle gets overshadowed by arbitrary project governance processes designed for yesteryear.

What is standing in the way of a product-driven versus a project-driven approach? Mostly organizational and financial legacy processes and mindsets. What can you do about that, other than articulating principles and facts? Ironically,[248] for a digital leader pushing for a change from project funding to product funding, physical construction efforts and their practices could be a working example of what I just described. When building a hotel, entertainment park or hospital, the construction teams don't have to break their efforts into mini-projects and justify, with funding requests, building every room or floor. They get the funding for the entire product and adjust as needed towards the end goal. Yes, they start with a design, but things change and evolve. Yes, overages happen (but in the digital model, it's a lot easier to adjust). And yes, finance departments are familiar with this approach.

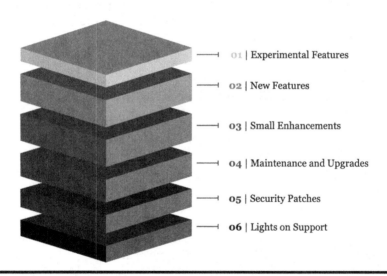

01 | Experimental Features

02 | New Features

03 | Small Enhancements

04 | Maintenance and Upgrades

05 | Security Patches

06 | Lights on Support

Figure 2.13   Product focused lifecycle.

In conclusion, don't manage digital through projects if you want a product that is well built, as well as supported and maintained. Digital is about experiences delivered by products, tuned over extended periods of time. With any other approach, quality, and fit problems will eventually be evident, especially to consumers.

Platform Versus Product – Build Platforms of Products

The consumer digital implementation ought to be a multi-channel platform[249] underpinning one or more products, that can be extended and reused.

These products could provide different functionality or serve different purposes: supporting consumers or staff, your individual B2C or B2B customers, or mobile and web for each, all operating on top of the same transactional and business rules-driven platform.

Platforms[250] are about reusability and economies of scale, but most of all they are about extensibility and opportunities for the future. Platforms can evolve and grow in somewhat unexpected but positive directions over time and that is the goal.

As such, when building your product(s), you ought to consider the evolution over time of your offering and focus on building a platform that you can use to expand your offering. Think big about your future evolution and, while you won't be building it all in one go and at the beginning, you must accept limitations to get things started, long-term you must think of how to grow the offering by building an expandable platform.

Product Brand and Company Brand

You build digital experiences for your customers, if that needs repeating, to enable and support them to consume your firm's (mostly) physical products and services. And so, your products and their brand[251] become part of the face of your company to the consumer.

The product and company brands are indelibly linked to each other. Normally, they support each other and reinforce each other in ways that customers *perceive* as natural and authentic. As such your digital product brand, for which you, as a digital product leader, are responsible for creating and developing, must reflect the perceptions of the company brand.

If the company stands for quality, customer focus, value, care, etc., then so must your product and the consumer's perception of it. The app stores are full of consumer feedback that say (maybe unfairly): "*How can such a great company like X have such a bad app?*" So, take note: If you work for a great brand, you must take extra care to avoid risking damaging its reputation with a bad digital product.

If the company has a sober reputation of being predictable in a boring way, your product probably should not show doodles, as it would be out of character (or be "off brand"). But if your company is the innovative startup that wants to change the world in a hurry, then by all means your digital product must reflect and reinforce that.

But brands are noticed only if they stand for something that is important or different that is worth remembering. An unremarkable company will find it hard to build a remarkable (in the sense of being noticed, remembered, used, and well regarded) digital product brand. Now, if the company takes serious steps to improve its brand somehow, your product brand will become important, and will support that improvement through consistency of message.

Of course, if the company brand is perceived as poor, your product, however great, probably won't be able to change that by itself, nor shake the negative influence of the brand perception onto your product. If nobody wants to buy or consume from the company, why would they bother with your digital product?

And for goodness' sake, choose a memorable name for your digital product, especially the app! A great name is a great start for a brand, especially in a crowded and noisy place like an app store. Don't call it "My *Company X* Mobile App".

Fight the Invariable "No, You Can't Do That"

For digital practitioners, always eager to provide consumers with the best experiences and willing to push the boundaries in a good and ethical way (see the section on ethics at the end of this chapter), there will be a moment when someone will tell you that you can't do what you need to do. That is the famous organizational risk aversion and inertia *"No, you can't do that!"*

Now, sometimes the pushback is legitimate. What you're trying to do, unknowingly, may be something that the regulators would come after you for with guns drawn or something that would allow criminals to use your product to scam your customers or would lead, in ways you haven't considered, to unethical outcomes. In those cases, you should listen to what others must say and weigh hard against any potential benefits. In my examples above, your decision should be indeed to ***not*** do it.

But then there will be those whose sole job is to preserve the status quo – those who would say *"we've been successful without what you want to do, why rock the boat?"* (to which you should say *"well, the boat is already taking in water faster than we can throw it out overboard"*).

The power of *"that is not how we do things around here"* should not be underestimated, but it should also not be accepted as the law of gravity – it can be defeated with perseverance, facts-informed-discussions, and proof of success.

In a previous life, I wanted to convert the digital platform my team and I built into an active-active operational mode. That is, parallel infrastructure running in multiple locations, serving requests independently across the internet.

Increased availability (unless all of the US internet was going down) and making use of infrastructure effectively versus an active-passive were very strong arguments for doing that. These days you get that from the cloud – with availability zones and regions – for *well designed and implemented* applications, but this was long before these days. I got a downright *"NO!"* from the networking team. You want to know why? Because they had other initiatives that were more important to *them* than this.

In all fairness, it's true that nobody at the time did what I wanted to do (I guess Andy Jassy was still cooking up his cloud capabilities at the time). So, the project did not happen when I wanted.

Guess what? I stuck with the idea and four years later when there was a data center migration initiative (still originally designed firm-wide to be active-passive), I pushed hard for the platform to be active-active, and I got that through. I would have to admit that in the intervening four years I a) kept the idea alive in senior executives' minds, b) built the applications in ways they could operate in such a mode, and c) built my team's readiness and credibility in a multitude of ways.

So, push back hard, don't take *no* as an answer when it makes no sense, and be ready with strong arguments. All of it will require sustained effort.

Which Comes First: The Product or the Process Transformation?

When you're advised by consultants on digital transformation they'll very likely recommend you start the process or business transformation first and then, once that is done, you bring the product to expose that transformed operational process to users. I guess, at some level, that may be intuitive: You don't start selling an electric car without charging stations and a business model to support charging.

However, there's a big problem with this prioritization and sequence approach. Without the product to *pull* the business along, whether due to organizational inertia and other priorities or lack of trust in the feasibility of the transformation or the product delivery, the organization will not start changing. They'll probably give you a polite version of *"call us when you have something for us to do something about"* – with the expectation that you'll never call them back as they expect you'll probably have nothing to show.[252] So, your product needs to become a towing hook for change.

Now, there will definitely be exceptions to this: either when the respective business unit's enlightened leader pushes for changes and they'll do whatever they need to coordinate with the digital team product delivery, or the business unit has severe problems – such as customers choosing not to purchase its services or products because of significant friction points.

There are two consequences here. **First**, it's usually up to the digital team to drive most of the transformation. Why them? Because they act on behalf of the customer and, if the customer needs something (that can be reasonably offered), they'll work to deliver it. **Second**, the digital team will use the product (in some advanced state of completion or maybe in a limited pilot with some real users) to drive the urgency of the change. The digital team will say: *"Here is our product, where is your process change?"*

And the digital team, which, remember, includes engineering, will then need to assist with whatever behind the system changes/upgrades/new implementations may be required to change broken operational processes: If your app or web site can now sell the firms' gizmos online, but the inventory system that was used for physical stores can't support online transactions (usually because of peak transactional volumes in the digital world that don't usually exist in the physical one[253]), then the backend system needs to be worked on – now with added urgency.

At this point, having heard the two arguments above, you'll probably say: *"I get why using the product to pull in the process change is needed, but isn't doing the product first and then waiting for the process transformation (probably through a technical systems uplift) to catch up unnecessarily inefficient and lengthy? And what about the Agile precept of minimizing work-in-progress when you have a whole product just sitting there?"* Of course, you would be right!

In a lot of situations, that long tail[254] of having to do all the other backend work that takes a long time can actually be mitigated. How?

First, process or technical workarounds,[255] while not pretty and increasing technical debt and possibly the operational load,[256] can support an early product launch.[257] The most common technical workaround is when you integrate with a replica of the transactional system, or when the digital service is supported from an off-line system; in both cases there may be outdated data challenges to be managed.

Second, it is possible that, for independent reasons (lack of business functionality, technical debt, etc.), that work is already in progress and maybe in an advanced state.

Outside systems work, what is left in that long tail is purely the organization's process change management. That, with enough effort, can be done in weeks, not months and possibly can be done gradually – for example, rolling out a capability incrementally to some locations or service providers.[258]

And the electric car analogy at the beginning of this section? The charger network was started *after* there was a car to sell and very likely funded *by* car sales.[259]

Long story short, use the availability of the product to drive the process change if the change is otherwise not forthcoming. It will do the trick nicely.

Are Your Products Ethical?

I placed this section on ethics towards the end of the chapter on product not because it's not important – it's very important – but to avoid the message being lost: Your product, whatever it does, must do it in the most ethical way possible from a consumer, employee, and other stakeholders' perspective. Ethical considerations extend not just to what your product actually does (like exposing or selling customer data to third parties) but also how your users may use the app (can it be used to bully other users or for illegal behaviors?) and what negative impacts may have for them (for example, driving addictive behaviors).

Beyond not doing harm, which is goal #1, ethics is about doing good. For example, by making sure your product supports disadvantaged people who may not be able to benefit from or afford your product's value, if it is (incorrectly) specifically designed only for the top-of-the-market (i.e., for richer people). Offering network-intensive digital products to people in areas with poor cellular reception or WIFI coverage is downright insensitive. How are those folks going to attend high bandwidth telehealth visits, especially when alternative transportation to an in-person visit is equally challenging?[260] Technology is supposed to make the world better.[261]

Making products that provide the best value in the most user-friendly way is not a license to overlook (potential) negative impacts.[262] What is ethical will be obvious most of the time, but it may be more difficult to discern in certain cases, especially with multi-purpose products and those open to large categories of consumers.[263] Keeping ethical issues in mind and having informed debates is important.

How ethical your product will be is a measure of the culture of your organization. If the organization doesn't care about ethics, that mindset will seep into your products, likely through pressure to cut corners. If that's what's happening, get a job elsewhere.

How Good Is Good Enough – Or When You Should Stop the Revolution

When you start, from scratch you will be in a mad rush to support as many of your consumers' needs, as well as possible. It will take you a good number of years to get in a decent place. You will probably have to catch up with what the rest of the world offers, for your consumers viewpoint. This is the *revolution* phase.

At some point though, you will probably meet your target customers' expectations reasonably well, in terms of both depth and breadth of experiences. Your efforts will start declining in returns, measured from your consumers point of view. Whatever you may add after that may become just clutter, reducing the value of what you have already provided. That is the point when it's natural that you should slow down, short of some extraordinary event that drives drastic new needs.

Slowing down doesn't mean stopping altogether, as the product is never finished. It just means doing less and more slowly and most likely focusing your team elsewhere. The product is mature and so is your team, foundations, and processes. That is natural and expected. In my career, it has happened everywhere that I've been and that was a sign that all previous efforts were successful. That is when the gradual *evolution* phase kicks in.

The question is: How do you know that you have reached that inflection point?[264]

Of course, one answer could be when the CFO/CEO/board says you can't spend any more money. Now, that is probably a bad situation because it is incongruent to your customer needs and thus probably arbitrary (although possibly legitimate given the firm's financial constraints). You should fight that by proving you're still providing meaningful value to you customers and, implicitly or explicitly, to the firm.

The more meaningful answer is by relying on both the vision and strategy and then the consumer. I suggested elsewhere in this book that you should start your strategy by defining how much you want to do for your customers – for example 80%, but not 100% of your customer needs (the percentages are subjective and driven by practical considerations). Are you there yet or close? If not, continue. If yes, slow down. Now, maybe since the strategy was defined, things have changed in terms of consumers' expectations, needs or business models and offerings[265] (for example, you now have physical stores not just online selling and consumers need to either order online and pick up in stores or buy in stores and deliver at home, etc.) or the marketplace at large. If so, you need to adjust the strategy accordingly, but making sure you don't do it just because you want to keep adding output.

The second part of the answer to the question of determining the inflection point is by evaluating meeting the target consumer's expectations: Do they have the majority of the capabilities that they value and use? Do they still struggle, in numbers and impacts, to do something important to them and their life stories? What do you hear from them, what do you see and measure? If the answer is yes, then you need to continue to fill in the gaps. But if the answer is *no* too many times you review this question and the needs are minor and incremental, that is when you, the transformational digital leader, needs to slow down and instead focus elsewhere. Yep, that time does arrive at some point, so be prepared for that.

That is also the point where you may need to rethink and restructure your team for a new reality. Some very talented team members will leave the team and even the company and that is OK. They can continue the revolution elsewhere and you should support that – you may even benefit from it yourself in the future as their consumer! Maybe they'll even go into healthcare and make the digital patient experience better when you next need a doctor?

Part III

The Digital Team

I strongly believe that missionaries make better products. They care more. For a missionary, it's not just about the business. There has to be a business and the business has to make sense, but that is not why you do it. You do it because you have something that motivates you.

Jeff Bezos

For any great product and experience to be created, all the ingredients discussed in this book – crisp vision, coherent and decisive strategy, design thinking approach, high-quality execution, etc. – must be great and come together in a cohesive and effective way.

But it all depends on one thing above everything else – the team that knows, learns, imagines, designs, solves, creates, and implements. This is the digital product team or the digital team in short.[1] They are the key to building up everything else, as without them *nothing* will ever happen.

The next chapter is about these wonderful people.

DOI: 10.4324/9781032644370-3

Chapter 3.1 The Digital Team Structure

What I'm best at doing is finding a group of talented people and making things with them.

Steve Jobs

For the first 35 years of software development, this is how things worked: marketing talked to potential customers and sales talked to existing customers and they each collected feature requirements.

The customer experience department used consultants and focus groups to glean what should be implemented. And when consumers were asked, they usually said one thing one day and one thing another.[2] Creative design was a separate team, usually an external creative/UI/UX agency. And "IT" implemented whatever it was required of them to "support the business." Different and disjointed internal teams were "contracting" with each other through formal requirements documents.

That is how we found ourselves with monstrous products almost impossible to use.

So, what changed? Three things. Technology has become a lot more ubiquitous and integrated, and it is a lot more important to design and manage it well. Then the Internet happened and that opened the firm's technology to consumers. And finally, powerful consumer devices like laptops and especially mobile phones burst onto the scene. With all these things happening, it became clear that the old ways simply could not scale and work well to meet consumer's expectations. So, we had to change.[3]

The approach that I have used that delivered good and great results was one with an integrated, stable long-term digital team, fully responsible for defining and implementing the digital product and the experiences it enables. This team delivers on all digital products and experiences. There are four components of this team.[4]

A **strong product management** capability that understands the customers and their needs. They're the ones who, as Steve Jobs once said, must start with the customer and walk back into the technology. They rally everyone else, are the closest to the customer, and are, ultimately, the keepers of the experience realm.

A **robust technology/engineering function**, using mobile and cloud, plus AI/ML for intelligent interactions. This team also participates in product research, evaluation, and debates, both experience and technology solutioning, and does it very well.

A **UI/UX design team** – remember UI/UX[5] is not only what the product looks like (and a good product must always look good), but *how* it works for the consumer.

Finally, a **structure to bring all this together**, operating efficiently and har-moniously[6] – organization design, roles, responsibilities, hierarchies, processes, communication, etc.

There are many ways to build this structure well, depending on the situation, but one rule prevails: these teams must never have divergent incentives, missions, and goals.[7] It's your role as a digital leader, through creating and implementing the proper organizational structure, as well as your constant presence and reinforcement, to make sure that disconnects never happen.

Digital Product Team Structure

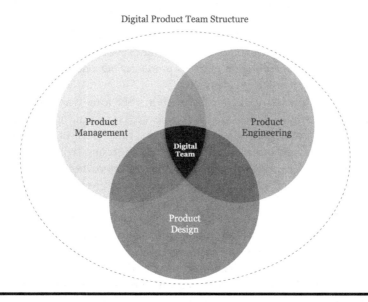

Figure 3.1   Digital team – intersection of product management, engineering, and design.

Before I go any further, let me enforce an important rule that, if not fol-lowed, will prevent all this from working well. I call these teams "components" of the digital team, *not separate* teams. While each has a dominant area of exper-tise and focus, they're all knowledgeable of and good at all functional aspects of the digital team. Yes, product managers may not know how to write code (although you would be surprised how many of them are actually former soft-ware engineers). Yes, engineers don't normally do consumer research, but they're avid users of digital experiences and are attuned to other users' needs and wants, so they are very informed and knowledgeable (as well as opinionated, which is good!). Same with creative designers – some have been involved in structures like these for long enough that they do design, user research, and they have seen what engineers can do, so they incorporate that in their thinking. The conclusion is simple: they all have great ownership, and you need to listen to them all.

In terms of designing the scope of each digital sub-team (if you have to have more than one), there are a few options, depending on the company, team size, or investment levels, as well as differentiation of products/sub-products or market segments.

You can have different teams focused on different products (e.g., the app/web for retail separate from the app/web for entertainment, or the app/web for HR vs. manufacturing, etc.), or on different customer segments (e.g., the app/web for B2C consumers separate from the app/web for B2B customers and the app/web for internal staff), or by digital channel (mobile vs. web). All these options are used and work for different companies, sometimes even a combination of models (different teams for different external products, but one team for multiple internal, employee-focused products, etc.).

Very likely when you start your digital efforts, the team is small enough and the focus is narrow enough that you have one team. As you scale up, though, you'll have to think of how to evolve, tune, and tweak over time.[8] And yes, the personality, experience, interest, and inclination, not to mention the team-playing ability of leaders and team members, sometimes can drive different approaches.

What are these folks like? People who are or can grow to be imaginative, solution-oriented, and problem-solving, working inventively around challenges of any sort, bursting with purposeful ideas they want to try out, courageous to take on challenges and risks, and curious and eager to understand the consumers and their problems, the company business as well as the technology.

These types of people always find a (good) way to solve anything. They are passionate about a better world, want to learn more in divergent fields, and optimistic that things will eventually turn out right. They constantly keep themselves abreast of new experiences and new technologies, even in unrelated domains and industries. They learn from their own experiences but also from others. They deeply, in their guts, empathize with the consumer and their problems – in the direst situations users may find themselves in[9] – and are always dedicated to the mission of supporting consumers with great products. They exhibit *esprit de corps* and thought leadership.

But the single rule for everyone is simple. They care deeply for their work and the customers' needs. Everything else, including learning what they don't know – and being at ease with that fact – is easy when they care. But if they don't care, it will show and consumers will notice.

And in case you think I'm asking you to search for digital unicorns, I'll say that you can find folks who, over time and with leadership effort and support, can grow and develop to be all that and more. Some have it in them but were never allowed or given the chance to show it – so find them.

Not everyone can or wants to become that. You, the leader, will have to weed out those and find the ones who can be that, get them on your bus, enable and empower them, and help them grow. One day you may work for one of them who has surpassed you. And that would be just fine, as you would have taught them well.

The Product Management Team

Be a creative person. Creativity equals connecting previously unrelated experiences and insights that others don't see.

Steve Jobs

So why don't we just execute exactly on what our business partners or consumer interviews tell us to do? Because business leaders or consumers can't design digital experiences. Most of the ultimately great solutions did not come from "the business" or consumers. Enter product management.

Product managers are the proxies for the customer or the end user. Their role is needed[10] on the team otherwise the customer's needs would get drowned out by the internal stakeholders' asks. At the table where business priorities are decided, they sit in the chair with "The Customer" tag on it and tell the user story.[11]

They research and find the needs, evaluate them with the rest of the digital team, create the definition of the product and features from the viewpoint of the consumer (aka user stories[12]). It's their job to ensure the product is successful, from a customer viewpoint, including post launch, enhanced, and sometimes adjusted through subsequent iterations and throughout its lifecycle. They do it through influence, not administrative oversight.

The product team works with the design team to make sure the experience is intuitive and usable, with engineering to get the product built according to the user stories and with marketing to help them craft the correct messaging (or even better, they'll be doing it themselves, unless organizational politics prevents them).

And, while looking at what others are doing is not necessarily the way to develop products, what customers experience *elsewhere* in their lives is definitely something the product team (and the digital team at large) should look at. Consumers expect similar convenience (we, humans, adjust easily to the good things) everywhere they go, so they'll judge your experience by the bar that Apple, Disney, Amex, and Amazon set. A mental model established elsewhere is *how* people will interact with your product.

They "own"[13] the product and have ownership[14] responsibilities. That simply means they'll do whatever is needed to design the product with the right features for the consumer – based on a deep understanding of the consumer – and get everything and everybody else going and make sure all is done the right way, from early understanding of the need, all the way to product messaging. In my digital teams, there are well-defined product managers that have these responsibilities, but I also look at everyone else in the digital team to also be "product" people.[15]

Truly special people. Applications welcome.[16]

Product Managers and Business Executives

> *It is always a team of people and the chemistry between that team of people, that makes great results.*

> **Steve Jobs**

Product managers will have to prove to the stakeholders whose support they need that they profoundly understand the business and industry, its goals and constraints, technology (present, future, and trends), and competitors, in addition to understanding the customer. They need to establish a mutual trust-based relationship so they can confidently communicate sometimes "no" answers to stakeholders.

Most product managers will have hierarchy titles no higher than director or assistant vice president and usually lower than the operations and business executives they work with. That is a power imbalance that, if not addressed, can lead to undue influence of business folks over what the consumer needs (remember, product managers are proxies for consumers).

For the **H**ighest **P**aid **P**erson **O**pinion (HIPPO) not to prevail, product managers need to come out not only very knowledgeable and prepared but with the full open and public support of the Chief Digital Information Officer (CDIO) – which in itself should be a very senior role in the organization. That should not be very difficult, as the CDIO should play the chief digital product officer role. The CDIO should be the one reaffirming to business leaders that consumers come first and that product managers act on behalf of consumers, and thus they need to be listened to when it comes to product decisions.

The Engineering Team

Whether code needs to be written, or components must be integrated, and the whole package must be deployed and managed appropriately, you need engineers on the team. And pretty good ones, at that. Hoping that someone else externally (like outsource development and integrator companies or product vendors) will completely do that for you and you don't need to manage engineers lead to largely mediocre and unsatisfactory outcomes for two major reasons.

First, splitting the vision, strategy, and design from execution is arbitrary – they're all part of the same whole – and you can't glue the two parts with a legal contract with a third (engineering) party that will probably not understand the vision, design, and consumer well enough and that, very likely, will suffer from agency, mostly profit but also possibly IP,[17] agendas.

Second, which sometimes comes as a surprise to some, is that talented and enthusiastic engineers sometimes come up with the best product, feature, or experience ideas and solutions – and that is because they're usually avid (and impatient with poor solutions) digital users themselves and also because they can think of solutions to support whatever product-related idea they may come up with.

Engineers, by definition, find solutions by writing code and/or integrating components in often creative and imaginative ways. You can empower them by always pushing technical decisions down to the lowest level that can make and implement them competently and timely.

Doing engineering well is hard,[18] especially for an organization that doesn't have any tradition of it, but that is no excuse for crimping your success from the get-go by not doing it. If you want quality engineering, go and build the capability as needed and don't take the easy way out of delegating the whole effort to external parties.[19]

There are many ways the engineering team can be structured, especially from an organizational reporting perspective. But the rule is simple: the engineers working directly on the digital product must be close to the product and creative people. Otherwise, you run the risks outlined above on using external third parties.

Specifically for engineering, you can organize the team into two major ways. The **first** is reflecting the modern layered architecture: the UI team (developing or integrating mobile apps and web pages), an experience service layer team (developing or assembling services that specifically support the UI layer and usually translate between the backend domain architecture and data model and what and how the consumer needs to consume data and transactions), the enterprise domain services (sitting in front of databases or systems of record), and the shared infrastructure team (providing the data center or cloud infrastructure services). The **second** is to have one single vertically integrated technical team for each distinct product.

The advantage of the former is the ability to scale teams independently and share artifacts between products, but it comes at the cost of increased coordination between teams. The advantage of the latter is simplified interactions but introduces challenges with scaling and requires engineers to master the full stack – from HTML/Javascript/Flutter all the way to cloud deployments and tools – which is very difficult to find.[20] Both models are viable if managed well, but all things being equal, I've seen better results with the first model.

In order to support digital, especially a fast introduction and evolution, your organization very likely must (re)build up its technology foundations. Cloud helps immensely, so do Agile, scalable reference architectures and application and provisioning infrastructure, but so does having robust and modern backend systems that you can integrate with. Trying to build a real-time digital experience depending on a 20-year-old batch system that has no APIs (or concept of them) is pretty much an exercise in pushing a rock up the hill – not impossible, but very hard and time-consuming, thus frustrating for the impatient digital folks and their customers.[21]

So, you as a CIO/CDIO must make sure that building the foundation is happening through either workarounds or expensive but necessary system upgrades.

The Designers Team[22]

A designer knows he has achieved perfection not when there's nothing left to add, but when there's nothing left to take away.

Antoine de Saint-Exupéry

There's a common misperception that user interface (UI) and user experience (UX)[23] are all about what the product looks like. And indeed, more tastefully looking products tend to be more successful, simply because most users, attracted by the looks, tend to be more forgiving of gaps and lapses, at least for a while – but not always and definitely not forever. So, by all measures, make beautiful products.

However, what is important in the long-term is how the product *works*[24] *and what it feels like to users.*[25] What emotions, good and hopefully great but also possibly bad, does it arouse? The product must create a feeling of serenity that it will help the consumer solve whatever problem they need solving, finding, and buying the right product at the last minute before a birthday they regrettably forgot about, or for getting medical care in the panic moments of a health emergency. Systems should perform like reassuring humans would – they provide what needs to be done and will confidently guide so that customers don't have to worry and stress about spurious details. They should convey the "Don't worry, I have you covered. All will be well" message.

There are many factors that influence designing a reassuring experience, some driven by assets or capabilities[26] or, on the contrary, by limitations or constraints.[27] The design and its quality are definitely the most important aspects to make the experience desirable.[28]

The designers have their focus on understanding what makes users feel good about a product and creating that simple, as friction-free as possible, usable interface that conveys that serenity and assurance. This definition is not what one could put in a job description to hire a designer, but it's certainly what must come out of the interview with a prospective candidate.

In addition to deep empathy,[29] great product interfaces require four other things.

First, an *obsessive attention to details*; small as each detail may be, in aggregate they can either build up to a great or, instead, an abysmal experience.

Second, a *deep expertise in consumers' mental models* of similar experiences and common design frameworks. Unless a very uncommon interaction model is the only way the product works for a very unusual application, always present to the user experience elements[30] that they're familiar with. Use as much of the conventions the platform your product is deployed on – Mac, Windows, iOS, Android, etc. – as you can.

Third, for designs to be valuable, designers must be *familiar with the technology and what it can do and how*. A cookbook writer must know how to cook, their recipes, and others', so they understand what works and what doesn't.

Fourth, designers must be *aware of the environment* their consumers and products operate in – what is special in that environment, unseen needs and opportunities, constraints, and limitations, what else in that space influences consumers, their needs, and their behaviors – and thus how they would, likely, use the product. This is what we call ethnography that, in most places is underrated, although it shouldn't be.

But I also learned, as a product designer, that in order to be great when designing specific products, you must constantly exercise your creative mind on *all* products you encounter, not just the ones you design and build yourself. For designers, every encounter with a product or experience is an opportunity to evaluate its qualities: how good or bad it is and why, and what would you do to make it better. As a bonus, not only does that mindset keep the creative muscle trained, but occasionally you learn new and better ways to do things in your own designs.[31]

User Research Product (Sub)-Team

Talking to consumers all the time requires skilled product management folks – or a specialized team of them – to keep the engagement going. You'll need to deliberately create that team for this dedicated purpose so you can learn all that you can about your customers. The day you stop talking to your customers and you stop watching what they do, then learning and adjusting your product, that is the day your product is starting to go down the drain.

Who are the people who would fit well into this team? Well, they need to be curious, solution-oriented, empathetic to the extreme while being realistic and knowledgeable of the grander vision and strategy, detail- and meaning oriented.

They'll need to figure out where your customer is and needs to go from there, in order to learn what should be offered next. If you have a physical operation like stores, entertainment parks,[32] doctors' offices, and urgent care centers, well, that is where these folks need to be on a constant basis, interacting with actual consumers trying to use your physical and digital products.

Somewhat out of the box, I look for my user research team to also do industry research: trends in consumer needs and wants, evolutions in user experience, industry or leading institutions' approaches to experience, new technologies to address known problems, etc.[33] Up to you if you want to put that scope elsewhere, but your digital team should have it *somewhere*.

Now, this team is not only expected to skillfully gather insights, but then analyze and make sense[34] of them, come up with proposals for improving the product and the experience. Those proposals can then can be taken through the evaluation and vetting process (discussed elsewhere in the book).

The "Other" Teams Are Very Important

Building digital experiences requires the support of other teams besides the digital team that can provide guidance, active engagement, and support on both business processes and goals. I include here the business stakeholders – who provide the physical service and product that the digital experience enables or supports – the legal and compliance team, who keep you and your product out of legal and compliance trouble,[35] procurement, who help you get the services and products needed for your own product, the human resources team who assist you in rearchitecting your team,[36] vendors, and partners who help with products and resources.[37]

Out of all these, the business stakeholders are the most important. Not because you should follow blindly what they say and want,[38] but because, in reality, you negotiate with them on *behalf* of your customers. That negotiation must be mutually satisfactory to lead to positive outcomes – they get business outcomes and results, and you (that is, your customers) get a better experience.

All these groups are important, and it's part of your job as a digital leader to get them aligned to your efforts. We will talk later in the book of very particular groups who have outsized beneficial impacts to your success, as they had for mine. But it's never easy, and at times it can be very frustrating to actively engage and enroll other teams in your efforts. That is when you must remember what you do is not a job; it's a mission.

Chapter 3.2 Digital Team Processes

The people who are crazy enough to think they can change the world are the ones who do.

Steve Jobs, Think Different Advert, 1997

New Team (aka Storming and Forming)

When you start from scratch and there's *no* digital team to speak of and yet there's a strong need for urgent delivery (driven by immediate consumers' needs), you, as a digital leader, will need to do three things.

First, and that is obvious, you'll need to assemble a digital team, the best one you can, given the circumstances. That doesn't sound cheerful, but it may be the only thing you can do with what you have. Well-functioning digital teams don't grow on trees, as they say, but you'll need to make do with what you have at the beginning while you patiently build your dream team.

And that leads to the **second** task at hand: you'll need to work hard and take that team and grow and evolve it over time. Define the structure and populate it. Create a team spirit. Help the team members grow in understanding and skill-set. As a leader, you'll need to be very hands-on[39] during this period. While you can and should delegate decisions and actions, expect that you'll need to step in often, while offering learning opportunities to your team members.

This is a time for you to be a mentor and a teacher, not a demanding leader. That will come later after you make the thoughtful investment in time and training. This is the time of less envisioning and strategizing (that you would have done earlier) and more sleeves-rolled-up doing.

Third, while you're doing all this, you'll need to appreciate the limitations that this team will have for a good while as they learn and adjust, individually and collectively. You'll have to help them through growing pains, while they come together (under your gentle but firm direction) and find their cadence and inner collaboration processes. And while all this is happening, you'll have to fill in for them, so be detail-oriented and prepared to put in the hard work.

Team Structure Evolves Over Time

I described the structure as roles and responsibilities, hierarchies, processes, procedures, communication channels, etc. Some of the roles and processes are detailed elsewhere in the book. For others, I will not go into deeper detail as they'll be different between organizations. But there are a couple of points worth making here.

First, each leader and team must find a good balance between a relatively stable structure and a constantly fluid one. With a too rigidly stable structure, the team's efforts are unnecessarily hampered when conditions, both inside[40] and outside[41] the team, change. On the other hand, constantly changing the structure will only ensure everybody is constantly confused about how they're supposed to operate.

Second, especially in a growing team, the structure will have to evolve in different ways over time. That's natural, expected, and needed. In one of the big initiatives I was responsible for years ago, the team went from a core team of 5–6 people (myself included) to some 150[42] in about a year. You don't operate a team of 150[43] or even 50 the same way you operate a team of 5, most of whom are all physically located in a small conference room and where everybody necessarily does a little bit of everything.

Growth is good when it's a reflection of the team successfully providing increased value (as long as it's not just inefficient bloat), but it has its challenges. Communication among more team members becomes more complicated and it can't continue to be done as a quick and impromptu huddle in that small conference room; instead, it needs to be done through tools,[44] protocols, and large town hall-like settings.

The bigger the project, the more likely that specialization of roles is required – engineering, product management, creative, a variety of specialized sub-teams, etc. Complex coordination mechanisms between multiple teams, possibly remote or global, will be required.

In those situations, the leader *and* the team must be prepared to look out for the need to evolve, with one eye on the present need and the other on the likely future need – to meet both at the same time, as much as possible, so the structure doesn't constantly change in a fast-growing team nor is stagnant. The leader must keep that duality in mind, but the discussions on why and how to best change must be collective and not come as leader's edicts and definitely not out of the blue.

For anyone who has experienced the camaraderie, diversity of work, and speed of execution of small teams, it could be sad and unnerving to go to what will inevitably be a slower and somewhat more impersonal structure as the team grows and gets more specialized. But changes will absolutely be required in order to deliver on increasingly bigger needs and products.

However, there are nice touches leaders can apply to still keep the humanity of interactions and team cohesion. I have always done a lot of town halls with my entire team or large chunks of it (used to be limited by how many people can fit in large auditoriums, usually 500, but Zoom helped with hybrid, both remote and in-person, approaches). My direct reports and theirs' do the same with their own teams.

Every year I do a "CDIO Awards" team-wide meeting to celebrate the best projects, teams, and products of that year. As a secondary benefit, more than once, the event planners, who never knew they had the talent and desire to become product managers in them – the event is a product, after all – become just that. Beside team celebration, fertile ground for product managers-to-be to find their calling.

Diverse Viewpoints Are Priceless

I have spoken and written elsewhere about the importance of having diverse viewpoints on the team – the digital product team or any other team. But I think it needs to be reiterated here. You need the diversity for two different reasons, both driven by logic.

First, because your (target) consumers are diverse – needs, wants, history, demography, race and gender, cultural, sexual orientation, etc. Only a team that is diverse can successfully identify, empathize, and be adequate proxies for your consumers.[45] That is not identity politics; it's a fact.

Second, people with diverse mindsets, experiences, expertise, and skills will be able to design, based exactly on familiarity with diversity, a more informed, imaginative, intelligent, and robust solution, one that can better satisfy your customer needs. And to satisfy your customer needs, you must have a strong digital product team.

Agree and Commit, Disagree and Commit, or Get Out of the Way[46]

There are multiple versions of this principle. But what they all mean is that there's a time to debate, when some agree and some disagree, then there's the time to decide, but once the decision is made, *everybody* commits to implementing it.

The decision cannot subsequently and constantly be revisited and re-litigated – *unless* there's *significant* new data that questions the decision in some fundamental way. Re-debating a decision already made kills positive forward movement and introduces a level of organizational politics that, over time, becomes absolutely toxic. Yes, some decisions may turn out to be wrong or slightly misdirected, but in those cases, experimenting, prototyping, launching, and learning are the way to settle arguments, learn, and improve – or change past decisions.

Where you will want to be to make progress toward great products and experiences is somewhere in between consensus, at one extreme, and disunity in commitment, at the other.

Without this principle working well in your organization, there's no moving forward and the organization is paralyzed. Not a good place to be.

Leaders need to make sure they create the conditions for an open and vigorous, data- and insights-based (not unfounded opinions) debate that informs the decision, but then they must also enforce[47] with all the team members that there will be no backroom conversations challenging the decision just because some folks don't like it, or it is not aligned with their narrow agendas. Those not liking the decision and not wanting to execute on it should find other employment.

While most people agree with the value of the outcome – decision and action – some have concerns about the debate process, specifically in extreme conflict-averse or command-and-control companies where some may not have the courage to speak up and debate, therefore depriving the decision of useful insights. Yes, those places exist. However, I would venture that it is not a problem of committing, but is a lack of company openness and team members' courage.

To those lacking the courage to express opinions, I offer one of Amazon's leadership principles: "Have Backbone; Disagree and Commit". If you have no backbone, you stand for nothing and you should expect nothing in return. Fortunately, missionaries – the ones your team is made of – always stand up for what is right.

Remote Teams and Team Members

With the pandemic, we have explored a fully remote model of work, at least for white-collar workers. But in truth, some of us have had remote teams for years – across the country or the globe. They may have worked in an office, but it was a *different office*.[48] Even in the same city, locations may have been miles apart.

Traditional agile development has always focused on team members being collocated with each other – as in the same office. The reasons were simple: collocation increases collaboration opportunities, serendipitous encounters lead to interesting and novel ideas, reduced reaction times, etc.

That ran afoul of the off-shore outsourcing model that many IT organizations have been following since the turn of the 21st century, for cost-saving or talent-availability purposes – given the difficulty of finding talent, especially in a narrow geographical location and also the availability of talent in different locales. Having remote teams and team members has been definitely attractive.

So, what's one to do? Here is what I would say.

While colocation benefits are real – in theory and *if* done well – the realities of distributed talent are more poignant, so, unless the team is small, a digital leader must get used to the idea of remote teams and team members, take advantage of the talent availability benefits, and work to mitigate any distance or time zone challenges.

Most of all, you need to improve communication through constant interactions. If you hadn't been doing it already, you must become a great "connector", ensuring that information flows to everyone needing it, including by creating occasions for serendipitous (remote) interactions.

Working Meetings Are to Get Results, They Are Not Social Events

Digital teams, once well stormed and formed, must find their natural rhythm. Part of that will be a cadence of meetings to discuss and debate user research findings, design and plan decisions, and delivery status updates. What those are will be subject to the individual team's situation, velocity, people, and styles.

I have a *monthly* meeting with all the digital stakeholders in the company so that everyone is clear about what the team is doing, why, and (*directionally*) when and in what order. This meeting is heavy on updates on status and plans but light on requests (that must follow the evaluation process discussed elsewhere).

The actual core team meets *twice a week* to discuss findings, features, UI/UX, and planning. This is the more strategic part of the digital product sausage-making. This can have other stakeholders for any high-level feedback.

For the upcoming one or two releases (three to six weeks), the team meets *daily* for status updates and tactical resolution of issues. The team will also use these meetings for any more strategic topics that may require a timely discussion and *immediate* decision.

In addition to these meetings, there are countless user research sessions and business process change management processes (multiple times a week plus impromptu issue-solving meetings).

Delivering digital at speed and with quality is definitely intense and time-demanding. If you don't appreciate that, either things will be slow or the resulting work will be of low quality or both.

Core Team Size: Large Crowds Are Not for Debates and Decisions

A question that is often on people's minds is how big should the team be? Usually, the question is about the core team that deliberates the consumer needs and product features and team activities.[49] The one that the chief product officer (i.e., the CDIO) should actively chair.

The answer is: as small as possible – 10–12 at maximum. The reason is simple: more than that number and the conversation becomes unwieldy and not very effective. The people at the (possibly virtual) table should be able to collect and rationalize the best points from their teams to be discussed in these meetings. The reality is that, even in the biggest and best companies that do product management well, their product decisioning teams are still small.[50]

Occasionally, especially in organizations that are fixated on broad participation and when stakeholder team members are worried about Fear of Missing Out(FOMO), these meetings can become larger. That is when finance, marketing, HR, operations, etc., can get involved. The interesting thing about this style of meeting is that, despite the multitude of participants, it's only still (the meaningful) handful that participates in the conversation. Those meetings provide the rest of the participants with a good understanding of the topics discussed and the actions agreed upon and timelines.

One could argue that for all those who don't provide value to the discussion, participation is a time-consuming way to get updates.

That is fine with me, as long as the team is moving ahead with quality and speed.

Chapter 3.3 Digital Leaders Managing Digital Teams

A leader takes people where they want to go. A great leader takes people where they don't necessarily want to go, but ought to be.

Rosalynn Carter

Recruiting and Retaining Talent (Aka *the* People)

Robust talent and great teams are really the most important assets to have. Not just for digital, but for any endeavor. I have always said that if I have the people and the teams,[51] I can figure out a way to do almost everything and with people, teams, and a vision, I can get the funding and the organizational green light to do it.

But it takes a lot of time and effort from you as a leader to build stable and well-functioning teams of highly talented and motivated individuals. Yet, it absolutely must be the end goal.

Building a digital process and technology expertise is a very big challenge, especially in organizations without a background in digital technologies and associated processes and tools. You can't retrain an entire non-digital workforce overnight, or even in a year, moving them from doing legacy product sustainment to modern digital product and development.

When you don't have the luxury of time for building the team organically – and most of the time you don't – you'll need to look outside for talent in the short term. Yet that is also challenging in talent-crunch times. Hiring talent externally will come with its own problems of having to build customer, product, process, and lay-of-the-land knowledge. Unfortunately, while you must do all that, consumers won't care about your challenges – they only care about what they're getting when they expect it.

The singular best way to attract and retain great talent is to have a compelling organizational vision and mission that people want to be associated with, even if implementation is over the horizon. Money is important, but most people are willing to forego some of that for a great cause, like "transforming healthcare through consumer centricity".

Select candidates carefully for strong technical talent but, most importantly, for growth *potential*. I try to imagine how candidates are going to rise to future challenges. Look for people who are curious and imaginative, willing to learn and grow, with strong values, as diverse as possible, and with a strong team work ethic.[52]

One interesting thing about recruiting is the fact that the world is relatively small, so there's a high chance that potential recruits will know about your organization and its values. If so, these elements will recruit for you, but only if the mission of your group and the firm's values are enlightening.

Hiring for "fit to culture" is a faulty approach, however well-intentioned it may sound, as it will lead to either reinforcing the past (possibly stagnant) culture on one end or discriminating against diversity at the other end. So, the only "fit" is to hire for potential and proven ability to learn and adapt and be excellent, while avoiding self-centered jerks (aka, the unredeemable).

As to interviewing, the more senior the role, the more conversations are needed to get the right evaluation. First impressions are at best 50% accurate, which is to say they can't be relied on. While the interview questions are designed to uncover important aspects of the candidates' skillsets and personalities, I don't believe in superscripting them, as that may miss both good and bad signs and facts that a more open, unexpected discussion can show. An open conversation where the candidate asks questions can show a lot of what they want or fear.

Now, to retain these great people, the culture must be true to its promise and not another facade for other organizational agendas. Don't advertise the goal of changing the world when your firm's goal is maximizing profit.[53] As a leader of the organization, be truthful to your word and keep the commitments. Invest time and effort in your people's development – mentor and teach them. As they grow, stretch them by gradually giving them more trust, standing, autonomy, and responsibilities.

At some point, the team and its leaders must deliver on the promise of an inspiring vision, hard as that may be. While most people signing up for great causes don't expect park promenades, they do look for great outcomes sooner rather than later. So, don't take too long to deliver.

It's also likely that along the way some folks realize they do not really want what they signed up for or they change their minds and leave. That is OK and not to be feared.

You must define the expectations for culture and values. A great clarification would be answering the question: *What does this team stand for?* (Customer-focus, exceptional engineering, execution excellence,[54] "do the right thing", caring for each other and for what they do, etc.). The team must have a set of clearly stated operating principles (not rules) that everybody must embody without thinking. The more powerful those principles, the easier it is to recruit like-minded folks into the team.

As a leader, you'll also need to guide and support your team members on their personal growth and aspirations. Their growth and career will always be their own responsibility, but you'll have to be there to support and guide them. Some of your original team members, from when the team was smaller, will grow with you and the organization, while others will not, either because they don't want to, or they love being an individual contributor or a small team leader.[55] And some want to grow but can't find it in themselves to be able to do it, no matter what you, as a leader, do.

Leaders Must Ensure the Best Ideas Will Win

Senior product executives must be closely and extensively involved in the digital design and development process. And, among other reasons, that is because they must ensure *the best possible idea wins*, theirs or anybody else's. It's their responsibility. Without that, politics and agendas, delays, and confusion can bog down the process of delivering fast – by sub-optimal decisions or "offline"[56] agreements.

As such, the role of the leader is threefold.

First, to provide the forum for informed but vigorous debates, where all meaningful viewpoints (from whatever levels) are expressed freely and fearlessly and evaluated on their fact-based merits. Especially for more junior folks, debating with someone that has Chief and Officer in their title can be intimidating. That Chief something Officer must make efforts to ask for those ideas by *encouraging* everybody to come up and express them. The executive must make sure all available data is considered, and all viewpoints are presented and argued on their merits and with arguments, not based on the power of the title. A little bit of humorous self-deprecation from the Chief something Officer doesn't hurt.

Now, as I said many times elsewhere, the sausage-making of figuring out and designing and implementing something is usually messy, but that is the most effective way to get great results.

The leader doesn't have to be right all the time; they just must have a successful team and product. That is what they're judged by.

Second, while the debate must be healthy, at some point someone will need to decide and possibly break a tie. Maybe sooner rather than later if that is what is required – but not too soon. Analysis paralysis is a corporate disease when leaders don't have the courage and determination to take calculated risks by making decisions. But making decisions *is the responsibility of the leader*. Sure, the leader must articulate how they made that decision – so everyone is clear and understands the weighting of arguments – but it should be always clear they made it because they believe, after open examination, that it is the best idea presented.

Finally, make no mistake, that digital executive has to know what they're talking about. They must themselves understand and empathize with the customer, they must develop a sense for the product, and they must put delivering the best product for consumers ahead of most other things, especially narrow agendas. And when they have gaps, they must develop a web of trusted advisors – hopefully the entire digital team – to rely on for honest, unfiltered, and competent advice and feedback.

Delegating Responsibility: You Can't Do It All by Yourself

As a senior executive, you get paid to make a small number of high-quality decisions.

Jeff Bezos

There will be many decisions to make, big and small, about your product. One leader cannot possibly make them all (and they should not even try) and so they need to delegate to others.

The rule on delegation is twofold and dictates the probable impact of each decision at hand.

First, if a decision is low-impact – to consumers or the company – or easily reversible, then the responsibility should be delegated to the lowest level in the team that is capable of making that decision fast and competently with the data they have. That is to benefit from a higher quality of detail in the decision-making process, as well as speed (so decisions are not bottlenecked). An added benefit is that delegating decisions will help those lower levels get more experience and confidence for when they become senior level and get to make big decisions.

If too many such decisions bubble up to senior roles, then either those lower levels are not provided with the right information and context, or they need help to grow professionally. That is where the digital leader and executive should focus, not making all the decisions themselves.

Second, if a decision is of high impact and difficult to walk back or recover from, then it needs to be made by the most senior leaders, after discussions and evaluation of data and options with the larger team. The decision maker needs to be transparent on the thought process used to derive that decision, otherwise they will come across to the rest of the team as arbitrary.[57] These decisions take time that should be taken to make the best of them. Fortunately, big and impactful decisions are usually not the majority.

But if it turns out that many such decisions need to be made constantly by senior executives, then either the vision or the strategy is not sufficiently clear – and the digital leader and the team need to step back and revisit those for clarity – or the leader doesn't delegate enough and effectively.

I take Jeff Bezos' reference to quality to also include impact. Leave less impactful decisions to others, but if you don't yet have those others, you need to compensate for them yourself – until you have them.

Notes

1. Some authors, probably more traveled than I, call this the product team. I choose to use Digital Team for two reasons. First, this team really is responsible for all things digital inside a company and in my experience that structure works well, for a variety of reasons. Second, the product team and product management can get confused and may imply that other critical teams to the digital product, such as engineering or creative, are separate and somehow not as important to the product management team, when in reality they're all sub-teams of one team. A great team.
2. See Tony Fadell's book, *Build*.
3. A lot of companies still work the old way. Look for bad digital products, and you'll identify those companies.
4. Remember though: there has to be a wise balance between the size of the team (as in a number of individual team members) that brings many voices, which is useful, and the overhead of communication and coordination among too many participants, which gets more complex with size. The more team members, the slower the team moves. I have seen, in organizations where everybody was devoured by FOMO (Fear Of Missing Out), committees of 40–50 people. They discuss (not so much as debate), they never reach any conclusive decisions, and they drive no progress. Avoid that model like the plague, as it's the antithesis of the fast and nimble product evolution that consumers expect. Any discussion must lead to a decision that must be outcome-oriented in some measurable fashion and binding.
5. UX (User eXperience) is about designing the experience of using a product. Good discussion on UI/UX can be found in *Bright Ideas for User Experience Designers* by Davis Travis/Userfocus.
6. By that I don't mean consensus as in long-term compromise – that is a recipe for mediocrity – but through a good and open debate where everyone has an equal voice, followed by firm decisions, commitment, and concerted action.
7. This is as much of an art as it is a science: to make sure you measure individuals and individual sub-team performance as well as the overall team performance. For example, you want your engineering team to have great technical designs, architecture, and implementation, but that needs to be woven in with the rest of product needs, sometimes accepting some technical debt that can be solved later for a feature the customers need immediately. Conversely, the product management team must understand when the engineering team must take the time to address technical debt or update a platform or patch a critical vulnerability. It's never one above the other (OK, maybe **security** is first, and the rest can wait).
8. But not *all* the time; otherwise, there's constant confusion, lack of focus, low morale, and inability to build enough expertise on the target consumers and the inner workings of the business unit supporting those consumers.

9. If you don't have that down to the last cell in your body empathy for your consumers, their problems and needs, you should go and design industrial automated machinery that nobody ever sees. The world would be a better place without heartless processes and pointless forms and consents that users have no choice but to accept blindly (when your life is at stake, can you really read and understand a 20-page legal disclaimer?). When a young child was snatched by an alligator at Walt Disney World in 2016, possibly some lawyers advised Disney not to accept any blame (it had never ever happened in the previous almost 50 years). (Disclaimer: I was not in the room where the discussions happened that night; I was on my patio hearing the helicopters desperately circling over the scene). Instead, Disney leaders never hid behind legalese and did the best that they could do in the circumstances (and the parents understood). You know why? Because everybody's heart was bleeding with pain for the loss as if it was their own child. Cold-hearted profits can wait. But empathy like that doesn't just miraculously emerge one night in a company and its leaders; it's carefully cultivated over years and decades in the team and company spirit. Walt Disney himself would have done the same as the leaders of the company did in 2016.

10. You must be realistic in that being the intermediary to the consumer is imperfect. Even if you, as a digital team member, are a consumer yourself, it doesn't mean you will perfectly represent what all the actual consumers need in all situations. But that doesn't mean you shouldn't try and, in the absence of any other data, that you shouldn't go with your instincts and adjust later.

11. My innovation team and I once did a presentation to the Chairman of Disney Parks on guests' (aka visitors) experiences enabled by emerging technologies. Absolutely everything we presented was exclusively about stories of guests in the parks. What they wanted, their friction points (yep, there were some, but we were actively trying to solve them), and what we would offer them to make their experience even more magical. I don't think we even put anywhere what technologies we were using, although I think the chairman did ask a few times.

12. The waterfall model called for these requirements, which basically meant a list of things the firm wanted.

13. Time to talk about the concept of product *owners*. In the early days of Agile, it was correctly identified that having users (that is, the business users) separate from the development team was inefficient. The product owner role was introduced to alleviate that problem, but they were still part of the "business" not the digital team. They were the folks whom an engineer could go to and ask, "Should this screen have these fields or those other fields" and the product owner would tell them what to do. The problem was, and still is, where this role is still defined this way, that the product owner was representing the business or organization and not the consumer. When the consumer became the rightful center of the experience with the ascent of product management discipline, this role was either folded inside the product team, representing the consumer, or removed altogether. In my current teams, the product owner is a position in the product management team hierarchy, usually owning one or more features and reporting to a product manager, who in turn reports to a group product manager, who in turn reports to

a product management director. The product owners do detailed user research and ethnography, together with a specialized user research team also under product management, and also write user stories.

14. Ownership here is about a state of mind rather than an organizational allocation of responsibilities. The commitment to own reflects ultimate accountability for outcomes, driving for results, irrespective of the formal job description, and organizational hierarchy.

15. Ironically, the Product Management Director in one of my teams has a computer science degree, although he has always been instinctively a product person.

16. Hiring talented product managers is among the most difficult recruiting I have had to do. The good news is that these unicorns can be trained by your staff, but that requires extra effort from digital leaders.

17. IP is Intellectual Property. Stuff that one has rights over, likely the ability to prevent others from using or to monetize to third parties.

18. Especially for CIOs/CTOs with no background in technology; yep, there are some like that.

19. That doesn't mean that you can employ every single engineer yourself. That would be beneficial as it would ensure continuity of knowledge, but in practice it may be difficult to find sufficient engineers to staff your team, especially in a time of demand surge, whether internally or marketwise. But if you must contract outside, make sure you control every aspect of the work – through reference architecture, standards and hands-on technical lead and architect oversight, source code and configuration repositories, tooling, etc. – and that you don't delegate wholesale. The criteria to determine if you control the engineering work and artifacts is simple: If your contractor, whether an individual or a subcontracting company, disappears tomorrow, can you recover by taking the code or whatever other artifacts to someone else or use internal resources and have no impacts?

20. If you can't find the full stack unicorn engineers, you could also conceivably staff dedicated engineers with each of the required skills in each team, but that would lead to poor utilization at different times.

21. And they should be impatient. The way I look at it, every month my digital experiences are not in the hands of consumers, it's another month they have poor experiences messing up their lives. Having said that, rushing in not fully baked experiences, however well-intentioned, also doesn't help them.

22. In many places, this team is called creative design. I don't like that name for two reasons. First, it's an oxymoron; if the design is not creative, i.e., imaginative, clever and smart, novel, bold, then it's just implementing rigid and inadequate templates. Second, I expect all digital team members to be creative (in the way I just described) for their domain (yes, I look at engineering to come up with creative solutions to the technical challenges the product has), so calling some people and not others creative is counterproductive.

23. For much more on UI/UX, see *The Basics of User Experience Design* by Interaction Design Foundation and *Graphic Design Rules* by Sean Adams, Peter Dawson, John Foster, and Tony Sedan.

24. Steve Jobs: "*Design is a funny word. Some people think design means how it looks. But of course, if you dig deeper, it's really how it works.*"

25. Thus, the user-centered moniker. Don't ask an operational leader to decide what the UX ought to be.
26. Great team, modern business systems and processes, etc.
27. If you must integrate with a backend system that is slow, the user experience will most likely be slow. I've had such limitations in all my work. Sometimes, though, workarounds are possible, and that is where the engineering team's imagination and skill can shine.
28. While coming up with a good or great design is a lot harder and takes longer than sloppily and knowingly putting together a bad one, the implementation takes about the same amount of time and that is where the big costs come from, not in design. So, do you want to avoid implementing the wrong design and then having to re-implement it better, which costs money? Then invest in good design from the beginning. Note, though, that I say *knowingly* bad design; I did not say not-tested design – you must test to find what the right design will turn out to be – and that is a great investment.
29. Empathy is a first-person, in-your-gut mindset. How would you feel using the product or having the users' needs, pains, and challenges? If you're in the middle of an entertainment park with your restless and tired kids in the middle of a hot afternoon, how would you feel if the app is not very helpful in finding the closest restroom or restaurant or exit? Sympathy is a third-person mindset – you understand what the other person thinks and feels at an intellectual level. There's no better proof of empathy than designing products that you yourself would want to use in times of a life-threatening emergency – like visiting an emergency room.
30. Buttons, fields, and screen functionality and navigation. If your platform requires a long press or double click or right click to get explanatory details, use that, and not swipe left just because you, as a user, like that better, for some bizarre reason. If the common user expectation is to go back one screen by clicking a left arrow in the top left corner, do that and not a right swipe. Etc. Different platforms may require different screen actions, which may drive more complicated coding, but it's worth doing.
31. Beware of copyright issues, though.
32. My emerging technology team at Disney Parks used to "shadow" park operators to see what their interactions with park guests were. We got surprising and invaluable insights.
33. It's usually hard to say if what other firms provide for common customers is relevant to yours. Just because the dominant players in your (relevant or adjacent) industry do something, it doesn't mean you'll have to ape their approach. But you should still keep an eye on them, to divine what could be useful to you and your customers. You can decide something makes no sense for you, but at least you're informed.
34. Sometimes what you learn about consumer behavior or needs doesn't seem to make much sense at first sight. That is a sign that you need to ask more and especially better questions of both consumers and the data that you have. Consumers rarely behave irrationally (although sometimes what they actually do is not what they say they'll do) when it comes to their own needs. Sometimes you must create experiments to understand more about what is happening.

35. But beware: these folks, although well-intentioned, are focused on eliminating negative outcomes – litigation or compliance fines – not creating positive outcomes for your consumers and business. They should advise on the decision, but not arbitrarily decide. Tony Fadell has a chapter in his book *Build* about this very aspect.
36. All leaders need to be architects of their organizations. If they fail to do so, the mission will most likely fail.
37. You can't build everything with your own (limited) resources. With that being said, the vision, strategy, execution, and control must be yours. External resources are extensions of your teams, not the brains of it.
38. Due to their status in the organization, these folks never get to experience the services the company offers *as their consumers do*. Let's be honest about it, as senior business executives, even as customers we get the secret entry with a red carpet, organized by our administrative assistants. So, they can never imagine how bad the experience is for regular customers or how it could be improved, especially if the change would be uncomfortable to their organizations' operations. And when the consumers don't come or stop coming, they look to marketing for *new* consumer acquisition (isn't *acquisition* a very sterile term? That is why (most of) these folks, as well-intentioned as they are, cannot be product managers. A few of them, with consumer or product sensitivities, *could* be, but not most. When I started using the healthcare services of the health system I was CDIO for, I just used whatever tools everybody had at their disposal, waited in the waiting room like everybody else, etc. I came out with a whole list of observations of friction points and possible solutions to fix them.
39. You should never be a hands-off, disconnected leader, no matter what maturity stage your team is at.
40. For example, the departure of important members from the team. Hierarchies must be adjusted, albeit temporarily, to keep the team operating. Some turnover is to be expected, but if there are constant and considerable changes in the team, beyond the initial phase of "storming and forming", then there may be a leadership, goals, or vision problem that absolutely needs to be addressed.
41. Such as changes to the marketplace or consumer expectations. Most companies saw massive changes due to the onset of the COVID pandemic.
42. It was a team of teams, comprising multiple studios/teams, each of which should be no bigger than 8–10 people, roughly as many as you can feed with two pizza boxes for lunch, as Jeff Bezos famously described Amazon's teams.
43. 150 is an interesting number for the size of the team. Studies have shown that number to be the maximum number of people human brains can know and still recognize reasonably well. Past that number, recollection and detail become spotty or null. So, if leaders want to know the team members under them well, that is the limit they can personally operate at. Of course, their overall team can be (much) bigger, but then they have to rely on their direct reports (and their direct reports) to know their 150 people).

44. The great news is that in recent years, tools such as Slack and Zoom have greatly enhanced our *ability* to communicate within large teams. But tools don't simply make for better and more efficient communication and collaborations by themselves. Some ground rules and protocols are needed.

45. I remember the story told by a senior leader about being invited to an executive marketing and product definition brainstorming session about a potential female consumer market opportunity in Southeast Asia. Everybody on the panel was a white, North American male. Suffice to say, none of them had any clues whatsoever about the needs and wants of that target customer demographic. Organizing something with that member composition is nothing but stupid, uninformed, impractical, and illogical. Either you want to serve your customer or your uninformed preconceptions, not both.

46. Scott McNealy, the former CEO of the legendary Sun Microsystems (now part of Oracle), is credited with using this statement. The "Get out of the way" part is vintage Scott: great leader, technologist, and human being.

47. Leaders must provide the environment for open debates, looking for and accepting feedback based on data, facts, and insights, but must also be firm and certainly decisive. That sounds like a contradiction, but it isn't. Still not easy.

48. Before the COVID pandemic, I had teams and team members in probably seven or eight different offices across the *globe.*

49. The size of the rest of the larger team doing the user research, design, technical solution and development, launch, and support is really defined by the requirements of the product.

50. Steve Jobs is famous for challenging the presence of anybody in a meeting who didn't really need to be present – i.e., providing direct value.

51. Beware, random groups of people don't make teams, they're just purposeless gatherings of people. A team is a group of people that share and work together toward common values, outcomes, and vision. Great talent is meaningful only as part of great teams, not individually.

52. When assembling a team, you ought to make sure the composition of the team doesn't dilute the commitment to the mission.

53. You have that situation often, especially in Silicon Valley.

54. The opposite of excellence is not a catastrophe – as that would eliminate weak players. It's slow-motion mediocrity that somehow tends to survive, presumably due to the absence of enough alternative excellence to crush it in the marketplace.

55. I had this wonderful team lead whom I hired in different jobs in two different companies in two different states. She was fantastic at what she did. She taught me and others the value of good preparation and readiness in case things did not work out as expected. She would say "What is your current plan and preparation? Have you tested that? What is your plan B? What could go wrong with what you're trying to do, and do you have a recovery plan for that?" But she never wanted to take the role of a director, no matter how much I and others tried to convince (read: beg) her. She just wanted to be the best at what she was. We all love you, Debbie.

56. Have you noticed how often teams and team members in meetings ask to move conversations "offline" any time there are vigorous debates, even when the whole purpose of those meetings is to debate? Sure, when the meeting drifts into debating

a topic that is merely tangential to the declared focus of the meeting and would derail the resolution of the main topic, then a separate conversation is the best approach. But even then, the "offline" should not be a backroom deal between select individuals, but another open debate with all interested and qualified team members. Another variant of this problematic behavior is in review or governance meetings – say budget reviews – where teams and individuals come with proposals in front of a select committee (how that committee is selected is a whole other discussion; suffice to say it represents organizational power structures). The presentation is done, some clarifying questions are asked, then the stakeholder of the proposal leaves the room (or drops off the video conference). The committee members then proceed to judge the proposal and decide to approve or reject – with the decision being communicated "offline" (i.e., not face-to-face, which means the requestors get the decision without much explanation). The problem with this approach is that the judgment is done in the absence of a vigorous back-and-forth debate that would get the best outcome, in an open way. Maybe you would then say: sure, not great for avoiding an open conversation, but this makes some sense as the committee reviews multiple competing proposals, and they need to see all of them to judge them comparatively (even that doesn't explain not going back face to face to the proponent on the proposal so they can make some sense out of the decision). But that's not it. You know the real reason the proposal supporter is removed from the committee? To avoid the debate that would make it awkward to say no and, as such to avoid hurt feelings! Do you think those who get what sounds like arbitrary "no" decisions don't have their feelings hurt, let alone lose faith in the rationality of the process shaken?

57. There could be situations where indeed the decisions will look (somewhat) arbitrary. That is the case where data and insights are insufficient, all options are somewhat equal, and a decision needs to be made in short order. Not making a decision is a decision in itself. In such situations, the approach is to use the result of the decision – for example, a feature – once implemented, as a way to further collect more data that was missing when making the decision and then adjust.

Part IV

Execution

There's a famous adagio that says *"vision/strategy without execution is just lunacy"*. Another variant is *"execution eats vision/strategy for breakfast"*. You get the idea. These statements remind all of us that the only purpose of vision and strategy is to be *executed towards something*, namely the product or service of sorts that customers use. No outcome, no value for the input.

Apparently, Jamie Dimon, CEO of JP Morgan Chase, is quoted as saying more than once: *"If I had to choose between exceptional vision/strategy, coupled with a lousy execution and a mediocre strategy coupled with a brilliant execution, I'll choose the latter"*. Meaning that you shouldn't expect the strategy to deliver when the execution fails. But he's definitely not advising for poor strategies as long execution is great.

However valuable these statements are (and they are), they may imply – for the purpose of making the importance of the role of (good/great) execution crystal clear – that vision/strategy and execution are independent from each other, and they flow from one to the other. The truth is a bit more complicated. There's a 1–1 relationship between strategy and execution, as they inform and influence each other. You execute on what you have chosen to do and not random things just because you can (see disciplined delivery versus featuritis[1] conversation elsewhere in the book).

You should chose to do only what you can execute on not what you *wished* you could execute on – for example, even if your customers could benefit the most from an internally developed product, if you don't have the team (or the time to build it) or the money, you'll have to settle in the short term for whatever you can buy on the market (however, you ought to put the effort to correct that limitation later).

With that clarification out of the way, let's look at how to make all the fundamental concepts we talked about in Chapter 1 happen through your digital team doing product delivery, using adjacent technologies, frameworks, tools, and navigating the firm.

Let's go and make the sausage.

          DOI: 10.4324/9781032644370-4

Chapter 4.1 Product Delivery

Always deliver more than expected.

Larry Page

Product delivery is the process of producing whatever was designed and getting it into the hands of consumers. This chapter will provide guidance on a number of concepts and processes to assist with that.

Plans Are Useless but Planning Is Indispensable[2]

Let's talk about a few unconventional things regarding planning – of activities, of releases, etc.

There's a famous adagio that says "*The best laid plans don't survive the encounter with reality*".[3] So, the first thing to ask, controversial as it may be to folks used to a certain routine, is "*why do we make plans in the first place?*"

One simple but shallow answer is because that is what we know to do, with the goal of getting the comfortable illusion of control, and illusion is it, over long periods of times and across experiences that we don't quite know much about, nor do we know how to implement. That's when plans get hopelessly out of whack with reality.

So, what to make of all this? To plan or not to plan?

The way I look at it, planning is valuable as long as the plans coming out of the process are not gospels to live or die for. It's valuable as it forces teams to think through all the pieces, their sequence, and dependencies to ship a product that consumers want and use. But there are several reasons why plans and planning feel so hopelessly disconnected from reality.

The way we tend to construct plans is problematic. We somehow decide at the very beginning of the process what we want/need to do, we associate with each deliverable an effort and time – all best-case scenarios – using PERT and GANTT[4] charts and project plans and all – all leading to approximating some delivery schedule. The mindset that we usually employ in this case is that we start with exactly what we want in great detail and assume we're going to be able to make that a reality – and resources availability (money, people, vendors, technology, processes), even occasional unexpected disturbances – all bent to our desires. That's wishful and delusional thinking that never happens in reality, resulting in objectively predictable disappointments.

A better approach is to start with the known or likely constraints[5] – people, money, process, technology, etc. – and figure out *what* you *could* potentially deliver, *how* and *when*. Simply put, the architecture and delivery of the product will be a function of your assets and constraints – current and future. For example, if you have the engineers today, you can deliver.[6] If you don't have them, you can't deliver.[7] Can you get your materials into your production or shop floor or not, but if not and you can't change that (at least not in the short term and not without delays), then you need to build your production and shop sales plan accordingly. As simple as that.

Agile methodologies always advise not to book your maximum number of resources[8] in a plan because at some point some disruption – some delayed critical dependency delivery – will come along and if your resources are fully booked, there's nowhere to absorb that gap from. But that still doesn't negate the need to start with constraints and build out from there.

Keep an Eye on Dependencies

There's a second consideration regarding plans, one that I briefly mentioned earlier. Even if you're doing all that we discussed in the previous section, if your components and teams have very tight dependencies[9] on each other, you're assured of having some unpleasant surprises in terms of one team's delay impacting others and ultimately the product launch.[10]

Loose dependencies between components and layers are a fundamental and well-known principle[11] of modern technical architecture. This allows changes in one component and layer to have minimal impacts on the rest of the system, leading to not only more resilient architecture and products, but less timeline impacts.

This leads to three action points.

First, break down the technical architecture into layers that can act semi-independently. Usually, the layers are user experience,[12] the experience service layer,[13] the shared services layer and then the system of record, database, or other integrations layer. You should be able to add and modify functional capabilities semi-independently at each layer.

Second, somewhat derived from the first point but at times separate, think of how to separate features and functionality in a release from each other in a way that you can release some parts even if others are delayed – sometimes critically delayed. For example, you should still be able to release the book-an-appointment feature even if real-time validation of the medical insurance, which was intended to be part of that flow, is not yet functional. Here, tools like *feature toggles*[14] are great, but the architecture of your product must be able to support it, not only technically but also in a way that makes sense from a consumer experience viewpoint.

Third, you need to watch for unnecessary or badly functioning dependencies between teams, as well as their deliverables, possibly driven by bandwidth or priority mismatches between teams. If the user research team is understaffed or allocated to some other work, your creative work cannot start beyond draft sketches and the engineering team cannot build beyond some basic work on interface contract or infrastructure provisioning (but that takes a minimal amount of time in the cloud).

The good news is that a mature and well-functioning digital team and process[15] will eventually reach a natural cadence of delivery and things will become more predictable and smoother. Yet don't expect that the team (and its team members and activities) will come together for a good while. With enough effort and discipline, you will get there.

We must be realistic that building products is neither a science, nor an art. In the end you, as the digital leader, must help your team to find their step and learn how to control and manage dependencies.

Flexible Roadmap

Let me start with this so we can get it out of the way: roadmaps *must* be decided by the digital team, based on prioritizing customer needs, feasibility, technical and operational readiness, etc., in alignment with the rest of organization.

Some organizations look at digital roadmaps as very rigid released plans, with strict sequence, cadence, and dates. To make things worse, these roadmaps extend sometimes to over a year.

I think that is a big mistake, simply because having detailed and committed plans to what is sometimes unknown – because it is yet to be researched and solutioned – or is potentially undeliverable (with the available technology or within the legal context) only leads to eventual disappointment and lack of credibility for everyone.

Instead, the way I think about roadmaps is more akin to a *guidance* of what the team *plans* to do and *roughly* when. Basically, a *prioritized* backlog with some *directional* dates (sometimes by quarter or even longer). Useful, again directionally, to the team and the organization at large so they can form an idea of what will possibly happen. General guidance, *not* rigid commitments.

The prioritization is around the highest benefit to the highest number of consumers, matched with the readiness of the discovery and the engineering feasibility, as evaluated at that point in time.

But the roadmap is fluid simply because of the unknowns. Sometimes what we thought can be done turns out to be more complicated to implement in the timeframe. Or what we believed were the user needs turn out to not be correct or to be incomplete. Knowing what is comparatively the highest value feature to deliver requires a lot of research and ideation work, which evolves over time. So, shifts, changes in a particular scope, and extensions of plan are natural when we're not ready to deliver something of value that will work.

Sometimes, new features that meet the litmus test of value, usability and feasibility come up naturally as part of the discovery, ahead of other features of less value/usability/feasibility. When that happens, engineering efforts are inserted in the roadmap ahead of the others. And that is OK.

One could say – and plenty of folks do say it – that this sounds like a license to never deliver anything or at least not on time. The antidote to that risk is that you always release *some feature* as long the criteria or value/usability/feasibility is met *at that particular point in time*. That is why you're always working in parallel (see release schedule section) in either a discovery or a solutioning phase that is ready for development.

And if there's absolutely nothing to replace a functional feature that can't be released in a particular iteration, then there's always the opportunity to clean up some technical or UI/UX debt and do some hardening – i.e., making the product more robust or resilient. No available bandwidth needs to be wasted – and rarely is – when you have a huge backlog.

Products, Sub-products, and Features

Features consist of functionality that allows a consumer to perform a particular action towards a desired outcome. They're useful constructs to manage the digital delivery vis-a-vis timeline, effort, and resources.

By themselves they're not what is important and they're definitely not a goal or purpose. The whole experience is what is important and that is usually built through multiple features working cohesively.

If a patient's desired outcome is to solve some ailment, the user will want to use a multi-purpose medical app (the product) that supports the self-scheduled journey/flow (the sub product) of finding a doctor, booking an appointment, checking-in, paying the bill, seeing the results of the visit and any associated prescriptions, and ordering the medication. Each of these are features.

In a single purpose app, the product and sub product usually are the same and they're built up by features. Sometimes sub-product and features are terms used interchangeably. Everything you put in front of a user extracts a cost of time, effort, and attention. You'll have to resist the temptation to add features just for the sake of it or because an important stakeholder thinks they are needed.

Releases – Real Developers Ship[16]

A release is putting new functionality in the form of features or products in the hands of real users. In truth, a product only becomes *the* product when consumers use it successfully[17] – any other time it's either a work-in-progress or a post-release failure (if it doesn't work).

A functional release contains one or more features that allow consumers to perform an action to interact, obtain, or purchase your organization's services or products. A non-functional release usually includes technical developments such as reducing tech debt, improving performance and availability, or improving the UI.

A rolling release plan – more precise for the immediate future (up to three releases) and more high-level and directional in the medium term – contains the sequence of releases and some approximate dates. As a release is rolled out, it drops from the plan and a new one at the far end of the plan is added.

You can either time-box or scope-base your releases. The former really means releasing whatever is ready – for the consumers to use well – at the end of the period you decided on.[18] The latter means waiting for all the features planned for the release to be ready before releasing.

While I would never support knowingly releasing functionality that is not ready for consumers to be able to use well,[19] I strongly support the time-boxing of releases. Why? Because it preserves the cadence discipline of regular releases, it forces the team to push themselves to work hard and creatively at improving their internal processes, it gets feedback sooner rather than later and it doesn't accumulate too much unreleased code that then collects technical and functional debt. If a feature planned for that release is not ready, then it won't be included in the release. The alternative may lead to endless delays with nothing released while code that could help users accumulates purposelessly.[20]

In either approach, though, there should be no long-term plan for releases (like for a whole year) as that is just an exercise in futility given how much you don't know and how much can change during that timeframe.

Minor or feature releases (FR) are evolutions of existing functionality, engineering enhancements, or bug fixes. A good release cadence is every two to three weeks. Major releases[21] (MR) launch major new pieces of functionality. A good sustained and sustainable cadence[22] is every two to three minor releases for each major release.

Production-quality prototypes, designed to validate assumptions, can either be introduced as part of major or minor releases – as long as they are clearly designated as temporary or beta – or be separate, offered in some way to separate audiences. Depending on the learning coming from them, they are likely re-released (after possible changes) as full features.

Pre-production (also known as shadow environment) testing (including for mobile apps, e.g., using Apple's TestFlight Production) ought to be used as soon as possible in the final testing process, using controlled test accounts. This will validate the production setup of your application and infrastructure.

I recommend a major whole-product user interface modernization (aka re-skin) every 18–24 months. This will keep the experience fresh and modern.

Technical debt[23] or temporary compromises are usually to be accepted when pushing hard to deliver fast – with the singular and notable exception of **security gaps**. Knowingly accept that bad security is a complete breach of trust of the consumer. They'll tolerate an honest gap in the functionality, but not you being reckless with their data. You should be in a different business altogether if you think putting consumers and their data at risk is acceptable to get a release out. It takes a lot of effort and maniacal focus to make sure compromising security doesn't happen, even unknowingly. But accumulating technical debt will eventually stop the product from evolving, if not addressed systematically[24] and timely.[25]

Figure 4.1 The infrastructure face of technical debt (author's collection).

However, you must resist the urge to measure progress strictly by frequency of releases.[26] Instead, think about speed from your *customer's point of view*. Are you helping them to achieve their goals quicker? Is releasing sooner providing a benefit to most of them who otherwise would struggle without it?

When a digital team establishes its *own* delivery and release date – give or take a few days, short of truly unpredictable events – then they must meet that date.[27] That date is, after all, estimated by the team itself, based on all the work that needs to be done, from user research all the way to launch preparation. A commitment, especially a self-imposed commitment, must be kept, or the team loses credibility.[28]

The only way to drive a sustained delivery pace is to establish a regular (as in daily) cadence of standing processes – reviews, meetings – where issues are discussed and resolved *fast*. If you want and need to move fast, you can't wait a week to assemble everybody who needs to provide input into a decision or solution. Preferably, those meetings should have the product executives (part of the digital team, not necessarily operational stakeholders) who may need to make hard decisions and break ties.[29] It is time intensive but is required to move fast and deliver quality products.

Releases should have an accountable[30] release manager or executive,[31] responsible to bring all pieces together in the timeframe. They could be a dedicated product manager who is well versed with the process. Just mechanically tracking items in a project plan doesn't cut it, so using traditional project managers won't work.

You Must Run Multiple Delivery Trains in Parallel

The simplest way to execute on the delivery process would be a single threaded flow: you do discovery for a feature, you design it, build it, test it, and release it and then its rinse and repeat with the next feature. Unfortunately, a single thread would be highly inefficient and slow in terms of output.

The problem with that approach is that while you're in one of those stages, each probably occupying one team's time, the other teams would not be very busy. For example, discovery is mostly the product management team, true with some participation from other digital teams, but other than the select members of those teams, the rest of their team members would be waiting for their turn to work. Similarly with the engineering delivery stage, where, while product management and design teams are involved closely, they wouldn't be fully utilized. This is not practical at all.

For resource efficiency and speed reasons, you will need to expedite the delivery by having multiple parallel delivery work streams, some creating new features – usually in different phases: one in discovery, one in solutioning, one in development, one in testing – and some improving on existing ones. For good measure, you can throw in a couple of technical spikes, trying or validating novel technical options. Continued improvements and enhancements and solving technical or experiential debt or user feedback are yet another. And, of course, another stream focuses on any issues with the product in production that must be addressed promptly.

Since resources are never sufficient to do all that could be done at any one time, you'll have to frequently prioritize what resources to dedicate to one stream versus another at that point in time – with one notable exception: if you have a critical bug in production that prevents consumers from successfully using a released feature, then that takes precedence over anything new, even if the new feature is what the CEO wants.

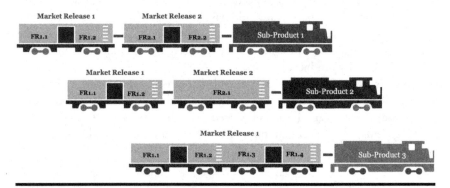

Figure 4.2   Multiple parallel delivery trains.

Each train is probably led by a different sub-team of your digital team, depending on how you decided to structure the team.[32]

All of this multi-train release process requires a structured yet flexible process and a lot of planning. And when one train is delayed, others may need to be pulled around to compensate and keep all tracks occupied.

Launch Plan and Preparation

The launch plan[33] refers to compiling and reviewing – from day one to launch D-day – the list of adjacent activities – i. e., all the other activities beside what we have been talking about so far – that need to happen to support each release.

The launch plan is required to ensure that nothing is missing, incomplete or inadequate and all the players – including and especially outside the digital team – have the necessary level of readiness to effectively support the release.

Many teams miss, or are not sufficiently focused on, these adjacent (but not less important) activities. That is where an integrated launch plan is highly valuable.

I will start this list with **marketing**,[34] specifically the readiness of any marketing campaign and its specific messaging that may have been planned to be executed at launch: TV and Internet or social media ads, flyers, promotional emails, targeted audience, updating existing web sites with the right messaging, etc. The marketing plan must be based on the product market strategy. Unfortunately, it is too often the case that marketing details, which should have been planned for from the beginning of the release and then continuously kept in sync with the evolution of the release, have not been.[35]

You need to make sure that **staff training and readiness** is at the needed level. If your upcoming release provides the customer with the ability to show up to an urgent care visit, having gone through (most of) the check-in activities at home or even in the lobby of the center, your staff members – which in a pre-release world would just hand over to the consumer a stack of paper forms – are knowledgeable of and ready for the new digital, non-paper, process. If not, awkward and frustrating situations will happen – they will still ask patients for paper forms! – diminishing the value of the release.[36]

It's equally important to make sure that the **support** teams are ready to help consumers through the new feature. Sometimes consumers do need to speak to or text a human[37] to ask a question about the digital experience, or about known gaps (unavoidable, but hopefully temporary).[38]. It is a terrible experience for a consumer to call the customer service number and the rep answering has no idea how to help, because they have not adequately been trained on the new capability. So, by all means, try your own dog food (customer support service) to see how well (if) it works.[39]

A higher-level variant of support is the **white glove/concierge support** that may be required in certain cases, depending on either the significant scope of the release or the customer's importance. These white glove support teams interact with the user in-person and make sure the experience, at least at launch, is well understood. They also have an important secondary role of observing how users interact with the product, providing informed feedback to the digital team for future tweaks.

Elsewhere I detail the importance of having metrics tracking the performance of the experience with consumers. Therefore, each release must have appropriate *system logging, on-going tracking*, and *reporting* ready at launch.

Any of these activities, however hard they're prepared for, may not be ready in time for the launch date. Not having the marketing ready can be disappointing but not a showstopper. Staff training, however, needs to be ready to avoid bad experiences, in which case you must delay the release if not ready. Once or twice it's OK – just don't make it a habit and instead plan the release properly.

Either You Shoot for Reliability or You Go Home

The promise of shiny new features can be alluring to the well-intentioned but naive digital team, especially when that feature is demanded by powerful operational stakeholders. I've seen the worst of crashes of products launched just before the December holiday season, despite them not being sufficiently bug-free and well tested, just because a powerful stakeholder wanted it to showcase the release in their annual bonus review and pressed for it to be included at the last moment.

While the digital team exhibits a high-level of urgency to deliver products and features so consumers can benefit as soon as possible, the release needs to happen when it's ready to deliver a great experience – and no sooner. Done-done, as they say.

No consumer will accept a crashing app that worked just fine before the new flashy feature was introduced but now it's unusable for most basic features. Consumers prefer the stability of what they have already over what they *could* potentially have in the new release. They may even not need or use that new feature anyway, at least not in the short delay before you could make it solid.

So the rule is simple: **Thou. Shall. Not. Put. Crap. In. Consumers. Hands**! It's disrespectful to release bad products to the extreme, let alone frustrating and a satisfaction- and loyalty-killer.

Reliability[40] of the product is at least as important as its features – if not more so.

Delivery Milestones and Deadlines

Waterfall methodologies[41] emphasized rigid project delivery plans and, implicitly, commitment to fixed milestones and deadlines, all decided at the beginning of the project. The assumption was that the project team knew in excruciating detail what needed to be done (including, supposedly what the customer wanted) and the actions needed to be executed to deliver that, including all project lifecycle phase durations.

But in reality, most of these commitments and dates were more or less wishful thinking (or I should say, forced thinking by business stakeholders). Of course, life has a habit of throwing curveballs even at the most disciplined practitioners, but here the problem was about starting with wrong assumptions and commitments, including that no *unexpected* events will ever happen.

When the delivery was committed "in stone" at the beginning of the project, what followed was either outright failure to deliver as committed or the attempt to recover through *death marches*.[42] More problematic: If one death march worked, it built a perverse organizational expectation that teams would do it repeatedly in subsequent cycles – misguided and counterproductive, to say the least.

With Agile methodologies, despite its many other benefits, unfortunately sometimes we went to the opposite extreme, where some teams had absolutely no commitments, even to *reasonable*[43] dates. This could happen because of the product team taking extravagant time to do their user research to define 99.99% correctly the customer needs, or the engineering team going by "*whatever (time) it takes, it takes*", etc. The result was that releases were not only impossible to predict, but they would stretch on forever. All until a high-powered business executive, exasperated by the delays, would force, you guess, the (in)famous death march. Back to where we started.

As you probably expect by now, the best way to plan is somewhere in the middle, with some interesting twists.

An agile (lower case A, as in "*delivered with agility*") effort should always split work in small chunks. Designing, solutioning, and delivering on small chunks is always more predictable, within a reasonable margin of precision (for an iteration, aka sprint, of three weeks, that margin would be less than a week). If a stakeholder wants to understand the release date of a product of feature, they'll plan around the cumulative ranges of the sprints on that release.

So, are milestones bad and unrealistic? Absolutely not, they are needed to establish a natural but robust cadence of delivery. When the team processes are still gelling, the digital leader must enforce ambitious-to-a-stretch goals on delivery dates. That establishes a culture of urgency among the team (after all, consumers need solutions to their current problems today and not next year), and it forces the team to be in the mindset of constantly and proactively finding optimization solutions (whether technology, process, or people)[44] to deliver sooner and better.

However, while the digital leader must know when to push hard, they also need to understand when to release the pressure before it becomes counter-productive. You don't want your team to be so desperate to escape pressure that they'll cut any and all corners,[45] including leaving the company or your team.

But you may argue, what if the release is something publicly announced months in advance, like the release of a new iOS version? There are two ways to make that work.

First, the stakeholders and the digital team can reprioritize other work. But it is important that all the stakeholder's (including the consumer, represented by the digital team) interests are considered fairly in any reprioritization exercise.

There is a **second** lever that can be applied. If it is not realistic to release the scope on time, then the scope can be tweaked (changed, reduced) to make the date for the remaining scope feasible. This is basically switching a scope-based plan for a date-based plan. Whatever is not making it for that date is being pushed to a later date. Even Apple does that sometimes with iOS releases, with delayed features.

Team Processes Cadence – Like Clockwork

Every project needs a heartbeat.

Tony Fadell

All well-functioning teams, once formed, must establish an optimal operating cadence – that is, their own internal predictable processes and task durations to perform specific activities. This starts to be built in the storming and forming stage – as fast as possible, but realistic – and gets refined over time.

Establishing a cadence is not about artificially accelerating delivery, it just means the team knowing how to deliver and how long it will take them. Developing this cadence is critical for them to be able to realistically commit to deliverables but also having the confidence[46] to deliver.

For the larger team – product management, front end, back end, and shared services engineering, not to mention third parties and business partners – to function well and deliver in a synchronized manner, all individual cadences must be harmonized.

Otherwise, it's like an orchestra where all the members are playing at different tempos. Making sure flexible processes for that coordination are in place is the role of the digital leader.

Testing – Make Sure Your Stuff Works the Way You Think It Works

Good tests kill flawed theories.

Karl Popper

Testing a system for correct operation against the user stories or requirements is probably something that all teams (hopefully) do by now. How much and how rigorous testing is needed depends on what the feature is but more (meaningful) testing is better, especially regression testing.[47]

Be prepared for comprehensive regression and new functionality testing. As the product gets bigger, automating regression testing becomes a running-or-crawling proposition, as without it, the more code and functionality you have, the slower manual regression testing and thus releasing becomes. Without regression testing there will be a Groundhog Day of old bugs previously fixed but somehow reintroduced in the codebase. Not pretty.

And there is also the misnamed user-acceptance-testing, which is basically business users testing the functionality as *proxies* for consumers. Usually this is manual and as such far from comprehensive, but it does catch interesting and sometimes subtle gaps in the product, the logic of operations, or hard to script conditions. In the old days, when "IT" was delivering to the business, this was viewed as a way to fulfill on the delivery contract. These days, though, it is about you wanting the business testers to test the product for business logic anomalies.

Whatever testing is done, it has to validate all the layers of the product, including correct integration with transactional backend systems.

Pilot Releases – Let Your Consumers Use Your Product

Having actual consumers use the product in real-life scenarios[48] is priceless. This is done with a (small) subset of users, sometimes employees who are actual consumers of the product themselves, other times enrolling in some manner several external users (i.e., true third-party consumers). The duration of this exercise can be anywhere between a couple of weeks to several months, depending on scope.

These are known as pilot releases and they're designed to provide feedback to the digital team for any small and last-minute tweaks of the product: UI/UX, some functionality, performance, etc. Even with extensive proofs of concept and prototyping exercises pilot trials can be surprisingly useful, although not for every release (they're expensive and time intensive), but just for the ones that are very significant and add/change significant functionality.

I have a hard rule: when introducing a brand-new product, whether internally developed or a vendor product,[49] I have my team do a pilot release to make sure we're still correct in our assessment of the product and use and, more importantly, we are addressing any last-minute issues.

Deciding on Build Versus Buy – Or Both

Usually this question is asked too early in the process of solutioning. The right question to ask is not whether we should buy or build but rather when one is optimal over the other. Sometimes a decision one way or another is forced upon you due to readiness limitations: The product and design teams can't design a product or can't imagine the experience and/or the engineering team can't build it – yet.

Short of that, the better approach is to define the product at a conceptual level – what it should be about, what it needs to do, and how it should deliver the desired outcomes by consumers. Only then the solutioning should be defining the best way to deliver that technically and financially – by building in-house or buying a product.

A lot of times it's not an "*or*" but rather an "*and*". The best solution is usually delivered through a combination of owned user experience but using, as much as possible, feasible and desirable, components from purchased vendor solutions, usually integrated at the API layer.

But for a team to make the right choices, it must have the readiness – that is, to be capable – to solution and implement in the best way possible, including building in-house – which is usually more difficult but more valuable (and sometimes cheaper and faster, surprisingly).

Buying could hold the promise of better, more mature, faster to implement, and cheaper, but that is not a given by any means. Many CIOs prefer that route, but they do so only because their organizations don't have the ability to build in-house, after years of faulty "*we're not a technology firm*" strategies or lack of efforts, at the notable expense of poor consumer experiences.

My advice is to be open to the best option but be ready to do the hard work.

On the Bleeding Edge of Technology? Not So Fast!

If you want to create great digital experiences surely you need sophisticated technology, especially on the bleeding edge, right?

Nope.

Sure, emerging technologies are a lot of fun for technologists to tinker with and for executives to talk about in articles and at conferences. But digital is all about the customer experience and not the technology. Sure, technology underpins everything digital and digital would not be possible without technology. But you don't need to bleed on the edge for that – pun intended.

As of a much of technology and digital leader that I am, if I evaluate an experience and that experience would be better for the consumer (or myself, as a consumer) without (much) technology, I'll go for the better experience and no technology.

So, any technology, especially the cutting edge, must be judged by how much better a customer experience will be *with* that technology than *without* it. The edginess of that technology must bring enough of a benefit to significantly compensate for any challenges and risks due to lack of maturity. If not, you should wait for it to mature or, alternatively, explicitly offer it only to early adopters as beta features.

At Disney Parks I led the emerging technologies team. We evaluated lots of technologies for readiness to meet some future need, but we always backed into those technologies coming from the desired experience. Problems to solve leading to a technology solution, not the other way around. We had two sliding time horizons for any technology we were looking at: immediate – that is, mature enough to possible deploy, should the opportunity arise, in the next 6–12 months – and then the speculative, beyond that time interval, technologies that we just kept an eye on. The maturity was evaluated not only on that technology merits, but on our own maturity to use and deploy it in a way that enriched the guest experience, production quality.

So, by all means, explore new technologies in the context of how they could make your experience better but wait, while preparing, for its and your maturity.

Version 1.0 *Is* a Big Deal

Irrespective of how you define what the version 1.0 of your product should be, here are the things you should do, expect, and prepare for.

First of all, that version, if you follow the incrementalism advice I give in this book, will not have anywhere near the features your consumers[50] will eventually find useful to effectively use the product. At least not to adopt in large numbers and at least not for most digital products. And that is fine. 1.0 is a statement of what it *will* be, not what it is.

You must go through version 1.0 to get to 2.0 and 3.0[51] (the product probably becomes really interesting at 3.0 and later). On the other hand, you want some adoption for 1.0, if nothing else but to get you some learnings for latter versions: If it is a new product, even minimal feedback can guide whether the market is really there for it. On the positive side, you also get some enthusiasts to promote the product (or I should say the promise of its future versions).

So, you should put out 1.0, but be prepared for negative comments like *"But it doesn't do x, y, z, so this is useless!"*[52] The feedback will not be universal, although probably dominant.[53] You may lose some consumers, disappointed that the product is not everything they want, but you'll probably get those back when you have a more interesting version (3.0?), if you do the right things between 1.0 and 3.0.

But make no mistake: 1.0 must have *something* about it to pique the interest and suggest future potential. Comparative to the competition, it must have something new and different for people to be interested, even if it's just a different way to present information or activities.[54]

Things will go much better if the market is really bare of any products to offer anything of interest, with your product offering something that is better than nothing. But not many markets are that barren, so don't count on it.

It's not a great description for your product to say *"it's better than nothing"* but you'll have to take all you can get and not be choosy. You're probably not

Steve Jobs and your product is not the iPhone. Ever for them, 1.0 was more hype than value.[55]

The one thing you *should* do, though, is take advantage of whoever tries and uses the product by communicating to them the *potential* for your product: that is, advertise inside and outside your product what is to come that will be of interest. This gives you the chance to keep whoever tries the product mildly interested to stay involved for 2.0 and 3.0. Not the committed and loyal users you're looking for, but better than advertising cold. iPhone 1.0 was that for Apple.

Now, the road from 1.0 to 2.0 and 3.0 is equally tricky. In those subsequent versions you must live up to whatever promise 1.0 had, otherwise you'll disappoint your enthusiasts and 1.0 trial users. You must be careful what you put in those subsequent versions, with the focus of relentlessly increasing the value of the product and retaining the promise and yet not lose whatever made 1.0 interesting.

Additionally, you'll have to carefully figure out how to scale from 1.0 to 2.0 and 3.0. Adding new features is not everything. Some of the value will come from fixing things that were annoying in 1.0 but early adopters gave you a pass on because, well, it was just 1.0. You won't get that pass anymore in 2.0 or 3.0.

Be prepared to put a lot of time and effort into 2.0 and 3.0.[56] For most people, "instant" success comes after years of efforts. Version 1 may have many minor versions: 1.1, 1.2, etc. – before it can graduate to 2.0. That graduation can't be arbitrary as it would mean nothing to users. There are no shortcuts with discerning customers, but there are many dead ends.[57]

Don't Surprise the Consumer in a Bad Way

No one likes to be surprised by bad news. We tell this to our children and to our employees. We prefer to hear early if something is not going as expected or will turn in a negative direction. For one, so we can compose our reaction. For another, so we can try to correct the situation.

Changing a product or its experience needs to be done thoughtfully, especially when it's used widely. Consumers prefer knowing in advance that a change in a product they depend on is coming, so they can be prepared when they use it next time.

One of the worst things for a consumer to experience is when they turn to your product in a personal crisis or time-constrained situation and find out that what they were familiar with is now completely changed and they need to figure out a new experience on the fly, when they really don't want to or can't. And if the new experience is only marginally better than the old one and yet requires a meaningful learning curve on a dime, then you really made a mistake.

But products and features need to evolve. So, what gives? My advice is two-fold.

First, give your customers early warning of what is coming, with enough time to prepare mentally. For example, *"we're redesigning this experience and a new experience will be available at the end of the quarter"*[58] or whenever. Or *"we're retiring this app on xx/yy/zzzz date and we will provide a new abc app"*. Etc. Add anything else they may need to know in advance of that change, like having to create new credentials (not a good experience, but sometimes technically unavoidable).

Second, when the time comes for the new product or feature or experience to be introduced, run it in parallel to the old one for a period, so consumers can still use the old one they're familiar with but with the full knowledge that they must switch at some date. Explain why you introduced the change (simplified, faster experience, more features that they'll appreciate, etc.) and tell them the deadline to fully switch to the new solution.[59]

That is especially important when the change is pretty drastic. This way, they're not left stranded with a new experience that they're not familiar with when they're in dire straits needing to use your product. This builds trust and avoids unnecessary frustrations and feelings of being disrespected.

Sure, there are situations when running both solutions in parallel for a while is not possible or very difficult. For example, your product was running on a platform that is shut down for independent reasons (yes, we all got that call about a vendor going bankrupt next week and stopping all services). But in most cases, you have time and options. Take them.

Measure and Adjust All the Time

Measuring the effectiveness of your product against consumer needs is critically important as it provides insights into what is working and what is not,[60] suggesting the likely needed adjustments. Not having visibility leaves you at the mercy of guessing and opinions.

However, it's important, before you go on a rampage of measuring, to decide what you want to learn from your measurements, what each metric means, and what you're going to do with the likely insights you'll get. Measuring the wrong thing leads to mistrust of data and its value, as well as a waste of time and implementation efforts. Not having a plan and an actual process to evaluate and then act upon those measurement insights is just going through the motions and ultimately pointless.

So, every time my team asks for a particular instrumentation, measurement or feedback, my question back to them is: *"What are you going to do with/about this particular piece of data?"* And that is not because I don't care for learning – I absolutely do – but to make sure the measurement or feedback is meaningful, useful, and usable. Otherwise, why do it – we have enough noise in the system so we should focus on the signal. It's surprising how often the answer you get to such a question is inconclusive or incomplete. Press until they have a clear view of action.

Engineering Spikes – How to Figure Out What Engineering Can Do

Sometimes, in order to figure out the feasibility of a technical solution or to actually figure out the actual technical solution, you'll need to try things out to see if they're possible and doable and, if so, how long would it *probably* take to deliver that solution to production quality.

This is what we call *engineering spikes*. They refer to spikes in engineering effort, usually out-of-band, outside the planned feature's architecting and development efforts. A lot of new solutions come out of these spikes. They're invaluable for evaluating the technical feasibility of your engineering efforts and your ability to correctly estimate your team's ability to deliver inside a delivery and release plan.

I can tell you that my teams have rarely not had such evaluation efforts going on in parallel with normal development.[61] And this is how we figured out if something would work and how to make it work.

Sometimes, they are modest trials for otherwise well-established techniques that the team has never used before. Maybe a new technology, API or vendor – all relatively low risk but needing to be tried, nevertheless. Others are untested approaches and technologies that have high risks for a production environment. With high risk comes high rewards –but not always.[62]

And that is worth trying if they benefit consumers and your organization.

When Things Go Bad – or Really, Really Bad

> *Character is built not in good times, but in bad times; not in a time of plenty, but in a time of adversity.*

> **Steve Jobs**

There will be many times when things go bad. Like when the product is not reaching your intended audience. Or when the adoption (people starting to use your product) or engagement (they keep using your product over time) is nowhere near what you expected and planned. Or when things are really bad:

Your product doesn't work when your consumers really need to do important things for their lives and well-being.

What are you, the leader, supposed to do?[63]

First and foremost, remember that however dark things are, you'll come out from under the cloud at some point. You must have the optimism to think about that and to impart that optimism to your team. People in despair have trouble recovering well from a bad situation. And how you recover from a bad situation is actually equally important, as a leader and team, to what led you there.[64]

As a leader of an organization in transformation, digital and otherwise, you took calculated risks which included the possibility of things going south and thus you should have prepared, at least mentally, but preferably with crisis procedures.

When things go wrong or really very wrong, as a leader, you need to be measured, composed, present, and involved, providing the sense of calm and structure, assessing the situation and plans, and making sure that the right people are in the right place and doing the right thing.

When all that is in place, you may need to assess your level of involvement. Sometimes you need to get out of the way, however unnatural that feels. Don't automatically assume that you necessarily need to be hands-on in addressing the issue yourself. Others may be better suited and it's your job to evaluate that. But be closely involved and take control if and when needed.

When your system, web site or app crashes, you need to focus on fixing it for your customers. Whatever happened (yes, even high availability cloud providers where your system is deployed can become unavailable sometimes, rare as it may be)[65] it's still ultimately your responsibility to address it and fix it. Blaming others and waiting for others to solve it for you won't cut it.

When what was fundamentally a brick-and-mortar retail business had to become fundamentally a digital business literally overnight due to Covid, despite its digital capability not technically being ready to support flash sales and when the first flash sale crashed the site, I had to accept the responsibility, despite having been in charge of that operation for less than two months. Another time, in one of my past assignments heading up, among other things, cyber security, we got a call from our contacts in the US Secret Service, that our credit card systems[66] had been hacked. I kept the team calm and focused on the problem and not the possible downsides, gathered as many facts as we had, mobilized all relevant resources, and planned to determine what the issue was. Based on that, we started the analysis. We got analysis details back, we analyzed and found the issue (it turned out to be a false alert, in full disclosure). Don't get me wrong, *it wasn't that my blood was not frozen in my veins*, but the operating word was "*projecting calm*", at least the perception of it, so my teams can perform as needed. When the Covid pandemic hit and upended an in-person model, in what felt like an apocalyptic time, like many others, we refocused on learning how to manage a mobile organization where people work from home.[67]

As a leader, you must find the power to control your panic and focus your team's efficient recovery efforts. You don't need an office to lead and manage, crisis or not. You have everything you need on the smartphone in your pocket. But if your digital product that provides critical services to your consumers becomes unavailable, all (your and everybody's) efforts need to be spent to correct the problem. You can't leave your consumer hanging dry or they'll do the same to you and your product next time.

Consumer loyalty, which is what you should strive for, is built on *consistent* great experiences over time. Fix the problem and then climb out of the hole with consumers through very structured and rigorous recovery plans,[68] followed by dogged but innovative solutions.

One thing I have learned from living through hurricanes in Central Florida: However bad they are, the sun will (eventually) shine again.[69]

Calm and optimism. Oregon Sequoias have stood for around 5,000 years.[70]

Post-Mortems Teach You Valuable Lessons – Learn Them

You can only connect dots backwards, not forwards.

Steve Jobs

The digital team is, by definition and need, a learning team. Learning comes from what happened, what went wrong, but also what went right and why.

The team must have regular meetings dedicated to evaluating those aspects. That should be followed very quickly with decisions on what tweaks need to be made – and there are always some, however small – and then implementing them. And if things have gone badly with your product release, while never focusing on blame, you ought to focus on learnings and adjustments. As well as *holding people accountable to change their behaviors in the future.*

I want to emphasize that without such evaluations, the team will not learn, and course correct. These evaluations are what people call *post-mortem* reviews – and while the term "mortem" seems drastic and macabre, or at least suggests something must have gone wrong – it just means learning about what happened recently – good or bad. Or maybe just effective and ineffective. This is about learning from what happened in the past to avoid a repeat or doing better in the future.

Phone Support for Digital Products – Yep, Still Important

Clearly, providing phone support for your digital product sounds like the antithesis of digital.

But here is the thing: I have talked about one of the most important rules of great consumer experiences being that the consumer must never be stranded or in a dead end when they're trying to perform an activity. Or when they don't know what they need to do next – because your experience at that iteration is still incomplete for all cases.

Equally, despite the best and most rigorous efforts to ensure that the digital product works flawlessly, at times there will be some people, however small the number, that cannot successfully execute their actions on the product. Sometimes the business process changes drastically and (almost) overnight (as happened with Covid-19) and your digital experiences are incomplete and need time to catch up. Or when you build something from scratch or an experience that has multiple parts, you're not going to have every piece built and well-functioning enough to satisfy every possible scenario in a way that your users will need on day one.

There will be gaps and parts missing and, regrettable as it is, you'll need to fall back on human intervention via a fully functioning call center, phone-based support to take care of customers in need. It's true, it doesn't necessarily need to be scaled up to take care of *all* the consumers and *all* their needs, but it should be able to support the (hopefully a) minority that needs support at least for a while, until your digital experiences comprehensiveness and quality makes most calls unnecessary.[71]

For that to work well, the phone support team must be equipped with the right tools and the right training to be able to take this task on.[72] I've seen situations where consumers were able to do more and knew more than the staff. But if neither the self-service experience (incomplete or not working) nor the call center (unequipped) can help, then the consumer is stuck in a dead end.

Don't leave consumers stranded. They'll go someplace else.

Chapter 4.2 User Experience Design

Good design is actually a lot harder to notice than poor design, in part because good designs fit our needs so well that the design is invisible, serving us without drawing attention to itself. Bad design, on the other hand, screams out its inadequacies, making itself very noticeable.

Don Norman

If you want to understand design – the *why*, before you can learn the *how* – you need to read Donald Norman's books, first *The Design of Everyday Things* (2013 edition), and then *Emotional Design*.

I have never met Don in person, and I only encountered his seminal work late in my ongoing technology and digital journey. The things he talks about not only made so much sense, but were very familiar to me, after many years of doing digital.[73] He articulates the concepts in ways that will significantly improve your understanding. His books (listed in the *Recommended Reading* section) ought to be a prerequisite for CDIOs.

This chapter is about the hands-on lessons I have personally learned about digital design.[74]

Interface Design and Implementation Are Two Faces of the Same Coin

Design is really an act of communication, which means having a deep understanding of the person with whom the designer is communicating.

Don Norman

Designers focus on two things: what the interface of a product looks like (aka UI) and how it works and feels for a user (aka UX). They put in their best efforts to ensure the experience they design is attractive, easy to use and intuitive.

It would follow that, having cracked what users would use through the design definition, their work is done, with the implicit assumption that the implementation will be faithful to that design.

However, digital designs are not just static works of art, however exquisitely they may be defined. Designs are not just pixel-perfect creations. Instead, they come to life when, and only when, they are working. That means they reflect the actual state, readiness and careful coordination of the myriad backend systems that support that interface – data stores, business logic, maybe even some clever AI.

As such, for products and their interfaces to work as designed, the implementation must faithfully and reliably support that design specification in its intent. The entire, sometimes complex, aggregation of systems that make the interface come alive must work in close coordination to make the design specification functions as designed. Of course, everything else behind the look and feel is probably the responsibility of technical architects – who have technical designs of their own – and engineers – who implement everything.

But the designer is still responsible for making sure that all that scaffolding – from their perspective – comes together to make their design UI/UX work as imagined. If dependencies and their implementation don't deliver, then the design of the interface must change – at least until the implementation becomes faithful to the design vision.

Think about a user screen design. It has information that comes probably from a multitude of backend systems, plus usually a number of controls (buttons, checkboxes, icons, etc.). They must all come together into a coherent whole. If the systems are slow, not available, or reliable, or not synchronized to provide the data, the interface will not work or not work well.

For example, if one of the items on the screen comes from a slow-response back-end system and that latency would impact the rendering of the entire screen, then the design must be changed to accommodate for that – render what's available fast and do an asynchronous (aka *lazy-loading*) for the slow item. Or pre-load it earlier before the screen must even be rendered. Or put in a separate screen altogether, etc. To make things even more ridiculous, sometimes that slow item may not even be relevant or used vis-a-vis the other elements on the screen.

Design and implementation are two faces of the same coin – the experience.

UX Design Constraints – How to Use Them to Make Your Product Better

A user interface is like a joke. If you have to explain it, it's not that good.

Martin Leblanc

Note that here I am using the word "constraints" not referring to limiting consumers actions, but in the engineering sense of the specifications that the design must deliver against.

Your design must ensure that features can be easily (as in no manuals required) found. Call that **discoverability**. If your consumers struggle to find what they need after a reasonable discovery effort around your product, then you have a big problem. There are two avenues to take here to enhance the discoverability of the design.

First, make sure you put the reference to the feature (aka Call To Action (CTA)) in a logical (i.e., from your consumers mental models, i.e., expectations viewpoint) *grouping* – all features related to categories of actions, like booking, checking-in, payments, accounts management, etc., being together. Also, depending on how important or how often the feature is used, put it at the right level of your interface – don't put the most used feature behind several menus and menu items Instead put it in the top level of your interface or the home screen/page.

A **second** approach is to put the CTA in *multiple* places in the interface, when a feature can reasonably be considered to be part of multiple groupings. But that should be used sparingly as users may get confused if their mental model doesn't put a feature in different categories, wondering if different CTAs for X are the same.

The interface and the product overall must ensure that consumers can fulfill their intended goals as they expect. If the interface tells them that an action – filling in fields in forms, booking, payment, updates, etc. – is successful, it must be so and in full. Call this **effectiveness**. The interface should assist in any way, including by preventing common errors from being made.[75]

Especially for situations where performing of an action very expeditiously is required – think tired kids in tow on a rainy afternoon in an amusement park or an urgent care – the interface must be able to accommodate **action-to-outcome speed**. I would argue that in this day and age even consumers sitting in their comfortable armchair at home expect to navigate a product in minimal steps, all fast to execute. Here you'll have to put effort into minimizing the number of screens, taps, and/or clicks needed to complete an action. Reusable do-it-once-reuse-many-times functionality (like saving profile, address, credit card, and insurance information) helps immensely.

Users become more adept and thus fast at using a well-designed interface when they can develop a mental model of how the product works and thus execute the required actions with speed and without a particular mental effort. Call that **mental model building**. For that to happen, the interface must be *consistent* and standard across different but highly similar actions, thus predictable, so, over several uses, it's easily learned and remembered. How we, as humans, learn something, is an interesting "feature" of our brains, but suffice to say it's by correlating to other similar memories, experiences, and models. That is why consistency, not just across your product, but across multiple products, is important – as long as it's not repeating bad experiences.

Visualizations – An Image Is Worth a Thousand Words

Sometimes text-based interfaces become too complicated or unintuitive to help users navigate the product and its features, especially on smaller screens.[76] In those cases, a visual representation of the data can be very useful, indeed a savior to the design. The most common scenario is that of selecting a place on a map.

The map is useful as it gives the user an *intuitive* representation of both locations and distances, in a user-friendlier way than a list of locations and distances could.

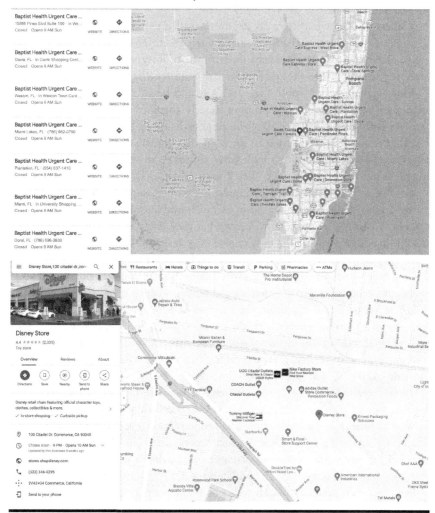

Figure 4.3   A picture is worth a thousand words (Google Maps).

You Must Design for What People Will Likely Do[77]

We must design for the way people behave, not for how we would wish them to behave.

Don Norman

What people will likely do is an exceedingly frustrating thing to anticipate. It's not just their preferences, but their constraints, mental models, and circumstances. And it may be different from one use of the product to another, by the *same* user. Go figure.

Understanding what users do requires detailed user research as well as ethnography (as different behaviors can happen in different contexts and situations), observing closely what they do with the prototype and the product, and analyzing insights from the system logs.[78] It requires *all* these together.

However much we would like, and it would be so much easier for us, our consumers will never use the product exactly the way we want it. That's not negative thinking, it's a fact. But the important thing to always remember is that they're not actually wrong to do what they do. It's not their fault, it's the design or the implementation's fault when things go in anticipated ways. It's the designer's job to give them what they'll naturally use. That is good design.[79]

So, the only realistic option is to make the product support what they'll likely do, by understanding *why* they do it, as much and as soon as possible. It's a lot harder than simply prescribing to users what they *ought* to do – which is pretty much impossible – but it's the only choice for a designer. For brain efficiency reasons, humans make simplifying assumptions about how things should work – and do elsewhere – and attempt to reuse those assumptions as much as possible. If your design and experience don't fit that mental model, then the product will fail.

There are plenty of videos on the Internet of people making fun of users for doing *seemingly* stupid things with the product. Well, don't be one of those who makes fun as, other than feeling good for one millisecond, it doesn't help you or your customers. In reality, it's the product limitations, whether functionality or confusing UI/UX, that forces people into doing what you don't expect.

Now, there will be those moments when you're damned if you do, damned if you don't, as they say. That is when about half of your users will want to do something in one way and the other half something totally opposite and the two expectations can't possibly be supported in the same product experience. In those cases, you may try extra hard to figure out a common denominator for the product experience to support both extremes, but if you can't find one, just resign yourself to be called an idiot by half of your customers, while the other half may not necessarily call you a hero.

Let's Debate Affordances – What You Can Do Versus How You Know What You Can Do

Affordances is a very peculiar word. The concept behind it is very powerful. However, in different places and at different times it has been used with subtly different meanings and as such there is confusion. I know I was confused when I encountered it in different writings.

The term was originally introduced in 1966 by James Gibson, a famous psychologist and it was used to define what the environment provides an animal. In this definition, an affordance is a relationship between the environment and the animal, not a property of either. In the human-made objects' realm, a chair allows (or *affords*) a human to sit on (and sitting is what in this book I call an outcome).

Don Norman, in the original version (1988) of his book *The Design of Everyday Things*, coming from the user design perspective, defined the term as the possibilities that are readily *perceived* that the object provides. In the chair example, a chair must be *perceived* by a human to provide the possibility of being sat on. If a human cannot figure out that a chair is a chair, it cannot be used (that is the definition you will mostly find used across many writings). Subtle distinction.

However, in the 2013 updated version of the same book, Don clarified the definition of affordances[80] aligning closer to the original Gibson[81] meaning: a chair affords a human to sit on, or move around unless it's royal throne etc. He introduced a second concept, signifiers, to help with the *perception* of the possibilities provided by an object (or user interface).

And that latter definition is what I use in my work and in this book: Affordances are what the product allows or *affords* the user to do with it. We all know that a door, once opened, affords one the ability to move from one space into another, spaces being delimited by walls. And we talked about the chair.

But in the digital experience design world I *choose* to use affordances as *what a product or features allows users to do*, in order to achieve an outcome.[82] It is true that in the strictest sense, product features are not affordances, as a product feature is the technical implementation of a way for users to get outcomes, while affordances are what users can do. Another subtle difference, but let's be honest, a consumer would not be able to distinguish between all the semantic and academic differences.

The more fundamental concept here is the user perception of affordances, more specifically the *mental model* around them. We have all learned as young children, through observation, what a door is and that a door is to be opened (and stay open), to be closed (and stay closed), and to be locked.

When either one is not available, it breaks the definition from the mental model. Why have a door you can never close – why not just an opening or archway? Why have a door you can never open – why not a wall? And if a bathroom door can't be locked, how is the privacy to be enforced against unwanted entry by others?

Now that we have settled how many imaginary creatures can dance on the tip of a pin, let's see why talking about affordances is useful.

Affordances or What You Can Do With a Product

For an airline app, affordances, in my definition, are the ability to book a flight, check-in, receive pre-board notifications, flight updates, probably on-board entertainment, plus the ability to see your reward points. For a hotel app, billing, check-in, check-out, maybe keyless entry, etc. For a retail app, the ability to buy products, have them shipped to whenever you need, pay, and then track the delivery.

In the digital realm, we have built mental models, through extrapolation from similar experiences, about what a particular app/web site should allow us to do – for example any retail site or app that lists products should have a checkout with the ability to buy, pay, and ship. Any unnatural limitations to our expectation will become confusing and frustrating, just like a door that can't open or close when we need it to.

What is the point of having an airline mobile app that doesn't provide flight updates, given the constant changes to schedules and gates,[83] when your mobile phone is what you're going to have with you in an airport to inform yourself? Or a hotel app where you can't see your upcoming stay and its details? Or a healthcare app that doesn't allow you to at least check your results – labs, tests, visit summaries –and your upcoming appointments. Or if a mobile app doesn't work well on cellular but only high bandwidth WIFI (which you mostly get at home, where a desktop web is better anyway, for screen size reasons). All sure recipes for user dissatisfaction.

Your app/web will not have all the features that all your users will need, at least not when you start from scratch. What it will have to have, though, sooner rather than later, is those features consumers expect to use the most and the soonest[84] – that their mental model predicts from an app like yours.[85] As such, you'll need to factor that set of expectations into your prioritized plans of what to provide and when.

Figure 4.4   No need for a door (author's collection).

Signifiers or What Tells Users How They Can Use Your Product

Signifiers, as a concept, are equally important as affordances for digital experiences, if not more. They're the interface indicators that allow the users to understand how to use your product.

To use one of Don Norman's favorite examples, public doors usually have a handle to be grabbed and pulled towards the user to open the door. From the other side, they usually have either push areas or push bars (that also unlock the door if it's locked on one side). Whether it's a handle to pull on or a push area to push on are what *signifies* (the signifiers) to the user what they can and need to do. This scheme corresponds to users' mental models (same discussion as in the earlier section of affordances). This way they can intuitively use the product, no instructions necessary and no new mental models to be memorized and recalled. Simple, right?

Well, the problem is that a lot of doors break the rule by offering the wrong signifier that leads to the incorrect action. For example, a door that only opens one way, but has pull handles on both sides, one to pull and one to push.[86] So, 50% of the time someone will be wrong and try to pull when they need to push or the other way around. And if it's a door you use reasonably often, but not constantly, now you'll have to remember what to do (push versus pull) so you don't look stupid half of the time.[87]

In digital interfaces, we have interface elements, such as clickable/tappable icons,[88] buttons, drop downs, checkboxes, swipes, scrolling approaches, input fields, etc. Those are affordances – they allow the user to perform an action. They have a deep functionality behind them.

But the state of each, the use of coloring schemes or fonts (normal, italic, bold, underlines, superscribed, etc.), even its presence or absence, labels, and notifications, are all signifiers. They tell the user something that they need to know or do (red is a problem, green means all OK, gray means action not possible, bold text means important, italic means information, superscribed means not available, etc.).

If a button is to be pressed, it should be colored or etched in a way that is obvious that it is to be pressed. If the feature is not available, it ought to be grayed out or removed altogether. If a list has more items than what the screen shows, it must either provide a fragment of the next item just above the fold or the horizontal sides of the screens to signify *"there's more"*. If something really needs explanation (preferably to be avoided) a tooltip to be pressed or clicked must be offered (and used only if the explanation is required for the current user). Whether input fields are mandatory or optional must be evident in some way (maybe they're in different color boxes). If you know people's favorites, show them first in a list – or have a "most used" list.

Consumers need to always be aware where they are in a process or flow (use breadcrumbs to provide flow progress) as well as what is going to happen next and overall, in the journey. Making it clear to them in some intuitive fashion helps them avoid mistakes and abandon flows. The solution should be predefined flows/journeys with predefined steps/tasks that consumers can pick, with the progress through the journey being tracked, with results from past steps and prompts for upcoming steps, maybe with dates for steps that can be adjusted automatically if the journey – or balance of it – is changed. That is, flows for an end outcome instead of disparate tasks that the user must know how to put together towards that outcome.

Now, not that having a 15-step flow is preferred,[89] even if described by the progress in a breadcrumbs flow at the top of the screen, but at least the breadcrumbs give the user an early indication on what is going to happen. Then they can abandon early if they can't go through the 15 steps. If all those steps are really needed, then provide the ability to the user to save the work and return later (*"Save draft"*) or provide the ability for each step to be done independently (demographics, saved payment options, preferences, delivery addresses, etc.).

At all times, the user must understand the result of an action – successful or failed – and thus the experience must provide meaningful and actionable feedback to the users. No feedback will prompt the users to repeat their action needlessly. Great feedback will provide user satisfaction.[90] But feedback must be used judiciously for when consumers expect it – like purchasing an item – and not merely when they close an information screen, for example (assuming there's no unsaved information on that screen that would be lost and whatever the content that screen has of importance).

Across different parts of the experience, signifiers and their behavior should be consistent.[91] Humans, mostly out of confusion, are prone to error – thus the design should start with the assumption that users will make mistakes and offer recovery options. There's no point in confusing them with inconsistency. And consistency, even if your app is used irregularly, creates mental models that can be applied easily and quickly to new features – provided they're also consistent with users' expectations. Consistency not only provides ease of use, but, through repeatability of at least satisfactory outcomes, they create trust. And trust is a critical element of consumer loyalty. As with everything in this book, this section is about focusing on consumers, their perceptions, and likely reactions – that is what great designers design for.

I could not end this section without a couple of examples of ridiculous signifiers – presumably required by corporate lawyers. Judge for yourselves.

Figure 4.5   Ridiculous signifiers – or seeing is believing (author's collection).

Avoid the "Big Brother" (System) Syndrome

Another problem to be avoided is that the product – and its backend records and business processes – "knows" more than the user. When all that knowledge and rules are applied to what the user is trying to do, it must be done transparently.

The platform smartness must help, not impair, or frustrate the user through its opacity (the customer will legitimately say *"why can't I do that or why is that not available?"*, with the undisclosed answer being *"because the product knows your account is not eligible, etc."*).

That transparency must be communicated in ways that the user can easily grasp. And the best way to do that is by showing what it does (*"Logging you in"*, *"Accessing your records"*, etc.) – which is a great strategy if an action takes longer than expected; The system showing what it's doing is a way to reassure that the system is not hung.[92]

And if your account is indeed not eligible,[93] make that obvious as early as possible, including explaining why. Even better, provide an alternative path for consumers to take (*"you can upgrade to the premium account that is eligible for this benefit"*).

When You Talk to Your Users, Call a Spade a Spade

The words[94] you use to call objects and actions in your experience are powerful signifiers that help – or confuse, if done incorrectly – the consumer's understanding of what they can do or are about to do. For example, I have seen plenty of user screens with a button in a notification window that said *"Cancel"*. Cancel what, the window (remove it from the screen) or the underlying action in progress that generated that message window?

If a feature is called *"Book Appointment"*, that signifies to the users they can book an appointment and be done with – fire and forget, so to speak in technology terms – and don't expect a separate, sometimes manual, staff review process that could change the outcome. If that is indeed the case, call that feature *"Request Appointment"*.

Design Systems – Or How You Ensure User Interface Consistency

All the visual interface signifiers and controls are usually brought together in a design system[95] – which basically is a collection of all the standard interface elements, what they look like, when are they to be used, i.e., in what circumstances and how they work. Importantly, the design system must be visually impaired-friendly.

While the design system can be custom to your product or company, it should still abide by the common standards users expect and definitely consistent with the underlying platform (iOS, Android, MacOS, etc.) standards.[96] Occasionally, I see an iOS app that has unexpected signifiers[97] – and that is usually a sign it is a port from another platform and reflects the dominant interface paradigm of that platform, not the one they're now deployed on. This must be avoided at all costs. It may require separate codebases for different platforms, but the benefits are high.

Chapter 4.3 Adoption and Retention

When the product is right, you don't have to be a great Marketer.

Lee Iacocca

Great! You've done your user research, you've designed and built a great product, now how are you supposed to get consumers to start using it and experience its value?

Your consumers, for their benefit and yours, must get to know about your product, in terms they can understand. If they don't know about you and your product, or they don't know what to make of your product, you're wasting your time – or theirs.

This is where market positioning, messaging, and other strategies of informing consumers come into play. Please note that while this chapter is placed after product delivery topics, it doesn't mean that this exercise can or should be done only at the end of the delivery process. The artifacts described here are usually living documents, starting early in the product lifecycle, and constantly updated throughout the process.

There are several adoption phases your product will go through. First, obtain awareness, when consumers will become aware the product exists but they're not ready to do anything about it or trust it yet. The next phase is where they download the app or find the web site. That is still not enough. Then they need to follow through with trying the app and/or the web, and probably invest time and effort in creating a login. This part is a big deal. The ultimate part is where they start using it effectively and then they *keep* on using it.

How you get from one end to the other is the focus of this chapter.

Adoption Lifecycle – Or Why Your Product Adoption Is Nothing Special

The standard adopter's cycle will also apply to your product: maximum adoption of 50–60% of all consumers; innovators (1–2%); early adopters (10%); early majority (25%); late majority (15%). You'll be crossing the chasm[98] when moving from early adopters into early majority.[99] Congratulations, you have made it. Now you'll have to worry about keeping your users.

You'll have to be patient as you navigate from the extreme left to the right. All products, no matter how successful they (eventually) are, go through this lifecycle. Most products from mere product mortals like us, will take quite a while to cross over.

And as you navigate that lifecycle, your product will need to evolve. The implementation bugs and limitations that innovators and early adopters tolerated, will not be acceptable to the majority. And poor user experience will delay even the laggards.

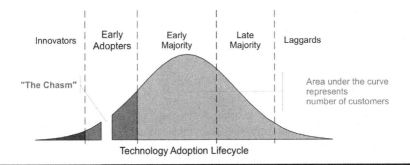

Figure 4.6 Technology adoption cycle curve. Craig Chelius, CC BY 3.0 <https://creativecommons.org/licenses/by/3.0>, via Wikimedia Commons

Product Positioning or the Right Thing for the Right Place

Having the best product means nothing if the people won't buy it.

Don Norman

Products, digital or physical,[100] must be defined by consumer needs. It is important what the consumers *think* your product's role in their life is and where it is supposed to offer value. That is product positioning and is obviously important, as, if your consumers don't know what to make of your product and in what situations to use and for what needs, they won't use it.[101]

There's another benefit to defining product positioning crisply: It provides clarity[102] to the product team about what they're trying to offer and therefore keeps product definition, engineering and marketing efforts focused.

Depending on the product and intended target customers, there can be myriads of ways to map product and features to customers.

Are you targeting busy shoppers that need to order something simply and quickly or connoisseurs who like to research extensively, compare, and contrast products? If the former, your product must be architected to show the most common or popular products first, at the lower end of the spectrum. If the latter, then the priority showing must be based on whatever special-interest customer user research indicates.

Is it for one-time customers or is it driven mostly by repeat and loyal customers? If the former, then the experience is simplified and probably non-authenticated (guest). If the latter, then customer preferences and previous purchases must inform the offering, at least with priority.

You get the idea.

It's OK to have situations where you are not positioned at all – that is where you don't want or can't provide value with your product.[103]

There is an obvious overlap between deciding who your target customers are and the product positioning. In the end, you would want to have the best and the most comprehensive product for the needs of your target customers – those who you are trying to please and retain.

Whether you decide to serve other customers besides your target customers is a choice, probably opportunistic – every firm wants a long relationship with a consumer, but most will serve one-time customers as well. But, even for repeat customers, you may decide, whether for commercial or technical reasons, that you will not be able to offer certain features. Just be clear what those are.

Messaging – You Must Be Clear What You Want to Say and When

> *To me, marketing is about values. This is a very complicated world, it's a very noisy world and we're not going to get a chance to get people to remember much about us. No company is. And so, we must be really clear on what we want them to know about us.*

Steve Jobs

Messaging is how you communicate to your consumers what your product does, in a way that speaks to their needs and wants, contextualized to what they are looking for in that moment, that they can mentally register successfully enough to adopt the product. That aspect is equally important, if not more, than market positioning. The former is about what you tell them, how and when; the latter is about what needs are fulfilled.

Given the different segmentation of the target costumers[104] and the different times in their lives and journeys that the product supports, what you communicate and advertise and how will be very different. A common denominator sounds good in principle – to those who don't want to do the detailed work of segregating messages – but it's not good for successfully *reaching* out to your customers.

Here is the thing: Consumers will notice your product if, when and where they can *match what the product messaging says it does in concrete, simple and direct ways, with what they think of or need at that moment, place, and context*. That is important for at least two reasons: increasing adoption through better contextual comprehension and providing understanding of the product.

Sure, a point could be made about consumers subconsciously noticing a message often enough that they then become interested in exploring it consciously.[105] The problem is that the subconscious mind is lazy enough to filter out the too many messages it constantly receives, especially in unexpected contexts.

It works for healthcare advertising in a healthcare context where awareness may be higher to anything healthcare (and even there, not if the focal point is pain), but it will not work if not in that specific context, for example in a sports context, where the mind focuses on the sports event and ignores adverts for hospitals (unless the consumer is afraid after the sporting event they may end up in a hospital, in which case they should pay attention, just to be prepared).[106]

Just because the marketing department purchased some advertising at a golf tournament, don't expect your (potential) consumers to notice any of the advertising and messages you put at that tournament about anything completely unrelated to golf – thus not registering what your product offers. And certainly, don't be under the illusion you're getting your advertising money's worth.[107]

That is especially true when the message the subconscious mind is *supposed* to absorb is not a very specific one. Here, broad advertising for an entire app that does all sorts of things, versus *"Four taps and you're in urgent care"* will not work particularly efficiently. The latter is most likely to be absorbed (because it's interesting or unusual or speaks to an ongoing consumer pain point) and to be recalled later when another message is encountered.

For brand-new products (or new to the consumer), the messaging focus should be in attracting the consumer to try the product, triggered from a particular feature or context.[108] If the consumer is interested, then it's a matter of maintaining and expanding the interest through whatever else the product offers that is now visible.

For an established product or one the consumer has been using, the focus should be on constantly reminding the user of the value of the product, including by advertising new (but relevant) features, to retain, and even expand, the engagement.

The most common tool to manage and clarify the messaging is what is known as the marketing messaging matrix:[109] Think of a two-dimensional table that would have on one dimension who you are trying to reach and for what needs, and on the other what you're going to convey to each about your product or feature.

For example, for a consumer trying to easily find a product on your website, the message would be one of speed (if that is what your product is good at), and the actual slogan would be *"No endless scrolling to find what you want"*.

If instead the product/feature is all about helping users make a complex buying decision, then the message should be about comprehensive information and research and the slogan would be *"We've done the thorough research, so you don't have to"* or something to that effect. Over time, the matrix evolves, for existing and new features.

The important thing to keep in mind about marketing messaging matrices, just like with the marketing process itself, is that they should be defined not at the very end when you're about to launch the product, but from the early stages of the process and throughout it, as it maintains clarity among team members of what you're trying to accomplish with the product. That way you don't move back and forth in the implementation between comprehensiveness and simplicity/speed, between search and browse, between easy access to a small subsection of information and transactions and an encyclopedia.

What makes focused and targeted messaging?[110] Targeted and focused doesn't mean referring to your product and everything that it does to anyone who may be looking any time for services in your industry. It means messaging at the time and place the consumer is mostly interested in and therefore likely to register the message.

For example, an email I receive from American Airlines about my upcoming travel promotes their app but speaks to how the app will benefit me *in the upcoming travel*: check-ing in, getting flight updates, getting on the plane, in-flight entertainment, etc.

It doesn't tell me that I can book other travel – I just did, now I'm focused on that trip. It doesn't tell me that I can share points or convert them. American Airlines do send me other blanket marketing emails to talk about all that. But not this one.

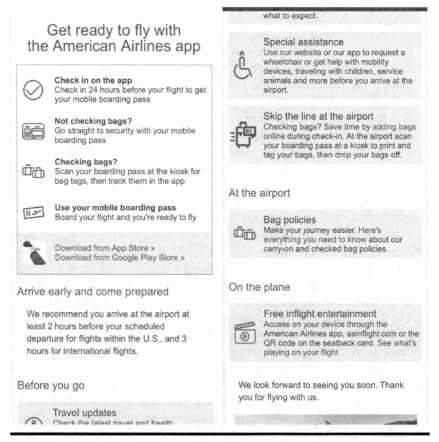

Figure 4.7   Targeted messaging from American Airlines (author's collection).

Hilton Hotels' email, again about my upcoming stay, advertises the app for keyless (in app) entry. Not that I can book stays elsewhere – which I have no interest in doing as I'm preparing for *this* stay.

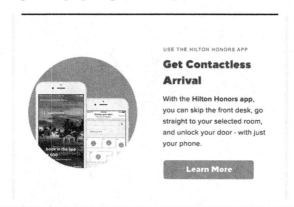

Figure 4.8   Targeted messaging from Hilton (author's collection).

At the un-targeted end of the spectrum, Gmail messaging makes no sense, as it advertises using their app when I happen to read their very email in *their* Gmail app – that shouts blanket advertising.

Figure 4.9   Un-targeted message from Gmail (author's collection).

The Amex wallet app recommends that I look up the charge details recorded in the app. Uber is advertising its services in the location where it knows I am now.

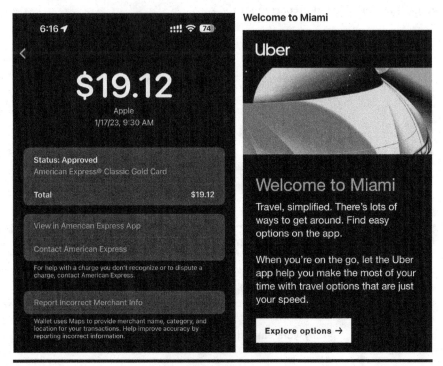

Figure 4.10   Messaging from American Express and Uber (author's collection).

That is what targeting messaging means. And with mobile, it's a lot about location.

In healthcare, it would mean in a PCP setting or Urgent Care Center visit, consumers are shown messages about check-in and registration in the waiting room, but about medical records in the visit room because they will need to check their medical and billing records after the visit.

And if you want further proof, here is Bob Stone's (famous marketing executive) formula for messaging.[111] First, focus the message on the most important *benefit* to the customer of your product or offering ("*Save precious time when you don't have it*"). Then reinforce that benefit in a way that is hard to miss ("*Four taps and you're in*"). Then explain in more detail how much better their experience/life is going to be ("*You'll get what you need faster so we can spend the saved time on more important things*"). Next, articulate what the experience would be without your product ("*Would you rather be at the back of the line filling paper forms?*"). Then summarize it all ("*Fast. Easy.*

Simple"). Finish with an easy call to action for next steps ("*Download our app XYZ*" with a link to app stores).[112]

But the number one rule of effective marketing and messaging is that it has to be all true, so you'd better be putting in the effort to make your product work as well as the messaging says it does!

Positioning Versus Competition

If you're competitor-focused, you must wait until there's a competitor doing something. Being customer-focused allows you to be more pioneering.

Jeff Bezos

As a matter of principle I don't believe that products should be defined by the competition but instead by the consumer and the market. Your competition may not be in the same product bracket as you, may have other strengths and weaknesses that don't apply to you and their customers may not be the same as yours.

You can maniacally focus on your consumers' needs or on your competitors' products, but not both at the same time. Better focus on customers and their needs and maybe adjust marginally to competitors' offerings.

However, where the competition is, how strong it is, and what capabilities it has should at least inform where your product and team need to focus strategically – if nothing other than establishing what consumers expect from *any* product similar to yours. If all the airline apps offer real-time flights updates and that is what all consumers now expect, then yours very likely will need to have that as well[113] – even if you're not hearing it in your user research as consumers will think of it as table stakes.

Evaluating advantages/disadvantages, strengths/weaknesses, as well as future roadmaps and potential of competitors – *all from the viewpoint of consumers* – could be valuable. But to be meaningful, it has to be viewed in the context of your intended or actual product competitive advantages.

When a competitor has defined in some unique way what the consumers *think* of that type of product, yet you plan to change your consumers mental model about your product, it's wise to understand what you're trying to move your consumers *from* (your competitor's model) in order to plan your positioning and messaging accordingly versus that established mental model.

But direct competitors are not the only place to look for inspiration on solutions. Consumers compare you with their experiences in any other domain, so any solution someone else has in a different but potentially similar industry is a good place to start. If a hotel has a great find-book-check-in-checkout-pay experience, that may apply to you in entertainment, retail, or healthcare.

In some contexts, and for some businesses, especially in hotly contested and competitive markets, I recommend defining a matrix that has your product's features versus the ones your competitors offer to consumers.[114] Beware, though, that this exercise focuses on understanding the competition[115] as described before and it doesn't lead to a feature-to-feature competition, where everybody is indistinguishable.

If your product is intended to provide services that every consumer could use, if no meaningful differentiation – whether better and more features, more intuitive UI/UX, etc. – can be accomplished versus the competition, then the focus is on the wrong market or product.

Word of Mouth (Or Social Media)

Word of mouth – customers telling other potential customers, whether in person (don't underestimate the size and influence of family and friend groups) or through media (email or more likely through social media) about a product, is the nirvana that all product managers dream of, especially if viral and preferably with no marketing expenditure.

Why? It's cheaper for one, but that's not only why it is very valuable. People trust other people, especially established users who experienced the product themselves, with their opinions and recommendations, way more than they trust yet another marketing campaign. If recommenders are both super fans[116] of your product *and* established influencers, you hit the jackpot.

However, such a feat is very difficult to achieve for most products, unless three things all happen: the product is very good (at addressing a pressing consumer need), refreshingly new, or significantly different. One or two will probably not suffice.

In order to benefit from a super fans channel, you will need to find the segment of consumers most likely to try the product *and* be willing to tell others about it. These are users turning into *evangelists* for your product. This is where understanding the market segment – where and who the consumers are – is very important.

If the product has innovative features or is new to a market, then early adopters are where to start. If new in the market but the functionality is mature (other products offering the same features), then word of mouth will be based solely on quality and customer satisfaction (if that's how you distinguish your product from others), but the adoption will be necessarily slower, as least at the beginning.

Social Media Influencers

A technique some companies use to advertise their product is to engage social media *influencers*. These are individuals who have a large number of followers that look for their opinions about social, environmental and, often, brand and product topics. If the influencer *chooses* to endorse a product or a brand, the company behind that brand or product can choose to reward them monetarily. Clearly, if the influencer cares about their own brand – i.e., what their followers think about them and their recommendations – and they do, then they'll be very careful with what they recommend to their followers. Somebody who is believed to just take money for any and all endorsements will gradually lose their followers and their brand value will eventually become zero.

However, an influencer who, after experiencing your product and brand themselves, is legitimately impressed by it enough to *choose* to advertise it to their followers, is an incredibly powerful vehicle to get your product advertised to other consumers. And it's worth at least as much as your traditional marketing, as long as it's credible with the audience.

Figure 4.11   A superfan advertising a digital product (author's collection).

Just make sure that you're prepared for the value of the influencer currency going up *or* down. Clearly, an influencer who becomes a widely popular star will project a halo effect on your brand and product – if they endorsed your product or brand reasonably recently. But equally, if the influencer decides to go off the deep end with deeply divisive and insulting opinions elsewhere while they also endorse you, that will eventually damage your product brand. So, you'll have to curate the influencers you reward carefully to avoid unpleasant surprises.

Now, how to decide who to proactively prompt to try your product and services and how to decide the value of their endorsements to your brand and product is more of an art than a science and requires carefully looking, finding, and cultivating influencers. The influencers and evangelists need your constant love, attention, time, and effort. They are expecting to have input into the product roadmap, which is not a bad thing at all, although it requires time and effort to engage. And remember, they endorse for the love of the product, not for the firms' other agendas, so don't take them for granted.

The easiest and most effective way to start finding evangelizers (as well as volunteer testers) is to enroll your employee base, assuming they're also customers. If they become converts to the product,[117] they'll tell others about it – both in personal settings *and* as part of their job – because they're enthusiastic as users and not because they're mandated by managers.

Having talked about the positives of evangelism, the lack of any is a big warning sign.[118] So, watch out for lack of genuine endorsements of any kind.

Focus Adoption Efforts on Your Targeted Consumers

I already talked about the goal of your product: creating loyalty through consistently great experiences, focusing on relationships, not just transactions.

The big trick here is to understand what drives that loyalty to your digital product by your target consumers. Simple, fast, short-to-the-point, secure, intuitive, reliable, user-friendly, consistent, etc. are all qualities usually applied to great products. But which of those qualities create loyalty in the long-term?

Your search may generate user satisfaction by returning the best-for-the-need results when customers don't know where to go, by understanding where they are now and where they (likely) need to go. The user making a booking by using your product may be rewarded by being offered appointments (or rides) sooner – so it should know when they travel or have medical conditions. Your payment process may support secure wallets when you know they're concerned about credit card theft. Quick in and out of physical premises is what busy people treasure – always.

Now, knowing what they prize most doesn't mean you're going to offer them only that, as, if the product offering is too narrow, they will not be interested in investing in the totality of your product. It just means you need to put extra effort into those qualitative areas to be even better.

It then makes sense that when you're trying to establish your (new) product, you should find ways to reach out to those loyal customers (loyal from either previous physical or digital great experiences) on the exact product aspects they value most.

I sometimes hear folks – including in healthcare, which is usually territory-bound – *switching* focus from loyalty to (new) customer *acquisition*,[119] especially during difficult economic times. Those marketers presumably promise the CEO new customers that are *additive* to the existing customer base. That may indeed be the case – good for them – but it will likely not be.

First, the most important customer is the one you already have – and must keep! – and not the one you're trying to get but you may not be able to. Acquiring a new customer is a lot more expensive than keeping an existing one.

Second, if you switch from customer loyalty to new customer acquisition, it's very likely that you'll lose focus on your existing customers and neglect them in ways big and small. You may get a new – and not yet loyal – customer but lose an existing, loyal one. That is a bad deal.

So, unless you're very well prepared to do both *very* well, keep your focus on your existing customers (and their families and friends) – especially in incredibly trust-based businesses.

Now that may sound easier than it is, especially if your customer is not needing to use your digital product right now (they just bought a car from you last week, visited your entertainment park last month, or had a triple bypass last year). In that situation, to keep on their radar, offer value and attract them to consuming *adjacent* services (if and only if they *need* to, as hopefully they don't continue to need traumatic surgeries, but they may still need follow-up visits and other medical services to enhance their health). So, focus on that category.

Then there are those consumers that you previously had and have since lost, either because of unpleasant interactions in the physical world or through subpar or incomplete digital experiences in the past. The latter is particularly going to happen when you build something from scratch and early adopters don't see exactly what they may need yet in the app or web, so they dismiss it outright in the future. They may not check back either because you don't continue to improve the digital experience or because they don't realize how fast you're moving (in my recent team's case, from very little to very much in some two short years). That category – and your data should tell you who they are – is to particularly be focused on, with the messaging being that the experience is much better now than earlier.

And then there are those who really have not heard about your digital experience. However you know who they are and when they don't use your digital product to interact with the firm, they are reachable with a simple message: "*Did you know you could do what you just did in a much better digital way?*" Identify who your customers have been and reach out to them first, but with very intelligent differentiated messaging.

But reach out you must, for their own benefit, as well as yours.

Even if you have done all this well, here is some bad news. Just as your firm needs to maintain the existing customer base, so do you, as a digital team and product. Don't assume that just because the users consumed your experience, even if they had a great one, they'll do it again. Time and non-use lead to the out-of-sight-out-mind-effect, so you'll have to keep communicating with your users, reminding them why your product is so beneficial (you probably have data on that, use it!) and what else they may miss, with your product improving significantly while they were not watching.

Use Focused Triggers to Spark Product Evaluation Interest

You promote your product – through advertising, inspired and well targeted messaging using the right messages in the right places for your prospective users to see, and being an adoption process. But what else could you do?

There are those consumers who will decide to buy or use a product based on careful consideration – they decide first they need a product, then they research options about different products, they may tentatively choose and then maybe try it and then decide to use/buy it. They may evaluate one product versus another based on a convincing advert they saw while researching.[120] Clearly, a larger effort put into careful evaluation is usually driven by a of larger magnitude commitment to a product: a house, a car, but also a computer or mobile phone platform. Clearly, buying a $0.99 app or downloading a free app in an app store would not be in that category.[121]

Then there are those who will just decide to go for a product after a very short evaluation. That could be the impulse-buying that stores actively exploit by deploying common products – batteries, magazines, for example – by the checkout. The location of those products is solely to remind shoppers of their other needs while waiting to pay but otherwise is unrelated to their other purchases.

But there's another type of trigger for adoption, and that is when a product use and advantages become obvious *while* performing a different but related operation, including a non-digital one. The product may be directly associated with the operation, or somewhat adjacent, but still close. In the absence of the need to execute that operation and the collocation of the information for the product, the product would either be ignored or not known altogether.

Think about this example. You show up at a restaurant and ask for a table. The staff informs you politely that you need a reservation that can be obtained easily on an app or web site that you didn't know about. If it's important to get into that restaurant or the restaurant is part of a chain that you care to patronize in the future, you'll download and use the app or the site – now that you know that is possible.

Another example would be when buying a product on the internet: You want that product and you could buy it in an unauthenticated way (guest purchase), but the site also advertises creating and using a digital account that promises to offer a variety of additional value points, maybe reward points, alerts and notifications of new or newly available products, the convenience of saving personal details such as address and credit cards for future easy reuse, or, even better, free shipping.[122] They may even call it a special membership, all driven by that digital account you create but otherwise wouldn't have. You may have encountered an advert for membership on a billboard on the highway, but probably had never registered it. Now, however, it makes sense because you link what you were doing to what you *could* be doing more.[123]

The trigger may be present in your own company through other communications with consumers – for example, a notification that your medical test results are now available can advertise[124] the convenience of accessing them through your mobile app at any time and any place.

A variant to this is when – in the case of mobile apps – the app detects the user is near a location belonging to a company – a store, an airport, a hotel, an urgent care facility, a hospital – and offers services through the app. Subscriptions – where appropriate[125] – and reminders for them are also a good way to enhance the digital engagement, not to mention providing convenience and a good revenue stream for the company. Think of medication refill reminders in the app. Of course, in all these cases the app must be installed in the first place, but these notifications constitute a nice way for the user to remember to use it and create stickiness in the long run.

The product adoption trigger effect is an important tool to expand the utilization of your digital product and should be consistently evaluated.

Changing Entrenched Consumer Habits Takes Time and Effort

The behavior of customers will never be transformed by a product whose design is based on an analysis of their past behavior.

Roger L Martin

By and large, people hate calling a customer service agent to obtain a product or a service – it's more cumbersome, the caller and the agent don't see the same details, there may be communication barriers, hours of operation are limited. In the end it works, but only with enough effort from both sides. And yet, even when a better (digital) product is available, the digital product uptake is frustratingly slow. Why?

One explanation is that the new product is not yet sufficiently known to consumers. This chapter is trying to help with that. Another explanation is that maybe the "better" part in *better product* is not accurate[126] and the product is more difficult to use than alternatives (say, calling).

But another explanation, most common, is that users are familiar with and trust the old options better. When the phone has been the main channel your consumers have used to reach your firm for decades, they're *mentally conditioned* to call. It will take a while and a lot of advertising, education, reminding and even overt incentives for them to switch to a digital product.[127] Introducing new habits and replacing old ones is hard.

The "trusting more" part speaks to two different aspects. The **first** is about trusting that the digital product *works* as advertised – and only through repeated flawless experience is that trust built up (and any mishaps encountered drives it back down).

The **second** aspect is more interesting: It's about the belief that when using an alternative, like talking to an agent in person or on the phone, consumers *think* they can extract a better resolution than through the digital product, either because they think the agent has access to more data (believing that some last item of a product in a warehouse or a forgotten slot available to see a physician[128] is only available to agents and not digital) or because they hope the agent empathizes with their situation enough to make some sort of exception. That is quite possibly the case – maybe the digital experience is not as comprehensive as the staffed systems,[129] but also because agents tend to make subjective exceptions (and some companies focused on exceptional customer service, like Apple or Disney, absolutely train their agents to be as accommodating as possible, short of outright abuse of the situation by the consumer), especially when the customers have mitigating circumstances.

That could be a problem for a digital adoption if the non-digital channel is preferred for that trust aspect as a matter of rule (as it was in the case of the 60–70% drop off mentioned earlier) and not just in truly exceptional circumstances (everybody wants a doctor appointment as soon as possible, whether they have medical reasons for an immediate visit or not).

There are two ways to deal with the problem. **First**, signify to the users that the channels are equivalent (what they see in the app or web is the same as the staff sees, if that is indeed the case). If that is not the case, work to expand the digital to offer the same access and functionality as the agent's (access to the same products or slots, etc.). **Second**, as the product matures, think of ways to provide intelligently differentiated treatment in the digital channel. Maybe you split the experience between normal processing and urgent or critical processing. For urgent, signify the importance of reasonable, fair use and then maybe ask for additional information (mobile location or sensors could maybe help for in-person situations) to have the system grant critical processing. Will some customers abuse that? Probably. Will most? Unlikely.[130]

In summary: Educate your users, have a great and trustworthy product, provide adequate functionality for most needs, and they'll leave poorer alternatives behind.

In the meantime, be very patient and persevere.

Communicating to the Customer – Not Too Little, Not Too Much

Once a consumer is on your platform, you must communicate (digitally or otherwise) with them in a consistent, useful, but not overwhelming manner. There are fundamentally two types of communications, depending on purpose.

First is what you would call *marketing* messages. These are adverts to customers about your firm's services and products, including digital ones, with the manifest intent to increase sales (or adoption/usage). They either speak to brand-new offerings or serve as a reminder of existing (and maybe older) offerings. Sometimes, an older offering that fell into disuse is relaunched, usually with some new features to make it attractive again. It's important that this type of message must be personalized to obtain maximum impact[131] but also that they need to be used sparingly.

Second is what you would call *servicing* messages. These are notification messages about (mostly digital, but not exclusively) past interactions, usually driven by users' actions – logins, credit cards charges, balances to be paid, payments due, changes of passwords or email/phone that increases security, confirmations of actions like booking, purchases, appointments, etc. – or about upcoming consumer actions – reminders to check-in or check-out or make payments. Borderline, I would add in this category messages sent to educate or remind users that there are simpler ways to interact with the firm services, like checking-in online. Why are these servicing and not marketing? Because they help users do what they would do anyway but better. They don't necessary serve the firm with improved sales.

How are these messages sent? A combination of (very) old fashioned snail mail (yep, really, some customers only see that, mostly for marketing) but mostly by email, text messaging and in-app notifications (mostly for servicing, given time sensitivity). Texts and in-app messaging must be used very judiciously, always only for servicing notifications and the most important ones at that, rarely for marketing. Why? Because they come with a level of real time urgency that few customers think should apply to intrusive marketing messages.[132]

In any period, the combination of both of these types can become unruly and lead to consumers ignoring even important notifications and thus missing actions they must take for their own benefit. The solution to overwhelming notifications is to provide in your digital experience a communications center where users can decide what messages they want to receive, of both types, and by what channel (mail, email, text, in-app messaging).[133] All marketing messages *must* be cancelable (and sometimes that is by regulation, but it always makes good sense), while most servicing messages *could* be cancelable – but not all, like notifications of user rights, rejection of submissions, etc., when the notification is required by law.

Providing this selection ability is the easy part. Modifying all your existing systems that may send a variety of notifications (usually enabled without proper governance in past years) to strictly enforce the selection is the more expensive part. Unfortunately, it must be done, either because laws or regulations require it or because customers tune out too much messaging and create problems for themselves and your firm.

How do you know when the many marketing messages are too many? When, whatever the notification channel, you notice a low and/or decreasing read rate (e.g., emails not opened).

But what if, even after customers choose to receive marketing messages, there are still too many messages – both servicing and marketing – to be effective? As a rule, servicing messaging takes absolute precedence over marketing, in the spirit of consumer's over firm's interest, but also due to legislation (no law requires you to send marketing messages). Then you must cut down on marketing – however hard is for some operational leaders interested in expanding the business.

The more strategic answer here is a firms' communications governance mechanism, where all the business units involved and interested in signaling to consumers about their offering, should come together regularly and decide what are the most important messages to go out in any period of time. And that governance forum must *balance* evaluating each proposed campaign based on the value to the entire firm (not just the value to the unit proposing it), keeping an eye on unexpected negative impacts (low-value offers drowning out high-value offers), on one hand, as well as the likely propensity of customers to take action on certain offers versus others (this is where insightful data analysis comes in handy), on the other.

Should You Only Implement and Advertise Profitable Features?

You may encounter a set of quite peculiar questions posed by marketing and other operations folks. The likes of: *"Shouldn't we only implement/advertise the digital product features that solely support the firm's profitable activities?"*

At this point in the book, I hope I have convinced you of the credo that the consumer must be at the center of digital and the firm benefits from that. But there is even more depth to that reasoning that I will address here.

Before I start, why is this section in the *Adoption* chapter and not the *Product* chapter? Because these questions are not really about product definition, which has well established rules, but a challenge to the product adoption when marketing and advertising for the product is misguidedly withheld. Marketing departments have their roots in the Sales departments of yesteryear (they used to be called that, the *Sales and Marketing Department*). So, it is natural for some marketing (and sales) folks to focus only on advertising profit-oriented sales.

However, consumers have their own priorities of what they want to get from a firm. They are not concerned about the firm's shareholders' dividends and share price or the management's bonuses. Nor about which services and products are (most, if at all) profitable. Only that they need them *if* everything else (including digital access) is right and they expect the firm to figure out how to deliver them in a sustainable way (but that's definitely not their concern). This should be self-evident but sometimes it is not, at least not to some folks.

Unless the firm sells only one product or provides only one service, some of the products and services are less profitable than others[134] or even not profitable[135] (aka *loss leaders*), yet they are still sold or provided.

Why in the world would a firm deliberately have *loss leaders*? Because they support the company's entire ecosystem. These firms want consumers, initially attracted to the firm by lower profitability or loss leader products, to start gravitating towards the rest of the company ecosystem of products and services, some presumably very profitable – and stay there permanently, through various incentives and memberships rewards, etc. If consumers are not attracted by the lower profit or loss leaders, they may never bother to look elsewhere in the company ecosystem and thus miss the rest of the offerings, some being very profitable. And to put the cherry on top of the cake, the rest of the offerings may be products that *they may not know yet that they want or need*, even if directly advertised (with advertising being missed, without a larger context and stickiness).

Want examples? The initial iPod launch was envisioned by Steve Jobs as a way to bring in customers into the Mac ecosystem. iTunes was deployed on Mac (much later than on Windows) for the same reason – and seems to have worked nicely for Apple. Amazon Alexa was launched not for users to check the weather – they could – but supposedly to order products from the Amazon marketplace. And there are many other such examples.[136]

Something else to think about in relation to an offering that is unprofitable: There is a fair chance that digital, through enhanced access, can make that offering profitable by either increasing sales (as the offering is now more visible and accessible) and/or decreased cost of sales (no phone reps needed to take orders for those products). So, it makes no sense not to digitally enable those.

But what if these unprofitable products are not loss leaders, that is, they do not attract other more profitable sales, neither can they be made profitable? Then just hiding them makes no sense for the firm and neither continuing to sell them – let other vendors, with possibly bigger economies of scale, sell them successfully – and focus your efforts on what can be both customer-desired and firm-profitable.

To summarize, consumers will use digital experiences that provide solutions for a variety of their needs in relation to the company, not just the "most profitable" for the firm. Unless they get those most wanted, they'll never get to the most profitable.

Marketing or How to Let the World Know About You

Marketing is about values, not products.

Steve Jobs

I assume some readers may wonder why I left the overall marketing efforts towards the end of this chapter on adoption. Isn't marketing supposed to sell the product?

Well, maybe, but not quite. There are a few reasons for that.

First, there are very few Nike's, Amex's, Disney's, Apple's that do marketing very well in ways that help both the consumer and the product/company, even for great products. Your digital product can't change that situation, so don't bet the farm on marketing-driven viral adoption of your product. I don't quite know why that is, but I suspect it has to do with the internal administrative processes that companies, even those with great marketing professionals, have for creating, reviewing, and approving marketing campaigns, channels, and messaging. And the result of those processes is indiscriminate marketing with bland messaging simplistically dumped onto consumers. The kind of marketing that human brains automatically filter out as noise.[137]

The **second** is that so many companies put truth-twisting marketing out there to the point that it is hard for consumers to trust *any* messages, so the marketing credibility is damaged for most products. When that happens, the problem is in reality the company culture and values.

Marketing is hard as it requires crisp clarity on the product, the consumer, the company and its brand, and the messaging, telling a full story (honestly and non-manipulatively) speaking to people's emotions,[138] desires and needs, and framing your product in their minds. All while having to make hard choices on how and what to do, based on customer data but also on the marketing and product team's knowledge and talents. Creativity[139] and boldness to try channels and messages that help (in an honest way) are a given. It also requires a dedication to the truth, if nothing else, as a sign of respect for consumers, the company, and their employees.

But sometimes the simplest messaging vehicles for putting your product out there in front of consumers work surprisingly well. For example, if you use a paper flier, it should have a reference to your digital product – even better, a QR code to your site or to the App Store that serves your mobile app. Every time you send a text notification or reminder, the reference to your digital product must be evident.

To the starting statements of this section, the answer is that I *do* believe in the value of product marketing, *if and when* done properly.[140] You need strong marketing to reach your audience in order to have a chance to prove your product value to your customers. Marketing can shape the consumers' perception, by applying to their emotions and by telling (truthful and meaningful) stories, of what your product is about, at least before they try it for the first time.

From there, the product and the feature should be their own marketing agents by providing value and usability. But products and features are not used if nobody knows about them and their value – they instead die in silence, to the desperation of the product team and to the loss of those consumers who might have otherwise benefited from it, had they known about it.

So, my best advice to digital leaders is to understand what is required for useful marketing and find great *product* marketers[141] to partner with. Then measure the marketing efforts and adjust as needed. Whomever does it, product marketing works *for* the product, not the other way around. For that to happen, marketers, above anything else, need to understand the market through targeted insights – that should be obvious but in many situations it's not the case – which really means understanding the target consumer in that market, the trends in consumer behaviors and interests and then articulating how the product is meaningful in supporting these.

It also requires understanding where consumers gravitate to – social media, news media, physical locations – to focus the marketing efforts on those places (of course with different messaging, as we discussed earlier). This is doing ethnography to design the marketing, not just the product. Too often the marketing messages are bland and uninspiring or in the wrong place solely because marketers simply don't understand the market and the consumers.[142] When that happens, it's worse than not doing any marketing at all, as you'll spend marketing campaign's funds, and you'll get nothing of value in return.

Marketers absolutely need to feel what consumers feel, as much as the product managers do. So, then the question is: should product managers be responsible for the product marketing? The answer is "preferably yes", with an internal organizational politics caveat: in most companies, the marketing department is historically a lot more established than digital product management – because of their historic focus on brand – and as such pulling product marketing into product management will be a tough political battle.

The only middle-ground solution I can offer in that situation, however imperfect, is that the marketing for the digital product is a joint responsibility between the digital product management and the marketing department.[143] Product managers provide the articulation of the product value (through their knowledge of consumers) and are involved in decisions on positioning, messaging, and marketing strategies and plans. The work must start from the early stages of product definition and continue throughout the launch and while in the hands of the consumers. Working together this way provides complementarity and usefulness. It does, however, require the two teams *wanting* to work together in ways that enhance the product and its appeal to the users and not worry about power and territory, as the weaker each team is in their own domain, the more defensive and non-collaborative they'll be. There are plenty of opportunities for miscommunication if team members are not open to the model.

Chapter 4.4 Tools and Frameworks

Give me six hours to chop down a tree and I will spend the first four sharpening the axe.

Abraham Lincoln

There are a number of tools, technologies, processes, practices and frameworks that, while not limited to digital, greatly enhance the chances of successful digital. They should be used extensively while doing digital. In truth it's hard to think how digital outcomes would be successful without them.

This chapter is a brief introduction to three important categories: the public cloud,[144] the Agile development frameworks and process automation.[145] Clearly, they're each big topics in themselves that merit deep dives – fortunately there are plenty of available materials elsewhere. Each will require a lot of attention and focus from the technology and digital teams and leaders.

Public Cloud Is More Than Someone Else's Servers

The public cloud is not merely someone else's compute and storage,[146] though that by itself is true, with benefits hard to replicate in one's own legacy data center for anyone who is not Apple or Meta (even they use public clouds for some products).

So, why should you use the public cloud? Those who use it will say (accurately, from my experience): faster speed-to-market, flexibility of implementation, superior resource management and provisioning automation and tooling, security tooling, and cost advantages.

On the business side, speed-to-market is probably the most important advantage that is not as easy to quantify as cost reductions but much more financially significant in the long-term. Coupled with the flexibility of solutions, it allows you to innovate and iterate for new products or solutions and then deliver a product or service to your customers a lot faster and sooner than otherwise possible, with in-house infrastructure that takes months to provision. Providing multi-zone/regions high availability, as well accommodating sudden traffic spikes through elastic scaling, means your solution will be available when your product sells unexpectedly well. And in a competitive market, fast, more, and better means better commercial survivability for your firm.

So, let me put it out there: *Thou shall deploy all your new digital and data/ML efforts straight into the cloud, exactly in order to take advantage of all that the cloud offers.* Yes, most of us did digital and data first in owned data centers (and then we migrated to a public cloud), but that was *years and years ago*, not in 2023 and beyond.[147]

What about migrating your old systems – some that your digital and data efforts may depend on – from your own data center to the public cloud? You ought to still migrate those for all the reasons mentioned earlier, but you need a strategy. Cloud is not a toaster you just plug in and works effortlessly – no enterprise system or technology is. The migration tends to be costly, requires a lot of effort and comes with some risk, so strategically building a robust plan – and tracking your progress to it – and ensuring that readiness is critical.

Migrating data centers and/or migrating from on-premises to the cloud, are probably the biggest foundational projects technology groups undertake. They're big, complex, with lots of moving parts – including running in two paradigms (on-premises and cloud) for a while, so preparation, planning, team and program management are super critical for the success. Plenty of risk of failure so, without these preparations there will be colossal challenges and impacts.

So, what are the important elements to have and do when migrating to the cloud?

- Establish a dedicated program management and engineering team.
- Take an inventory of all the systems, technologies, and architectures.
- Build a Reference Architecture[148] for each class of applications and systems.
- Prototype and pilot with each class of applications the migration and redeployment in the cloud. How you deploy and configure older applications in the cloud is probably going to be different.
- Build a robust yet flexible plan and obtain funding for the entire effort. Flexibility will be required as there are going to be many unexpected schedule and prioritization changes over what will be a two–three-year migration time horizon.
- Align with application stakeholders on the migration process, factoring in the normal business functionality changes that the systems undertake in their normal operations.
- Monitor, track, manage, and adjust the program closely.

You'll likely hear some people saying that unless you completely rearchitect every single application and system that you currently have in your data center to be cloud native when you move it to the cloud, you will miss the full value – with the undertone that you failed if you didn't. It's true you may miss *some* value, but there are *several* serious caveats to their statements.

First, rearchitecting and reimplementing *everything* when you migrate is *very* expensive and time intensive. You'll spend a decade[149] and a fortune to do that, all while you'll be trying to deliver all sorts of other value to the firm – such as doing digital or even regular functional updates and enhancements.[150] In the meantime, you get no reprieve from your basic on-premises challenges – such as having to upgrade your computing, storage and networking hardware, and data center facilities as well as having to revamp your (likely) outdated security protocols and systems – with no benefit from the cloud.

Second, not every system needs to be cloud native – I've seen systems not evolving for years that don't necessarily benefit in any way from being cloud native, but they do benefit from the basics of cloud. You'd be wasting money if you insist in rearchitecting those in the absence of any other reason.

Third, sometimes it is easier to rearchitect an application or system *once* it is in the cloud – simply because of the tools the public cloud providers offer out of the box.

Fourth, rearchitecting an application to be cloud native may be more effective to do either part of a functional redesign or enhancement instead of during the migration. Timing of that may be different than your cloud-migration plan.

I talked about security tooling as a benefit for cloud. Is the cloud really more secure than your own data center? Well, any deployment can be more secure (better protected and defended) or less, all depending on the efforts and paranoid due diligence applied to it, whether cloud or on-premises. But all efforts being equal, *two* aspects favor cloud.

First, public clouds come with a plethora of security tool and structures, expensive and difficult to replicate in an owned datacenter – and that is both native tools provided by the cloud providers as well as those offered in cloud marketplaces.

Second, older data centers and systems, built in the days of barely incipient security threats and with inadequate (bolt-on, not organic) investments since, tend to have massive security gaps, so the comfort of having control of your own data and systems is misplaced and underestimates the security gaps of those facilities. It's like feeling more secure because you can hold water in your own sieve better than in Jeff Bezos' bucket.

It is, however, true that consolidating compute capabilities under public provider capabilities could in theory increase the blast radius of a potentially systemic and successful attack on one of the cloud providers, but we must balance that with the constant stream of successful attacks on owned data center vulnerabilities – in effect we would be replacing a high-probability constant distributed risk with a low-probability but higher-impact centralized risk.

Finally, you may also have heard that cloud is more expensive than your own data-center costs. This has not been true in my experience, when you factor everything in – infrastructure, facilities, and labor costs, including opportunity costs for the executive focus,[151] etc. Even factoring the cloud provider's profit margin, the difference between the cloud providers operational economies of scale, volume-discounted infrastructure[152] and automation and yours, you will be more expensive than they are.

But there is a shred of truth to *potentially* higher costs for the cloud: In the cloud it is a lot easier to provision infrastructure fast (on premise there is usually a capital approval process and procurement that controls and drastically slows down the capacity additions). If you don't need that infrastructure or don't control its growth, it will be wasted and be unnecessarily expensive. The good news is that cloud providers provide plenty of out of the box tools to monitor, manage, and correctly size your cloud infrastructure and services, so all you must do is put a little bit of focus on using those tools. Those efforts will make a huge difference.

Agile Frameworks Must Be (Lowercase) Agile

Normally, in most books, this section would be about the **A**gile (*capital A*) framework. But the point I will be making here is one about *being* agile (lowercase a) as in *operating* in an agile *fashion*, irrespective of which particular framework you use, as long it's focused on *agility*.[153] So, whatever agile framework you decide to use for your digital efforts, it will be fine as long as you do it well and don't follow a waterfall methodology.[154]

In the waterfall paradigm, all requirements and all the design were done at the very beginning of the project, then the development started and then the capability was delivered in one go, maybe a year or two later. I call this the Big Bang methodology. There are usually two big problems with this approach. **First**, things change in that year and what gets delivered is not what is needed when it gets to be delivered and thus work may need to be redone. And **second**, you only get the functionality, in its entirety, at the *very end* of the process.

In contrast, with agile methodologies, you structure your process in short iterations – understanding the need, designing, developing, and releasing often, and not allowing unreleased code to accumulate.[155] Agility is particularly crucial for developing digital experiences in no small part because it allows fast iterations of try-learn-repeat when it's not clear what the consumer needs. You get something (parts of a larger capability) released often and sooner, the users get to see it and ask for tweaks, you discover and fix problems earlier and in small increments.

But what if you're starting your product from scratch and at the beginning it only has one or two features out of the many that will (eventually) make the product valuable to consumers but those one or two features may not make the product interesting enough to keep consumers involved? If that is your case, you ought to still release but maybe only to your employees who don't mind an incomplete product and are happy to test whatever is released. The other alternative, that I prefer, is to still release to consumers but show what else is coming, so consumers understand the plan and stay engaged.

In terms of process, operating in autonomous teams, each fully responsible for a feature in a larger product, eliminates the coordination overhead and friction between teams that otherwise would be responsible for pieces of the same feature. The downside is that the internal friction removed could be pushed onto external customers in the form of many uncoordinated features and integrations being offered. And yet, for consumers, the overall product experience and not individual features are what's important. That is where the product managers must step in to alleviate any such problems.

Automating the Drudge Work

Automation replaces manual steps with a piece of software[156] that follows some rules or models (including Machine Learning).[157]

Usually, those steps are part of a rules-based script that human operators follow that can then be defined in software. Where that machine learning part comes into play is when the steps and tasks are not documented and then we use machine learning algorithms to, well, learn exactly how that process functions in real life, what is done when and based on seemingly what rules, that then the model can execute, possibly with self-correction.

There are many places where automation can be deployed: Technology team operations should be first in line, to reduce technology delivery time to market and improve systems quality.

Then there's business process automation, that usually has significant operational benefits in terms of reduced costs and improved efficiency – good for the company – and reduced time to process goods and services – good for customers.

Whether introducing automation is technically part of digital or not can be debated but it's particularly important in order to enable self-service consumer digital experiences. If, for every type of purchase or booking of a product or service, a human must manually check inventory or validate a credit card or insurance,[158] that user experience is stunted and not in real time.

As such, it's very much for the digital team to drive, if not implement, automation behind their apps and web pages and in front of backend processes. That may slow down the digital releases when focus is diverted to automation – sometimes unavoidably but manageable.

I recommend digital leaders put automation efforts – some having nothing to do with digital consumer experiences – into separate and dedicated work streams.

And those business processes? Don't automate an inefficient business process just because that's the process that you have (likely) inherited. Reengineer that process first and then automate it. In truth, most times only after process reengineering the automation becomes feasible.

Consumers Don't Care About Your Maturity Matrix

Any respectable book about transformation and change is supposed to talk about the maturity (or readiness) capability matrix, depicting the journey from minimal readiness for a particular capability or product all the way to what is considered (at the moment of describing it) the ultimate goal, adding where the company or product is on that path – like the map you find in malls that have a big sign saying "*You are here*".

Consultants love graphing this journey, I suspect, because they relish showing the company or product in lower maturity levels, in order to highlight the need for their services to help bring it up higher. If you're Apple and the maturity matrix is for an operating system, I doubt the consultants would bother highlighting that iOS and MacOS are at the very top, where there's seemingly not much to catch up to.

Management consulting practices aside, sometimes this artifact is useful to honestly highlight to the executive committee or board how much work you still must do and, more importantly, how much money you need to get to the top of the journey.

I don't find this type of artifact very useful, besides rallying the troops and getting the funding part. Why? Because it's graphed against generic targets of readiness and maturity. Focusing on grand generic targets and not particular consumer needs is not really useful.

Instead, the way to make this tool more useful is to depict consumer needs and your team journey to fully build up to them. That approach has its own two problems: It implies you know at the beginning of your product journey what all the needs are and the trajectory to get there but ignores the fact that customers' expectations and needs change and evolve constantly and your product also has to constantly evolve. So, what is even the end point of that journey, other than the end point described high-level by the vision?

With all these caveats and gyrations, in my opinion, the value is modest other than visually rallying the troops about how behind you may be and the board on how much more funding you still need (Yes, I have built and use them myself for these exact purposes). So, have one, but don't get fixated on it.

Focus on the consumer needs instead.

Chapter 4.5 Innovation

Sometimes when you innovate, you make mistakes. It's best to admit them quickly and get on with improving your other innovations.

Steve Jobs

Innovation[159] is matching a new solution to a problem in a way that creates value to someone (customers, employees, etc.). It must be used by someone, otherwise it's just a curiosity.

We're innovating because we want – proactive, preferably – or we must – reactive, but not a good situation to be in – to make things better. And if we're innovating for fun yet we still meet the value criteria, that is even better. *"It's kind of fun to do the impossible"*, Walt Disney used to say.

Before I start, let's clarify what the difference between innovation and invention is.

Simply put, *innovation* is about creating something new (to the company or the industry) from pieces that in themselves don't have to be new. *Invention* is about creating something that did not exist before. Innovations and inventions support each other, for example innovating in a business process using a technology recently invented. It leads that innovation tends to lend itself to incremental approaches.

There's a perception among senior leaders that, in order to start and do digital successfully, you must innovate through edge, emerging, or disruptive technologies.[160]

I don't think that is correct or even wise – and I say this as one who ran the Emerging Technologies Group at Disney Parks (the opportunities to solve there at the edge of technology were very different than the digital transformation of an average firm). The most positive impact, at least for the first couple of years of doing digital, comes from relatively widely available and used technology (mobile, web, personalization, and ML) and well-known processes (design thinking), frameworks (Agile), or tools ecosystem (cloud).

Quite frankly innovating business processes (how the organization operates) and model (what it does), uniquely enabled by digital technologies, is where the big bang really is. (If all that digital is used for is to digitize a bunch of forms, some value but not very much will come out of it.) Later, innovation will come from introducing new features that may be new to the company or the industry, sometimes supported by new technologies, but rarely bleeding edge.

With all that being said, I will be remiss if I did not talk at a high-level about the innovation process, focusing on a number of aspects that I think are fundamental to the success of innovation but are not well understood or adapted.

Prerequisites or What Is Needed to Get Started

If you stop innovating, you'll die. Maybe not immediately, but if all you do is optimize your existing solutions and you stop innovating, it's only a matter of time before you're someone else's lunch.

Marty Cagan

Once a need to innovate has been identified, there are five major pillars that are important, in my experience, to the success and stability of innovation.

People – curious explorers, learners, versatile, accepting uncertainty, optimistic, self-motivated, diverse in skillsets and experiences and very good at what they do.

Organizational culture – one that supports innovation and change or at least is not hostile to it.

Leadership – that provides guidance, cover and support, especially during the early vulnerable stages and during the inevitable setbacks. As widespread as innovation has to be, leadership has a surprisingly oversized role – without its support, nothing even starts, let alone succeeds.

Approach or methodology – what mechanisms, approaches, and processes are going to be used to get from need to solution to execution and to launch. Normally the right word here would be structured process but sometimes the word "process" has overhead, or rigidity connotations associated with it so I'm not going to use it. You need something but nothing overbearing by any means. The fundamental characteristic of the approach is a *bias for action*[161] – start doing something right away, not spending months on planning that may be rendered useless by what you'll learn later.

(Some) **Funding** – it's a mistake to believe innovation, at least in the early stages, requires a lot of funding. In truth, too much funding only creates opportunities for scope creep beyond the original identified need, so I'll adapt the original adagio about innovation to "*scarcity is the mother of innovation*". Nevertheless, some dedicated funding is definitely good to have.

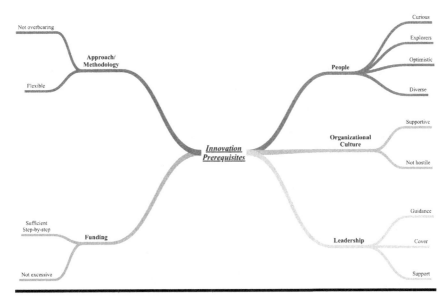

Figure 4.12   Innovation prerequisites tree.

Ground Principles

> *We believe that we are on the face of the earth to make great products and that's not changing, We are constantly focusing on innovating. We believe in the simple, not the complex. We believe that we need to own and control the primary technologies behind the products that we make and participate only in markets where we can make a significant contribution. We believe in saying no to thousands of projects so that we can really focus on the few that are truly important and meaningful to us.*
>
> **Tim Cook**

There are three fundamental *principles* of innovation that I always talk about and without which I don't see how innovation can ever be successful. There may be others, so feel free to add, but my advice is to at least follow these three.

Incremental and iterative through multiple cycles. The cycle is Ideation -> Solution -> Prototyping and piloting -> Feedback -> Adjusting -> Productization -> Rinse and repeat.

The corollary of that is: *"Get it out"* – at first at small scale – beats *"get it perfect"*.

Experimenting. The road to innovation success is about experimenting, failing, learning, adjusting, and repeating. Expect to fail – a lot – while trying – but preferably early in the process, fast and before spending plenty of money. But that is good because failing means learning and getting better. But fail small through small iterations and learn after each. Failure in itself is not good, unless you learn from it. Failing larger than needed is not good.

Execution. There is a strong misconception that creativity (in the sense of coming up with brilliant ideas that no one else thought of) is singularly the most important aspect of innovation. That is patently false: innovation almost never fails due to a lack of creativity (as defined above). Ideas are a dime a dozen.[162] In my experience, innovation projects fail almost always because of a lack of discipline in pushing it through or poor execution. Successful innovation does require a lot of focus and relentlessness in execution and, yes, being creative but in how to *overcome* challenges.

All this should sound familiar by now because doing digital *is* about innovation.

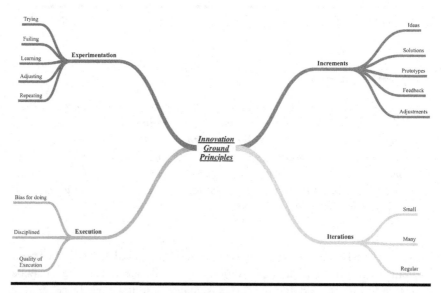

Figure 4.13   Innovation ground principles tree.

Should You Do a *Skunkworks*?

You can read more about the origins of this name turned organizational principle in Ben R. Rich's book.[163] In short, it's about Lockheed establishing a secret team of great technologists to build special planes[164] during WWII.

What made this team special is that they were operating outside corporate bureaucratic processes, usually breaking rules, in search of remarkable outcomes.

Over the years, this approach gained traction in various enterprises, when the main organizational processes were too oppressive and hostile for fast-paced innovation or, at least, with processes too cumbersome to follow. For action-biased leaders, it has therefore been attractive to develop an administratively unencumbered team that is free to innovate out of the limelight[165] – aka a Skunkworks – with the goal of developing remarkably innovative products. For all intents and purposes, these internal innovation teams are startups inside established organizations – aka *intrapreneurs*[166] – fighting with the rest of the company for everything, from budget to office space to access to systems and technologies to recognition.

I built at least two or three of these groups and they indeed developed extraordinary concepts, head and shoulders above whatever else comparable the rest of the organization realistically accomplished.

However, there is a big challenge with these arrangements that every leader going down this road must be prepared for. Whatever these groups create *must* have a path to evolution into the mainstream, either in the existing business lines, or as a separate business unit. Each option will require an incredible amount of organizational effort and political savviness from the leader to make it happen.

Furthermore, what is required from the innovation group leader is not what the typical *intrapreneur* would normally be interested in spending most of their time and effort on – that is creating products rather than maneuvering through politics and bureaucracy. Yet, it is those latter aspects that are critical to the long-term success of this approach. Ken Johnson, Ben Rich, and their successors were masters of working those processes, plus the Navy's and the Air Force's (the customers).[167] Skunkworks-like leaders not mastering the bureaucratic landscape is a main reason that for each example of it being successful, there are a thousand others that die silent and frustrating deaths.

Now, while digital product innovation may be easier to build than supersonic planes – which is what Skunkworks does – it will still need the support of the organization – funding, marketing, and advertising, etc. – to come to market, if it is to have even minimal chances of commercial success.

One of the more successful ways to enroll the rest of the organization to support innovation efforts is to create *demo areas* to showcase the results of the innovation teamwork in ways that everyone becomes enthused. It works wonders when people, even those normally opposed to innovation and change, see the fruit of the team's work, but that demo must be followed with reminders and signs of progress, otherwise their enthusiasm may wane.

Figure 4.14   Innovation showcase lab (author's collection).

So, my advice is: Do it when you must, but have a path at some point to make it mainstream.[168]

Notes

1. See a discussion of proliferation of unneeded features that he calls *featuritis* in Don Norman's *The Design of Everyday Things*: "*Featuritis is an insidious disease, difficult to eradicate, impossible to vaccinate against*".
2. Dwight Eisenhower.
3. Modernized version for civilian purposes of strategist Helmuth von Moltke's "*No battle plan survives contact with the enemy*".
4. PERT: Program evaluation and review technique (PERT) is a project management tool for representing the required tasks for a project. More at https://en.wikipedia.org/wiki/Program_evaluation_and_review_technique.
   GANTT (not GANNT): A project management tool representing project schedule using bar charts graphs. More at https://en.wikipedia.org/wiki/Gantt_chart
5. Even in the absence of a devastating pandemic, people get flu in the winter and miss workdays. And their kids get the flu, and they should definitely tend to their kids ahead of an arbitrary delivery schedule.
6. This is why agile methodologies, especially *Kanban*, are important. The available team can just pick the next item in the prioritized list they can deliver on.

7. This doesn't mean you're a victim of your circumstances. Smart approaches can be deployed to improve your delivery. Some may take time and changes (that hopefully you'll make to be more resilient and that is what postmortems are for) but at any one point you must accept and adjust to your constraints.
8. Usual recommendation is 80%.
9. You can't build the first floor of a building without having built the foundations.
10. To be honest here, if what you're delivering and how (the technology and process) is relatively well exercised from past experience, you'll be able to minimize the variability of delivery. Call it a well-honed process of practice or "*being in the flow*" as a team.
11. As a digital leader, you still need to make sure this principle is followed in the technical design. A variety of situations, as well as convenience, may lead to this principle not being followed rigorously.
12. UI/UX, that is delivered by the web or mobile layer.
13. Where aggregation of data and activities to support the UI/UX layer take place and in front of shared service or domain data layer.
14. Switches to turn on/off pieces of functionality.
15. Process means how things really happen, driven by a well-functioning team, not some heavy handed, rigid governance.
16. A take on Steve Jobs "*Real Artists Ship!*"
17. Wait, what about the principle of putting products and features out early so you can learn from consumers? Well, there's a difference between putting features that fail to work as promised and products that work well but may require tweaks to make them a better fit, more useful or interesting. It's the difference, for example, between an app failing to get you on a flight when boarding versus an app where the boarding pass is more taps away than it needs to be.
18. This usually means cutting off from the release whatever features are not ready. On-off toggles do wonders for that purpose, although they need management over time or otherwise, they become unwieldy.
19. See the *Testing* section later in the book.
20. This is the principle of releasing soon and often.
21. Whether a release is major or minor will likely have implications on your launch plan and preparation.
22. Sustained and sustainable are critical attributes here. Death marches to meet some arbitrary release date are not only unsustainable, but are followed by longer cycles, as everyone needs more time to recover after the dreadful death march, so the purpose of forcing more features out in a period of time is defeated. Besides, as I tell my team: "*We're not in the sweat shop business*". Nobody should be. Yes, I lived through project release death marches, and I may have even, regrettably, driven some. But those need to only happen in absolutely exceptional situations when there is no way out and not as a matter of rule. They're counterproductive with your team and they can be avoided through better and realistic planning, coupled with efficient process and tooling.
23. Inconsistent architecture that can't evolve well or code that is fragile (breaks easily with small changes) and thus is hard to maintain and built upon.
24. If truly unavoidable, either structure the scope of each release to address previously accumulated technical debt or force "hardening sprints".

25. Before it completely crashes on you in a future release.

26. However, adherence to a cadence in the long-term is beneficial. I articulated earlier why time-boxing your releases forces the team to think inventively how to be more efficient.

27. The power to decide what to release (based on the customer value, usability, feasibility, business value) and when comes with great *responsibility,* which requires great *accountability.* Without that, nobody will accept the digital product team's authority (*on behalf of the customer*) and autonomy. Nobody argues with success, but everybody attacks failure.

28. Which also means that commitments must not be made based on spurious organizational deadlines. If needed, the scope of the release may be marginally adjusted, but not the core. Even Apple sometimes delays features from their yearly iOS releases – although I'm sure they don't take that lightly.

29. I, as the most senior digital product executive, have daily, one hour, sometimes longer, product release meetings with my team to review status, progress, and solve issues. (Yes, I have many other responsibilities – non-digital releases, systems availability, systems and users support, "IT" helpdesk, security, etc. – and similar cadence of involvement in each. But digital is as important, if not more, than others.). If needed, these digital meetings also become brainstorming or design meetings when unexpected issues arise, and a decision is needed fast. These meetings are to evaluate together *as a team* what we need to do, not for me as the most senior executive to dictate random orders to the rest of the team. But sometimes I am the tie breaker. Somebody has to be.

30. They can be dedicated resources or designated by rotation by release.

31. In a previous engagement, we had probably one of the richest in functionality mobile apps that I have ever seen, reflective of an incredibly rich and magical physical experience. Coordinating releases when probably ten different teams were working on different features and at different architecture layers was not for the faint of heart. So, while we rotated the executives in charge of releases, in the end we settled on one executive who was both very good at it and also very strict in keeping the strands together and on time – or risked being descoped, which both the consumers and the operational partners disliked.

32. See Chapter 3.1 about the digital team structure.

33. Feel free to call it a check list.

34. We will talk about marketing and messaging later in the book.

35. And yes, reviewing the plan also provides an opportunity to validate that the messaging is still focused, and it makes sense – preferably done starting early and then continuously, but better late than never.

36. I sometimes have a similar problem with hotels. Although I check-in using their app in advance, including selecting a room and getting a digital key, if I need something at the reception desk, they seem to want to do a full check-in again. Yes, the credit card is in the digital profile. Baffling.

37. See more about phone support in the *Phone Support for Digital Products* section later in the chapter.

38. Realistically, any complex enough digital capabilities will have gaps in what they offer that will need to be covered by human intervention. Not a matter of if, but

rather how few, how inconsequential, and how well they will be covered by human supporting processes.

39. Whenever I have a product that has a customer support process or I own that support team, I always call the support team to understand how well they respond to customer queries. I started this when I was responsible for the digital platform at Amex. I used to call the technology on-call teams to make sure they answer and are at their best. Now, sometimes the agents freak out when they figure out who I am, but until that point it's always informative.

40. The quality of a system to perform as and when expected.

41. I talk here about waterfall in the past tense as it is no longer the dominant delivery methodology in most places. But it is still used by some companies.

42. For more, see *Death March*, by Edward Yourdon and *The Mythical Man-Month*, by Fred Brooks.

43. Now, *reasonable* is a dangerously vague world. When I started in healthcare and presented to the board the 3-year digital vision, exemplified with what the consumers will experience and roughly in what cadence, the feedback I got was *"this is fantastic, everything that we need and want, but why can't you do it in 9–12 months?"* Now *that* is unreasonable! I knew of no enterprise, even some with successful digital products and larger and more mature teams that could do all that – not just write code, but do all the user research, an innovative design, built on top of creaky old systems which may have been implemented when Bill Gates was still CEO of Microsoft, change business processes, etc. Especially not when starting from scratch, including assembling a team where there was none. And that is exactly how you determine what's reasonable for you: what you saw/see good organizations do elsewhere, adjusting for your scope, resources, talent, etc. Is it subjective and experience-dependent? Of course, but it is a good predictor, when you start and have no experience of your team and its cadence. Later, when you would have delivered a number of releases, you start using that experience, building a baseline that can define *reasonable* much more precisely and objectively. And absolutely you must improve on that baseline constantly by looking at improvement opportunities.

44. This is about teams looking for constant improvement in their activities. At least at the beginning, there are a lot of opportunities for the team to function better. This also includes the team constantly and firmly holding others that are dependencies accountable for their own committed deliverables. Can't tell you how many times I have heard teams and team members say: *"I asked my dependency, but I did not hear back, so I'm waiting for an answer"*. To which the answer should be: *"How long are you going to wait? Have we followed up? Have you escalated?"*

45. For strong leaders, especially in weak organizations, where people are used to just taking orders and then muddling through on executing them, there's a real danger of a disconnect between the leader 's direction and what the teams can and will deliver, and what they're able and willing to communicate, with unpleasant surprises for both. In such situations, the leader must be crisp in expectations and the evaluation of plans and spend time closely evaluating progress and be ready to reassess plans for course corrections. Long-term, both the leader and the team must develop reciprocal understanding and protocols for alignment.

46. But beware, confidence is not the same as being right, just *feeling* right. As Daniel Kahneman said in *Thinking, Fast and Slow*: *"Declarations of high confidence mainly tell you that an individual has constructed a coherent story in his mind, not necessarily that the story is true"*.

47. Testing functionally that existed in users' hands before the upcoming release being launched.

48. Prototyping and proof-of-concept tests, discussed in Chapter 2.4, are about trying different designs with users for feedback on how the design could work or how the system should perform, versus whether it performs as designed.

49. Don't trust vendors' brochureware. Maybe well-intentioned, but usually misleading and papering over gaps and problems. So, *"Trust but Verify"*.

50. See the discussion on target consumers in Chapter 2 – *2.2 Consumer – Who Is Your Target Consumer* section.

51. Or whatever version numbering scheme you use for your product's incremental releases.

52. That type of feedback will diminish as you add features. Then the feedback moves to *"it doesn't exactly do what I want it to do"* (probably without telling you why that is) which you will need to fix through constant research and improvement.

53. This gives you an idea how it feels to be an all-in entrepreneur who puts everything into getting something out, against all odds, and then gets such feedback. Whether entrepreneur or CDIO at version 1.0, it takes nerves of steel not to get discouraged.

54. Avoid gimmickry that you can't live up to later on, otherwise you'll really poison the well with users.

55. No copy and paste capability. No app store. No custom apps.

56. Not that you shouldn't continue to do so after 3.0. But 3.0 is probably an inflection point.

57. If they decide, at 2.0 or 3.0, that your product is not worth it, they'll most likely not be freely coming back to it in the future, unless forced to by events.

58. Some of us may have seen Hulu's app's recent notification (April 2023) to users that navigation will be moving to the left side of the app. Great example of what I'm talking about here.

59. I've used this strategy multiple times with significant changes or a new product replacing a well-known product. Each time, to my (pleasant) surprise, we got little to no complaints when we finally switched off the old product. I credit early warnings and parallel runs for that smooth transition.

60. As the saying goes: *"You can't manage what you don't measure"*.

61. One of them was about evaluating how we would be implementing a relatively exotic person-identification system involving FaceTime-like face recognition linked to a person's identity.

62. If emerging technologies, see the caveats in *On the Bleeding Edge of Technology* in this chapter.

63. Bob Iger, of Walt Disney Co fame, in his book, *The Ride of a Lifetime* has a great writeup on leadership in a crisis.

64. See the story of the Tylenol recall by Johnson & Johnson in the 1980s.

65. Just look up BGP vulnerabilities and outages.

66. A heart stopping moment for everyone in charge of systems and data security.
67. That was after a whole year of bi-weekly transatlantic flights to make sure I was in person where one of my teams were.
68. Benjamin Franklin: "*Never ruin an apology with an excuse*".
69. Colin Powell: "*It ain't as bad as you think. It will look better in the morning*".
70. At least, until humans, foolishly, started cutting them down.
71. Short of truly bizarre corner cases, which may not be worth the product investment to take care of.
72. Sometimes digital investments to support consumer self-service experiences immediately starve investment in staff (and call centers), which is right in the long-term but only after a lag dependent on digital maturity.
73. Yes, I have always been baffled and annoyed about the inconsistent signifiers of opening a door.
74. Plus, it allows me to complain about things that I have complained about for years, which is always a lot of fun.
75. I have seen situations such as when a date field that allowed a non-date format to be entered and submitted generated a silent error in the back end that the user never saw but that prevented the operation from being fulfilled. And the user was never told that the whole transaction was not happening.
76. That may go against the ChatGPT frenzy, which of course, has a text-based interface. You can describe, in text, the action that you want performed, including booking hotel or airline tickets, etc. It is dubious, though, that that interface is faster to use than a graphical interface, one well designed. That is not to say that a text/chat-based interface, or driven by voice, could not be offered as an alternative for those who would prefer it.
77. See also https://hbr.org/2022/05/designing-work-that-people-love.
78. Instrumentation for insights from systems logs will be gradual as you develop your features, transactions and ultimately journeys. As with everything else, you will need to prioritize what to instrument and thus track and monitor. And then you'll have to determine what the signals mean. For example, when we introduced a certain type of transaction – booking primary care physician visits – we evaluated that the uptake was rather modest. We instrumented more within the journey and only then we figured out that consumers were dropping off when they were seeing availability too far into the future – months – yet they were expecting to be able to access that care no later the following week.
79. Someone once said that good design sells by making and keeping people happy.
80. There is another concept around affordances: hierarchy or layers (remember the *Thinking in Layers* section?). A house affords one to protect oneself against the elements, but elsewhere in the hierarchy a door affords one to enter the house. An app or web site affords one a collection of actions, a feature affords one the ability to obtain an outcome, like booking or checking in.
81. The two have known and debated with each other for a long time, according to Don.
82. If you search the internet, you will find plenty of posts (one is here https://uxdesign .cc/what-is-an-affordance-6b60f2de79f2) stating that the two are different. These posts, however, usually use Don Norman's 1988, not his 2013, definition.

83. I won't name the actual airline and its app, but you can probably guess. Or maybe not, as there is more than one not providing that information, now that I think about it!

84. What users expect the soonest is about prioritization. Sometimes there are feasibility limitations of one kind of another that may prevent you from providing the minimum expected features. Not a great situation.

85. Features must reuse or build mental models so when the consumer uses them, they are no different than the expectation of knowing how to open a door. Build your product features so well that it will be self-evident for consumers to expect them and use them as easily as opening a door.

86. We *all* encounter the problem *all the time*. I guess not all designers read Don's books.

87. Interesting use case of affordances needing signifiers for humans to make sense of. Have you even been to a modernist office (tech companies' office come to mind) that seems to have a strange interior staircase? Why strange? Because 1) it sometimes goes nowhere; 2) has steps that seem to be very tall (maybe two feet) that are difficult to climb; 3) there is a parallel normal staircase (regular height steps) that leads to the main staircase steps. If you have seen it being used, you would have understood this strange staircase is not a staircase after all, but a sitting area for workers to work on their laptops, similar to a stadium or amphitheater. But unlike those two, this one doesn't seem to face a stage or main action area and it doesn't have seats. Confusing as it's not intuitive. What some places do is add signifiers – in the form of either cushions (useful to soften the hard surface) or simply mats to signal individual seats.

88. Icons are metaphors for real objects or actions – that is, using some known imagery to imply something else from the physical world but similar to the virtual world. Metaphors are very powerful as they can short-circuit a long analysis and replace it with a reflex. Humans have always understood reality through metaphors. Some change over time – a rotary dial imagery that used to signify a phone means nothing to any of us, even those who actually used those awkward things a very long time ago. There is a whole discussion on skeuomorphism, if you're interested, but that is for another place. You should define intuitive and meaningful metaphors for activities to introduce new and contemporary features to users.

89. Overly complicated user flows and actions are usually a sign of overly (as in unnecessarily) complicated dysfunctional business processes, not digital teams' mistakes (those can usually be fixed relatively fast). Some of the complexity comes from operational leaders not being able or not willing to streamline their processes – yet otherwise ultimately good for their operations and business, independent of digital. They can also be a sign of a dysfunctional larger enterprise structure, processes, and agendas and whether by experiencing digital or physical products, customer usually suffer from that dysfunction.

90. LinkedIn recently introduced a tasteful sound when posting something successfully, even though the screen shows the success of that action. Although duplicative, it's satisfying through its quality and taste. Inexpensive enhancement providing oversized satisfaction. It also shows attention to detail.

91. Understanding that sometimes the design system evolves, and new standards are applied gradually. Eventually it needs to be applied consistently and that should be part of the modernization roadmap.
92. With that said, your design and implementation should avoid, if at all possible, long periods of time when the system is busy with itself rather than the user.
93. Healthcare example: If you're looking for doctors and your insurance is not accepted by some doctors in the list, they should either not be shown or be grayed out with an explanation of sorts. Don't allow the patient to go through the entire process just to tell them after submitting the request that the insurance doesn't cover it.
94. The words you use always matter and influence the perception of your message. But it's always a matter of quality and simplicity, never of quantity of words.
95. The more sophisticated digital organizations design their own. These are pretty extensive and support each company's design philosophy and branding. Big names like Apple, Google, Microsoft, and Disney have their own. My teams have created several over the years. For anybody not willing or able to invest in building their own design system, there are some open-source ones available. For example, Carbon from IBM https://carbondesignsystem.com/
96. This is not about the look or style (as important as those are, as nobody wants to use an ugly experience), but the feel and operation. If one platform has a swipe as a rule of navigating screens, for example, and another doesn't, users on that other platform won't expect to use that action. Preferable to avoid, unless you add a signifier that somehow signals what to do. But then you're back to manuals or overly busy interfaces.
97. Could be as simple as icons used on one platform are different than the equivalent ones on the other platform. Icons need to quickly express something; they should not be something that an unfamiliar user must use a search engine for.
98. See *Crossing the Chasm* by Geoffrey A Moore.
99. Percentages of each category of adopters may vary by your product type, industry, etc.
100. Let us also not forget those products that are at the intersection of digital and physical: consumers use a digital tool, most often a mobile app, to influence the operation of a physical object, like opening your hotel, home, or car door with a mobile app. Disney Parks Play app is a wonderful example of that cross-paradigm.
101. You may have heard about the product/market fit. That is when the customers are interested in your product enough to (try to) use it.
102. Clarity means less possible alternatives which leads to less confusion.
103. Depending on your vision and strategy, these no-shows may become future roadmap items.
104. Remember that your target consumers are usually more than one category and segment.
105. It's estimated that humans' attention spans to digital experiences is now less than one minute and decreasing.
106. Please don't go to events where your main concern is in which hospital you're going to end up at. Hospitals are the place where people with no other health choice *must* go. They're designed to the extreme to save lives, not compensate for bad choices.

107. A famous example is the man in a gorilla suit crossing the basketball court when the ball is played, and nobody notices. Why? Because the focus of everybody's attention is on the ball, not the rest of the court.

108. Think of a conversation at a hotel desk, when you are *about to* go to open the door to get into your room: "*With our hotel app, you can open your room door with your phone and not worry about losing keys, would you like to try that?*" Don't you think you will notice that better than an out-of-the-blue offer for a room in a hotel across the world?

109. For more on this tool, see Tony Fadell's discussion in his book, *Build*.

110. A topic I often have debates on with marketing folks.

111. See Bob Stone: *Successful Direct Marketing Methods* 8th Edition. Examples are mine (but inspired by his model), as his writing was before the age of digital.

112. These examples would be for a mobile app that simplifies a process of sorts.

113. Yet not all do, to the dismay of frequent travelers!

114. Make sure you're addressing the same target consumers. The features may be used by *their* consumers, but those consumers may not be by yours.

115. And possibly identifies consumer needs that your team somehow missed in their ethnography. And just because they offer a feature, it doesn't automatically mean it's useful. Everyone can suffer from featuritis; no point in copying that.

116. See Brittany Hodak's book *Creating Superfans* for a lot more on this topic.

117. If your own employees don't want to use your product, let alone evangelize it, you may have a big problem on your hands. Either the product is bad, not valuable, or merely uninteresting, or you haven't enrolled your employees in your digital efforts, or your employee base doesn't care about your company and consumers. I don't recollect any Disney Parks or Amex employee who was *not* a superfan of both the company and its products and services *and* were not users (and volunteer testers) of the digital product.

    Employees not caring for the product or the company is something no digital experience, no matter how brilliant, can solve for and it will become obvious to your customers, once they interact with your employees in some setting. Companies with employees *not* caring about customers will go bankrupt, unless they're monopolies.

118. See Britany Hodak in her book *Creating Superfans*.

119. I hate that industry word, as if customers can be acquired (aka purchased) like inanimate objects.

120. This is also known as the *Hook* or *Hooked* model (I hate that word as it implies some sort of addiction and indeed it was conceived that way) developed by Nir Eyal. In this example, the advert is an external Hook trigger or *actuator*.

121. Products have other costs beyond price, mainly in the form of investment of time and effort required to use them. A friend once gifted me his golf clubs and despite free executive access to golf courses at the time (yes, being a Disney senior executive has its perks), I never felt the time I would need to invest to even learn the game, let alone play 9-holes to be worth it. The clubs are still in my garage, never used.

122. Amazon Prime is a prime (pun intended) example.

123. Internal trigger in the *Hook Model* parlance.

124. Preferably, try not to advertise to a user who is already using your digital product. Then the effectiveness of a trigger becomes a nuisance.

125. You must always provide a convenient and easy way for your consumers to cancel their subscriptions.

126. I have seen perfectly usable flows having a 60–70% drop off rate at the 4th step (out of 5). That insight, when analyzed, probably corroborated through additional data, can suggest solutions. The team must build detailed signals into the product to understand the user journey and where most users drop off.

127. Some customers, especially the less technology proficient or for single transactions, will never do.

128. That is usually correct, as slots are reserved for patients with special urgent needs, short of emergency.

129. Digital experiences, especially while they're maturing, tend to be more limited and somewhat more rigid in what they offer – there's no mobile app that I know of *yet* that you can beg to give you better seats or medical appointments sooner.

130. If customers actually abuse that, that's probably a sign of an unrelated business problem or opportunity: You don't have enough product or services to sell to meet the demand.

131. That being said, unless you are Facebook, I would be very conservative on how much you stalk the consumer for best personalization. Just because there are many data brokers out there offering all sorts of insights about customers, don't fall for it. The criteria would be: Would you want any firm to use all that information about you to send you offers?

132. Unfortunately, some companies still think it's OK to send real-time marketing messages by in-app notifications or text, to the bafflement of users.

133. Most companies use a combination of both physical and digital notifications to reduce the load on each channel and thus improve acceptance and consumption.

134. Most of the firm's products and services are *not* the "most profitable". Maybe equally profitable.

135. Obviously, it doesn't follow that a firm must have unprofitable offerings, just that some are. It also doesn't mean the firm should not try to become more efficient through various improvements and thus make those profitable.

136. Do you know what the number one feature used in digital apps for healthcare is? Checking lab results. Number two? Viewing already scheduled appointments (*not* making new ones). Neither makes money for the company per se. But nobody will use a digital experience solely to make MRI appointments (those are high profit margin) without access to basic needed features.

137. On a web page, say news or search, usually there are adverts on the right-hand side of the web page. How often do you register those messages? Even when they're interspersed with the content of interest, the brain just jumps over adverts and no amount of animation, blinking, flashing can change that. Plus, do you really want your product to go out to consumers in one of those awful snippets?

138. Always speak to your customers in plain language. Use your grandma as the tester for your messaging.

139. A lot has been written about creativity. Most common discussions make it something that you either have or you don't. In reality, just like any muscle that

can be trained carefully and constantly, you can become more creative by making efforts to be creative. I always had a knack for coming up with ideas and solutions, but if I left it at that and had not carefully learned and practiced, I wouldn't have been able to accomplish what I have. Am I a Steve Jobs or Tony Fadell? Absolutely not, but I strive to be every day. In addition, as a digital leader, it's incumbent upon you to create an intellectually safe environment where people are encouraged and guided to learn how to create ideas and think them through. In a recent digital team meeting, one of the business stakeholders, whom I invited to participate for their know-how and to keep themselves up to speed with what we're doing, caught me by surprise when they started ideating and offering tentative solutions. What is more important, they caught *themselves* doing it. In time that moment led to that person building more creative muscles and, with it, more confidence and courage. Wonderful! What more can I hope for? For much more on nurturing creativity, see *Creative Confidence* by Tom and David Kelley of IDEO fame.

140. Steve Jobs is reported to have personally reviewed every brand and product marketing campaign for Apple. If he found the time to do it, I would think most other CEOs should do it as well. But I'm not a CEO to judge. For more, see *Think Simple* by Ken Segall.

141. Product and brand marketing, while obviously related, are different and specialists in each probably don't do particularly well in the other area.

142. Look for uninspired and unfocused "our product XYZ does everything for you" messages on billboards on main streets and avenues that nobody registers, and you'll know what I mean.

143. Martina Lauchengco's book *Loved* has a great chapter on how to make the product management team's relationship with the marketing team work, not just occasionally, but on-going.

144. Amazon Web Services (AWS), Microsoft Azure, Google Cloud (GCP), Oracle Cloud Infrastructure (OCI) are those I am familiar with in the US and most of the western world and parts of Asia/Pacific (they have data centers across the world). But there are other, smaller providers, such as IBM Cloud. China has its own providers.

145. I will also talk about the maturity matrix in this chapter, but as an anti-pattern.

146. I've been using this phrase extensively when talking about cloud at different events, with the difference that instead of "someone" I used Jeff Bezos' name.

147. I followed this rule in healthcare after 2021, when we developed the first cloud reference architecture. Before that, as digital was started before cloud offerings were matured, we started by deploying in on promise data centers, but we migrated our assets after 2017.

148. Defines how the apps will be architected, deployed and managed.

149. A balanced approach, combining rearchitecting of some applications while lifting-and-shifting others, ought to normally take no more than two to three years, depending on focus and funding. Yes, a large number of applications and systems would take longer to migrate than fewer, but also likely you'll have a bigger team and funding. Still basically two to three years. If the plan is taking longer than three years, you need to reassess your readiness or commitment and then get back to that interval. Economics, the firm and customers can't wait more than three years.

150. Coordinating and synchronizing your applications cloud migration efforts with regular systems releases is not an easy exercise. You will need to decide whether you combine functional releases with cloud migration or if you keep them separate on an application by application and release by release basis.

151. Do you really want to focus your firm's attention on keeping your servers and networking hardware firmware updated or do you want to focus on delivering value to your consumers? Do you want to spend time managing facilities personnel or digital product managers? I vote for the latter 100%.

152. When you buy 1,000 servers and the cloud providers buy 1,000,000, your costs per server will clearly be higher. When Google and others use sophisticated ML models to optimize data center air conditioning and energy consumption and your data center uses Windows 2007 terminals to manually do the same (real case), you'll be more expensive.

153. For how to do Agile best, refer to *Doing Agile Right* by Darrell Rigby.

154. One note about SAFE. This is an Agile sprint-of-sprints framework designed to coordinate very large projects that have many dependencies, components, and teams working on potentially different projects and on misaligned timelines. At times, grand projects such as these are inevitable when the product is massive – think the yearly iOS releases (note: I have no idea whether Apple uses SAFE for iOS releases, although I can surmise, they do). The SAFE framework can help to some extent on very large, multi-team projects. But I have also seen organizations trying to adopt and use SAFE even when the magnitude, complexity, or number of dependencies were not large enough to warrant it and thus a simple Agile approach would have done. Because SAFE has a lot more rituals than other Agile methodologies, in order to deal with complexity, it would require a lot more effort that may not be needed.

155. If you can't always release to the consumers in very small increments, at least you should still have the code be production ready at the end of each sprint as if you're ready to deploy at any moment.

156. Technologies supporting this need have been around for a while. In recent years, a class of applications called Robotic Process Automation (RPA) have shown great results. In case you're wondering about the term "robotic", it's meant to mean automated. UIPath seems to be a leader as of 2022.

157. I spoke at an Intelligent Automation Exchange conference mid 2023. What is Intelligent Automation you may ask (unless you attended my session, and you now know?). Well, it is about using machine learning. We technologists are very good at creating these catchphrases for our inventions.

158. Healthcare is particularly affected by this problem. In most systems, medical insurance validation is done manually. Patients provide the insurance in the digital flow, but they'll probably get a call from a representative to go over insurance details. That is not very self-service, is it?

159. There are a several frameworks that have been developed over time to enhance the success of innovation efforts. Clayton Christensen, Larry Keeley, OECD, Jake Neilson, Fran Johansson, etc., have all developed such frameworks by defining different types of innovation and how to approach each. I won't go into too much detail here but they're all useful for at least being familiar with their guidance.

160. I talk elsewhere about whether you need to use bleeding-edge emerging technologies. But innovation does not require such technologies. You can easily innovate with what you have in your trusted and reliable technologies toolbox. Just look at Apple, who take their time, compared to others, to mature their technologies, long after others blew it with immature implementations.
161. See the *Ship It!* book by Jared Richardson, Will Gwaltney, Jr., focused on developers.
162. It's very useful when you have a hundred of them, not just one. Put them in a backlog that you can curate – or reject – later and don't forget about them.
163. Ben R. Rich – *Skunk Works: A Personal Memoir of My Years at Lockheed.*
164. The most striking of them being SR-71, Blackbird. But also, the (in)famous U2s.
165. At least until they are ready to survive the inertia and bureaucracy when they are revealed to the world.
166. An *intrapreneur* (I think Eric Reis can be credited with that term) is a corporate executive who displays all the qualities and behaviors usually associated with an entrepreneur, starting a small company: focus on outcomes against all odds and not politics.
167. Ben Rich and his predecessor Kelly Johnson did it brilliantly, so it's possible. But definitely not easy.
168. Eric Reyes in his book *Lean Startup* talks about strategies for success.

Part V

Digital Leaders

A true leader has the confidence to stand alone, the courage to make tough decisions, and the compassion to listen to the needs of others.

Douglas MacArthur

Leaders, especially in a big transformation, have an outsized influence over how things turn out and whether their organizations thrive by providing true value to their customers. Why is that?

No, not because they have the administrative power over organizations, people, and funding – they may have some, but not as much and as permanent as people think, anyway. Or because they have important sounding titles and bigger salaries.

Not because they do it all by themselves – they absolutely don't. Organizations and their needed transformations have a myriad of levers to pull that no leader knows all.

And also, not because they have all the answers to every question – they don't, and they may not even know all the questions to ask at all times.

So, why are leaders that important, then?

Simply put, because by definition their job is to *lead*, sometimes from the front, when the transformation starts and the team and its processes are still forming; sometimes from the back when pieces come together and others can lead from the front, needing just light guidance on the direction.

They are the ones to crystallize a vision that everyone else rallies behind based on conviction. They are to shape a culture that drives change, and they put everything in place for their teams to do their jobs as unobstructed as possible. They must build the organization and grow other leaders.

And when things turn out well, their teams must get the credit. But when things don't work, leaders must take the fall.

Singularly the most difficult job to have, but indispensable.

DOI: 10.4324/9781032644370-5

Chapter 5.1 Who Should Lead Digital?

Leadership is about recognizing that there's a greatness in everyone and your job is to create an environment where that greatness can emerge.

Coach Bill Campbell

Who Else If Not You?

This will be a biased answer to a potentially politically charged question. So, here it is. There are usually two ways that companies have approached digital.

The first approach is very distributed, especially when starting the digital effort, where everybody and everywhere inside an organization tries to do a bit of digital. Only some efforts succeed and that, at least compared to complete non-action, is good because it establishes digital as feasible, although probably not very successful. But even those that succeed suffer collectively from a lack of focus and coherence due to the fragmentation of the experience that becomes obvious to consumers who expect to be able to interact consistently with products and services from the entire company, not just one unit.

To compensate for the gaps, a second approach appeared, with the Chief Digital Officer (CDO) (whether called that or equivalent) role being created, whose first order of business is creating a comprehensive and coherent vision and strategy for digital for the *entire* firm. Only the CDO and their team can create that vision and strategy through focus, expertise, and an across-the-board, broad overview. But the CDO is not only responsible for vision and strategy, but, equally importantly, for building a coherent team, centered around the three indispensable pillars: product management, engineering, and creativity. It's very valuable when the CDO is the deeply involved chief product manager, as well as chief simplifier, chief bureaucratic barriers remover, and chief tiebreaker.

The structure being led by a CDO is what I believe is the only one that can be successful, when most companies – other than the top tier that has started on the digital journey some years ago and invested appropriately – are starting the evolution toward digital and they are still too unsure or misaligned on how to proceed with digital. In those cases, one person or organization or office (the Chief Digital Officer) is usually the path to the fastest and most coherent evolution.

As digital becomes more bread-and-butter and becomes part of the natural operation of an organization, just like with AI/ML, that responsibility can conceivably be distributed throughout the organization. Then the only thing left for the Chief Digital Officer's role is a coordination and governance role. But most organizations are nowhere near that point.

CIO vs CDO vs CDIO: Our Origin Story

Once upon a time we had "IT"[1] that was focused on running systems for the business to operate: financial systems, Enterprise Medical Record (EMR), Manufacturing Resource Planning (MRP), Enterprise Resource Planning (ERP), Human Resources (HR), etc. In that world, the Chief Information Officer (CIO) was told what they needed to implement, and they were expected to run the systems well and constantly reduce the cost of running them. Call that the traditional CIO, usually reporting to the CFO.

Then digital, which involves a lot of sophisticated technology but also deep consumer and business understanding in one package, came along. The technology may have fit[2] into the traditional CIO space, but not the rest. So, most companies created a new role, the Chief Digital Officer (CDO). I call this the first generation of CDOs. This role was to be understood as a digital product management leader role, in the beginning staffed with folks with a marketing background and sometimes reporting to the Marketing department. And the understanding was that the CDO, usually a peer of the CIO, would tell the CIO what to do, in terms of digital.

The problem with that arrangement was that, in many cases, the CIO and "IT" in general did not have the expertise, processes, and mindset for building digital assets. So, a second generation of CDOs started appearing, with the difference from the previous generation being that they also owned the technology and the engineering teams to build *digital* assets. But the CIO and "IT" were still in the picture as they owned the business systems that the digital assets needed to integrate with.

That arrangement was superior to the traditional CIO (non-digital) or the product marketing CDO setups. Many companies still operate this way, but then two other problems started developing.

The **first** was one of priority misalignment between the two roles. I have seen a situation when the CIOs #1 initiative was the CDO's #57 and the CDO team was a critical dependency for the CIO initiative. Endless friction and tension abounded. The **second** one was of incentives. The CIO was still measured on operational efficiency, while the CDO was evaluated on putting out as many new digital features as possible, some increasing costs.[3] More friction and tension.

In the meantime, a separate development was taking place. Digital aside, "IT" was also evolving, first by moving away from old technologies and processes to new ones that are basically the same technologies and processes digital assets use – Internet, distributed systems, APIs, cloud, etc. The second evolution was that some of the folks in "IT", users of commercial digital assets themselves and practitioners of agile processes, were *very* attuned to the *what* and *how* of digital.

Enter the relatively recent development: combining the CIO and CDO roles into a Chief Digital and Information Officer (CDIO) role, mostly by the CIO elevating focus and expertise into the digital area. The drive is simple: digital, as experiential as it is, is fundamentally intertwined with technology, so two different leaders would just ensure misalignments.

For example, as I write this, I own all information technology capabilities (i.e., a traditional role of a CIO that obviously is important and takes a good chunk of time). But fundamentally, my focus is equally on the Chief Digital Officer activities, driving digital transformation – for customers and the business.

This combined role works much better, but it's a very hard one to do, with the person in that seat having to flex from pedestrian issues like desktop replacements all the way to expertly designing for consumer needs and savvy business transformation. In order to be successful, the CDIO must apply themselves to this new world and develop the aptitude for *both* experience and the technology space.

The only way to be motivated to do this complex and challenging job is to serenely accept the mundane and boring – yes, the CDIO still needs to get on a call to support their team trying to recover from some outage – (but important) parts of the job and get professional satisfaction from the really interesting, consumer-facing, and business parts. Both are important and, while at times one may need more attention, over time both must be serviced well.

So, who are the customers for a CDIO? On the one hand, the digital consumers (the CDO part), on the other, all the internal consumers of technology (the CIO part) – your payroll system still needs to churn out payroll checks and deposits, preferably digitally.

Chapter 5.2 Expectations of Digital Leaders

Fortune favors the bold.

Latin proverb

Digital Leader's Mindset: Leadership Qualities Are Going to Make It or Break It

Building digital, especially from scratch, and driving a digital transformation require some very specific leadership qualities.

Leadership is one of the most difficult missions to do well because it requires tremendous awareness and willingness to learn and adapt. *Situational leadership*[4] – that is, adapting the leadership style, methods, and approaches to the particular situation at hand – is critical. There is a special mindset built by several leadership qualities that are critical to the success of any leader[5].

First and foremost, a **maniacal focus on the customer** (internal *and* external) and their needs. That should not be a surprise; most of this book is about meeting the consumer's needs. The modern CDIO needs to also be a Chief Digital Product Officer and a Chief Digital Business Officer.

Driving ruthless prioritization of capabilities by value.[6] Not everything must be done or is worth doing from a perspective of value to the customer. Not everything has to be done *right now*. In any situation, it's fundamental to prioritize where to allocate the effort, money, and assets, in order to both solve immediate issues and meet long-term goals. Equally important is staying focused and not getting distracted by new shiny things. And what you choose to do and not do and why must be crystal clear to everybody in the team.

Communicating (veering into evangelizing) broadly and as often as possible[7] about why, what, how, and when on everything digital to as much as possible of the organization. True, there's no such thing as overcommunicating in times of a transformation and none of us do enough of it. Digital is change and communication is one of the most important rules of change management. Communication must be done with facts and numbers to compensate for alternative realities brought up by those opposed to change, but also by appealing to people's positive emotions and enthusiasm.

Understand how to **balance customer needs with the organizational needs**, but never put the latter above the former. Happy customers eventually lead to financially successful organizations, rarely the other way around. One must be very aware and constantly push back against the usually strong pull by organizations to focus on internal operations' wants versus the customers'. The best path is to find ways to meet both: for example, consumer self-service saves a lot of back-office work.

Digital requires a business transformation and change because it is about transforming how consumers interact with the business and how the business adjusts to that. And since the CDIO drives digital, clearly, they must **actively drive change**,[8] shoulder-to-shoulder with operational leaders. What this means in practice is that they must be very involved in the mechanics of the changes driven by digital and not just say "this is digital, you all go and figure out what you need to do".

With the digital product management and technology behind them as assets to be used, CDIOs must be **business and process re-engineering leaders**. That is less of a personal choice than it is one of the mandates and realistic needs. Sometimes that involvement is not technically about digital but improving processes through automation or system and capability improvement,[9] which is the traditional domain of traditional CIOs.[10]

As a CDIO, you must be a **decisive decision-maker**, because often you'll have to make hard decisions in order to break down a stalemate and move things forward. Not making a decision or at least not within the necessary timeframe is also a decision of sorts, but usually one that doesn't help.

You should not be afraid to do that based on whatever data and instincts (read applied previous experience) you have at that moment. Just be ready to explain to everyone how and why you made that decision. The added value of explaining it is that in the process of articulating to others, you'll re-validate in your own mind your arguments and the validity of your decision.

Leaders with the vision, imagination, and the willingness and ability to put an insane amount of energy to **push through despite organizational inertia**, having the optimism that doing the right thing is the only path forward to be successful for customers and, long-term, for the company.

But I don't want to create the impression that being a digital leader is all about seemingly abstract concepts like vision, strategy, and evangelizing. It is that, but combined with a **relentless application to delivering outcomes** toward that vision, which often requires that the CDIO rolls up their sleeves and goes into details, defining and architecting but also fixing and solving mundane problems.

You, the digital leader, are not the oracle of Delphi[11] to have all the answers all the time – no leader ever does – but you are supposed to **put the necessary ingredients together,** so your consumers can use something that makes their lives easier.[12]

And sometimes you'll need to do a lot **more listening than talking,** and even when talking, you'll need to make sure you are the last to speak *after* more junior participants – or they will never be comfortable expressing their honest opinions.

In approaching the mission, you're not a bureaucratic executive, you're a startup entrepreneur – or more precisely, an ***intrapreneur*** – but one attuned to the organization's processes and politics.

Success in business, and especially during transformation, is predicated by the **courage** to make changes and doing things differently and doing different things than in the past. Fear of change rather than courage to change will doom any transformation and, in the long-term, any business.

Finally, **optimism and perseverance** are mandatory. A positive outlook and attitude are some of the most important qualities a leader in a transformational or crisis moment must have. A crisis will have the urgency of war and wars need to be won. Optimism is not about expecting no challenges along the journey, but that they can be overcome with the right approaches. Leadership is about followers[13] and nobody follows a doom-and-gloom leader, definitely not during difficult times.

What about **relationships**? They are important for any leader to successfully exercise all the qualities described above. These relationships need to be invested in and nurtured over time. But some relationships are going to be a lot more important than others for transformation leaders. Which ones are those? **First**, the relationship with their own leader – possibly the CEO of the company or of the business unit – as without a great relationship and alignment of minds, operating through difficult times will be hard to do effectively. **Next** are relationships with the Board, its technology and digital committee, as well as the firm's Senior Executive Committee (usually chaired by the CEO), as they will have to create the organizational conditions and incentives for digital to happen and be successful (more on that in Chapter 6). **Third**, the business stakeholders and partners that have to join the digital efforts by transforming their businesses and processes. **Finally**, the digital leader's peers (if different than the Senior Executive Committee members) – digital will need their support on everyday matters that can quickly add up to big needs.

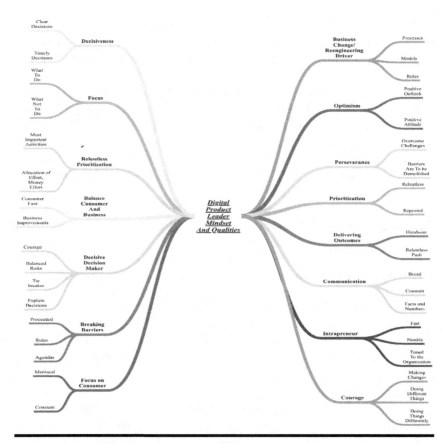

Figure 5.1 Digital product leader qualities and mindset tree.

Managing Expectations: People Want the Future Yesterday

It's always critically important, especially when establishing a digital program and starting a digital transformation, to precisely define the expectations the organization ought to have about you as a product executive and about your team. This is about aligning the vision but also the strategy with the organization's expectations.

There could be two diametrically opposite expectations between what you can do and what the organization expects you to do.

First, an unrealistic expectation of an accelerated timeframe and ambitious scope. The firm may expect a fully blown digital experience out of nothing in six months, preferably with little investment. That is usually true with a firm that has no experience of how digital products are built. That same organization is also the one that constantly listens to vendors' siren songs of wonderful results delivered "right away".

The way to deal with this is to articulate the process and likely timeline and refer to other examples in the industry and their timelines. Here I like to remind people that the first iPhone launched in 2007, revolutionary as it was, did not have cut and paste – something that editor programs in computers had since the 1970's. Or an app store – until a year after its launch.

Second, at the other end of the spectrum but equally problematic, is the expectation of long execution times – especially from supporting functions like HR, Finance, Procurement, and Legal, which will feel no need for accelerated administrative support for digital. If you're trying to release every three weeks (with a lead time of, say another five or six) but Legal + Finance + Procurement takes 90 days to approve a contract for a new piece of technology that you want to introduce for that three-week release, you'll know what I mean.

The solution is similar to the unrealistically short timeline expectations: articulate how the slow administrative process, in aggregate, will delay your work, resulting in customers having to wait – and then wait some more.

This is where a separate administrative track for digital and digital transformation – which I will talk more about in the next chapter – becomes critical to you moving fast enough to catch up with the world, to start with, keep up, and then get ahead.

(Over)Communicating and Evangelizing Is the Digital Leader's Job

There are industries[14] which, from a perspective of technology and digital maturity, are where other leading industries were 5, 10, or even 15 years ago, simply because, while those others were focusing on agile, digital, machine learning, and cloud, the laggards were still struggling with implementing the basics – or not paying any attention to what other industries and their customers were doing.

If you're in one of those laggard industries finally awakening to the need for digital, there will be a lot of evangelizing, teaching, and proving to be done by digital leaders.

Even in the best of situations, a digital evolution is a steep learning curve for everybody. That is why helping people understand the *what* and *how* is invaluable. I have meetings where people not familiar with digital and design thinking, including business and operations folks, learn "how the digital sausage is made".[15] I want to go fast, faster than those people are used to, and by them seeing how detailed yet fast the process is, they're able to adjust. Yep, it's pretty intense learning.

Digital will drive significant changes to the firms' processes, which is hard to sell in successful organizations that see no reason to change, based on past successes. That is exactly the symptom that Professor Clayton's Innovator's Dilemma talked about. He also spoke about when organizations succumb to that symptom and don't change.[16] So, unfortunately as it may feel, it's the digital leaders' job to tell that story of change and describe the path to the digital future.

But communicating is not just about showing the destination, it is also about showing the path and proving it can be done by having small successes at the beginning but successful and meaningful successes, leading to ever larger ones.[17] Trust must be earned, with people seeing the process developing and being successful over time. It's hard for people to argue with success, so prove the success of your approach.

Clearly, a mindset can't be switched on overnight, especially where there's no history. It has to be developed and nurtured over time, from developing a vision and a strategy for digital that articulates *what*, *why*, and *how*.

Change Management or How to Get Everybody to Change

> *The secret to change is to focus all of your energy not on fighting the old but on building the new.*
>
> **Socrates**

Let's say that from tomorrow onwards there's a new business process or model introduced to support a digital experience feature. Could it be as simple as stopping requiring your consumers to do paperwork, well, on paper? How is your staff supposed to know how to adjust their daily activities to support that new process?

The answer is, of course, change management, which is basically all the steps operational teams must take and the pieces required to prepare for the upcoming change. How much change management one must do obviously depends on what the change is – how much and how different than the status quo.

But, whether by underestimation or oversight,[18] probably most of us do too little of it, so the organization is not quite ready for the change moment when the time comes.[19] That usually leads to both consumer and staff confusion and dissatisfaction when the gaps between what it is and what it should be become apparent to them.

When manual models are replaced with digital or automated processes, it will be important for the digital team to do the same internal user research and design activities as for consumers. Then they need to map the differences between as-is and to-be and chart the process of change, communication, and training.

We just said that change management is about the staff both knowing *about* the change and *how to adjust* for it. It's also important that they understand *why* something is changing; first, so they align better to it, second so they appreciate it more, both leading to better transition and post-transition performance.[20]

There is ample literature on change management,[21] mostly focused on large-scale organizational change. However, even preparing for a smaller change requires a considerable effort and determination to succeed. The most important aspect to remember is that changing processes and business models is first about changing *mindsets and culture* and only after about the mechanics of the new process. And the more entrenched the mindset and culture are – and they absolutely are, in big or long-established organizations and even startups created around a singular culture that now needs evolving – the harder the effort to manage change will be.

Notes

1. You may wonder why I put IT (Information Technology) in quotes. The first is that traditional organization doesn't really exist anymore, because of the reasons described in the book. Second, because, technically, it describes an organization focused mostly on data center systems and desktops, and yet, with the massive increase in data-center grade computing everywhere in operations (have you noticed how many medical devices are *everywhere* in hospitals, all running standard OSs and connecting to the general network? Usually 10/bed), most IT organizations deal with *Operational* Technologies as well. And yes, also because we think we graduated from the stereotype of the IT technician who just fixed desktops (still needed, but not the main focus) in a long-gone era. No offense to those folks, I was one thirty plus years ago when I installed the first network linking desktops for the company I worked for. I prefer the term Technology and Digital. These folks deserve some respect.
2. On paper, at least. Running age-old mainframes efficiently and constantly focusing on reducing operating costs is not exactly the same as building digital applications in the cloud, with technologies changing every 3–5 years.
3. That is, measured on output. We talked about why that is problematic due to a host of other issues.
4. I learned this important concept at American Express. It was instilled in and expected of all leaders.
5. For much more, I recommend Bob Iger's book, *The Ride of a Lifetime*.
6. If your technology team is good at delivering with quality – and that is what you should strive for – you'll one day be deluged with requests to fix anything under the sun that is broken (and there's a lot in any company). Unless you resist trying to fix everything, you'll fail and nothing will be accomplished, not even the things you could fix. Prioritize, prioritize, prioritize.

7. Overcommunicating is about repeating incessantly the story until everybody hears it and, most importantly, understands it at a deep level.

8. If there's someone else in the organization actively driving the change, that is great; the CDIO doesn't have to do it all. But if there isn't, then the CDIO must absolutely take that mantle and run with it.

   Tony Fadell calls these hard driving leaders that drive forward with the mission in mind first and foremost *"mission-driven a**holes"* – they'll challenge the organization's approach for the right reasons, but they'll never challenge people's honest motives. Get used to being called that – I have been called that more times than I can remember.

9. Some authors include automation under the digital transformation umbrella. I don't, but in the end that's just semantics. It needs to be done, so the decision is how to manage the work streams and focus.

10. Another reason for the CDO to also be the CIO.

11. Leadership is a lonely endeavor, but you would be well served to have a "kitchen cabinet" of advisors to give you honest feedback and input. Assembling that group is priceless but requires careful selection based on extreme competence, mutual trust, and willingness to speak up with tough feedback. Take the tough feedback as tough love, or rather the dedication to the manifest mission you and that group serve.

12. Shep Hyken's *The Convenience Revolution: "Make the Customer's Day a Little Easier".*

13. Aka, other people freely wanting to follow a leader because of the mission or message of that leader.

14. Healthcare is notably one of them, as we all experience as patients.

15. I use this imagery a lot, not because I particularly like eating or making sausages, but because it describes a messy, hands-on activity that produces something great.

16. Where are Kodak, Digital Equipment Corporation, Silicon Graphics, Sun Microsystems, Data General, now? Even the once mighty IBM with a former 70% market share?

17. I don't mean larger and larger toward a Big Bang. Just more and faster increments in wider scope.

18. See the section on release launch planning and preparation.

19. These are those stories about call center or on-the-ground personnel having no idea about some new digital feature available to consumers. Don't be that story.

20. When starting change management discussions, I always start with the big, industry-at-large trends and then go into what it means for the firm and then for the individual team. Context from big to small is important.

21. For more information, I recommend searching on the internet for PDCA and especially OPDCA.

Part VI

The Larger Organization

I think a successful company is one where everybody owns the same mission. Out of necessity, we divide ourselves up into discipline groups. But the goal when you're actually doing the work is to somehow forget what discipline group you're in and come together. So, in that sense, nobody should own user experience; everybody should own it.

Don Norman

I said earlier that digital transformation is neither about digital technology – although that is the fundamental ingredient and enabler – nor just digitizing manual processes – although that is useful sometimes.

The difference between Amazon and Sears is *not* a mobile app. In the case of Amazon, it's about using the *flywheel as a virtuous cycle business model.*[1]

When you look at it from that perspective, digital transformation is a very tall order, especially for traditional organizations that haven't changed very much in a long time. Besides, any business transformation is very difficult for most organizations[2] – too much history of legacy mindsets, processes, and agendas.

But without the organization changing and being actively supportive, digital cannot be successful. So, what would be required for an organization's full support of digital?

First, the **support of the Board, the CEO, and the senior executive level**. Difficult organizational decisions will need to be made along the way – balancing between the consumers' needs and the firm's or internal groups – that will require that level of executive involvement and action. If operations and finance priorities always win, digital will be useless. The senior executives and the Board would be the ones to decide on priorities.

DOI: 10.4324/9781032644370-6

Dedicated, streamlined special enterprise processes and resources to minimize delays and overhead in the digital team organizational needs, balanced with some minimally necessary controls to ensure results are still delivered. Put simply, without dedicated processes, digital will die the silent death of a thousand (organizational) cuts.

Dedicated multi-year budgets and commitments. The transformation must be sustained throughout good years and bad and through complex budgeting cycles; otherwise, it also would suffer the death of a thousand cuts, with the digital team trying to obtain funding for each piece of the transformation.

Culture change and change management are driven by dedicated digital product leaders with a digital innovation mindset. The organization must be managed, guided, and, at times, pushed and pulled to change in a structured way.

Chapter 6.1 Enterprise Processes

Coming together is a beginning, staying together is progress and working together is success.

Henry Ford

Board and Executive Steering Committee Support

For a CDIO and thus digital to be successful, there has to be an unequivocal mandate coming from the board, the CEO, and the Executive Steering committee. And the mandate can't be a one-time announcement that everybody forgets about two weeks after, but a clear and sustained support that carries through the inevitably difficult times and decisions.

Digital transformation will require operational leaders to change and transform their processes. And all of that is for the good of the customers and the company, not for the CDIO.[3] The message and incentives to those leaders to change must come from the CEO and the Executive Committee; otherwise, the enterprise, between operations and digital, operates as a house divided and nothing good happens. For all that to happen, the CDIO must do sustained evangelizing work with these bodies.

Digital must be understood in the larger context of consumer needs and wants and the overall economic and social environment. Sometimes that means the CDIO must educate the board and senior executives, possibly starting with a "Let me tell you what digital and digital transformation really are". Without that, it will all sound like an expensive, shiny technical boondoggle.

Goals, vision, and strategy must be made crisp, clear, and aligned so there are no surprises on either side. What you're going to do, at a high level, without committing to low-level details and delivery dates and how. Make sure you talk about what you're not going to do, articulating why.

Evolution and progress must be clearly articulated, together with what is next and any other updates or changes. For example, I present to the entire board at least *once a year* on the status of the digital efforts and our high-level plans for the upcoming period (usually six months to a year). The Technology and Digital Board Committee gets a similar but more detailed update every *quarter* (together with security and a rotation of other updates); to the other executives, more often and on opportune dates.[4] Sometimes that support must come in the form of big but needed budgets, big increases in headcount[5] (when you have very little coachable talent on staff), and big compensation packages to recruit and retain the kind of talent nobody else in the organization knows they need in order to do great things.

If you can't get the unwavering support described here, you're in the wrong place and you're set up for failure.

Investment, Budgeting, and Funding

The most important thing is to know what you can't know, and we can't know in advance which of our ideas will work with customers and which won't. So, we approach discovery with the mindset that many, if not most, of our ideas won't work out.[6]

Marc Andreessen

Dedicated multi-year budgets and commitments to sustain digital efforts throughout good years and bad are critical, otherwise it will be the death of a thousand cuts for the digital team if they are required to obtain funding for each feature. Digital transformation is a long-term investment, not a singular expense in one year.

The biggest challenge when asking for a dedicated budget is the expectation of a short-term return on investment, unambiguously articulated in a traditional CBA. Something like this: *$X invested in digital will drive $Y incremental profit through increased sales, where Y > X, preferably in year one.* That is something that CFOs expect from investment evaluations. But there are three major problems with this type of expectation, mostly due to a timing viewpoint. Yes, digital does create value of the type described above for the firm, through the customers; however, *when* that value materializes is another matter.

First, especially when you start on your digital journey, simply because you don't have the history to see what works, that immediate results expectation is unrealistic. Experience and opportunities to tweak come later as you learn, but while you do that, you can't expect significant benefits.

One of the interesting things about creating digital experiences, like with any innovation at scale, is that you don't really know what will work – I don't want to panic CFOs here, but besides fundamental features like access or check-in or your record and account, a not insignificant number of your digital ideas will not be big successes with your users, at least not at the first iteration. As such, there's quite a bit of experimentation, tweaking, and tuning.

Second, unless your digital product *is* the product that your company sells versus supporting a different product or service – event tickets, resort stays, and entertainment park visits, healthcare appointments – the impact digital makes to the firm's bottom line is dependent on how the firm's operations can take advantage of it. If the firm doesn't have enough to sell what the customers want or it is of poor value or disrepute, there is nothing digital can do. Digital and operations influence and impact each other. Yes, digital leaders, in their roles as business leaders, must try to influence these operational decisions and activities, but they have limits.

Instead, you must work that backwards, from the investment to the benefit: *if I have these digital capabilities, what could I do in the operational and business models' space to make a positive financial impact?* To make an analogy, a bigger door allows more people to get in, but if the room or house you're trying to get those people into is too small or has too slow of a throughput, you're not going to make a difference. You must make the house bigger or preferably support faster traffic.[7]

Third, it is to be expected that the digital transformation will eventually require a lot of investment, both financial and in organizational focus, not just for the technical implementation (most of the time the effort is not about technical investment and size,[8] but process and organizational change management). It requires a high capacity to absorb financial and operational risk.

Organizations must be prepared for digital to introduce operational inefficiencies – in the beginning, as with introducing any change. Moving from one S curve[9] to another introduces inefficiencies at first, but then the improvement is exponential. And slow at first is OK, because then we can subsequently apply other methods – like process reengineering and automation – to solve for those initial inefficiencies. We can't get everything for nothing – at least not day 1.

Then there is always resistance to digital transformation as with any change and large-scale transformation. People are naturally averse to change.

Finally, digital may change reasonably working non-digital processes (at least working today), so people will need to be convinced of the need for and value of changing away from the status quo.

Administrative Processes or How to Avoid Death by a Thousand Cuts

Administrative processes are used by many of an organization's departments such as human resources, finance, legal, procurement, etc., to help run the business and are critical for the efficient functioning of any enterprise.

The problem, from digital's perspective, with all these processes is that they have been tuned for the normal, steady state of operations of the enterprise and not for a somewhat turbulent period of change that a digital/business transformation really entails. The steady state assumes certain predictability, standardization, strictness, and, yes, lack of urgency, which transformation moments don't have or can't afford.

As such, it's *imperative* for the timeliness of introducing digital that special processes are enabled to support the digital efforts, focused on expedited timeliness and accounting for the inevitable unknown of something new and unpredictable.

That may sound unfair to those who need to navigate the process for the normal operations of the business, but they must remember that the unknowns of a transformation and the stakes are very different than steady-state business. They also should understand that at some point digital will become another component of the organization's operations and will follow the same rules as everyone else – but not before.

Drive for Simplicity: Simple Is Exquisitely Beautiful

Simple can be harder than complex. You must work hard to get your thinking clean to make it simple. But it's worth it in the end, because once you get there, you can move mountains.

Steve Jobs

We talked about product simplicity earlier in the *Product* section. We need to now talk about business and organizational simplicity. Product and process simplicity are necessarily interrelated, and both are critically important for a great digital experience.

Simplicity is one of the hardest goals that we humans can accomplish. Even when we start simple and clear, without relentless effort to keep it that way, our organizational creations tend to become unnecessarily complicated and ultimately complex. And complexity is easy as it simply creeps up, usually in the absence of clear actions to prevent it.[10] It's faster to be complex than it's to be simple.[11]

Fairly frequently, when digital product teams are trying to design consumer experiences, they are interfacing with seriously convoluted organizational processes that are governed by quirky and awkward rules that no one can remember the reason for. Trying to design an experience around such processes will lead to almost impractical user flows that would just turn an inefficient manual process into an inefficient digitized process.

Designing digital products defined by simplicity – which, when materialized as convenience, is what consumers want – in a hopelessly complicated organization is very, very hard. The rust under the polish will eventually show through. The organization must reengineer its processes, which it should do for a host of other, non-digital reasons.

And this is the biggest takeaway of digital transformation – you'll have to change (and definitely simplify and streamline) processes and business rules. But digital practitioners beware: most organizations instinctively resist the change and the simplification, for a variety of reasons – mostly comfort with the status quo and fear of the unknown. Pushback notwithstanding, the digital leader must nevertheless drive change and simplification of processes and rules – or risk a mediocre digital experience.

This leads to another conundrum for the digital product team: finding a balance between pushing for changing enough of the business to make the consumer experience valuable and even delightful, and doing it fast enough, on the one hand, and getting bogged down in extended process reengineering and automation efforts, to the detriment of advancing digital as fast as consumers need it to be, on the other.

The approach I try to take here is to separate the digital experience work streams from the process reengineering and automation streams. While they interact with each other, they usually require different teams and technologies, so splitting the two is usually feasible and practical. And just as digital advancement is iterative, so is process reengineering and automation. Do as much as you can, live with imperfections, and then come back later to do more. Rinse and repeat, continuously.

If one must absolutely choose speed of digital versus speed of business process change – due to time, money, or people constraints – I strongly recommend always focusing on doing as much as possible on the consumer experience first and the remaining as needed on the rest. That is simply because consumers pay the bills by choosing to show up at your doorstep and the internal kludge[12] – technical debt and systems, inefficient processes, etc. – can be fixed later – as long as you don't forget about them, and you have a plan to address them later.

Simplicity is not just a goal. It's the guiding North Star.

Notes

1. See "The Ultimate Guide to the Amazon Flywheel Model for 2023", by Werner Geyser at https://influencermarketinghub.com/amazon-flywheel/ . For a more detailed analysis of the concept, also see "Turning the Flywheel: A Monograph to Accompany Good to Great (Good to Great, 6), February 26, 2019, by Jim Collins available on, well, Amazon at https://www.amazon.com/Turning -Flywheel-Monograph-Accompany-Great/dp/0062933795/ref=sr_1_3?crid =18CT8SLGB5YZW&keywords=amazon+flywheel+book&qid=1680884115 &sprefix=amazon+flywheel+book,aps,142&sr=8-3
2. Healthcare in particular.
3. This is a very important point. When the CDIO becomes the agent of change and promoter of products, which they should, it is easy for the organization to think in terms of "the CDIO's digital agenda", with a connotation of self-serving interest.

4. While we're at it, I also recommend a parallel update on security, either by you or your CISO.
5. This doesn't necessarily mean hiring from the outside although you'll probably have to do that if you start with no digital talent. Even if you reallocate from other parts of the organization, those folks will likely be backfilled in the short term.
6. Translation: don't book the investment in a digital product on the balance sheet until you know it actually works and thus is an asset to the organization.
7. By the way, faster traffic, aka throughput, in this context is not just about profit, but delivering value to more people sooner – and in healthcare that means more lives saved.
8. Most of the time you don't compete with the entire might of Microsoft or Google, just with a team not much bigger than yours. But possibly much more experienced.
9. Think of your efforts vs outcomes starting on a graph in the lower left corner of an S, starting slow, then going up the semi-vertical side of the S and then slowing down at the top side.
10. See *Think Simple* by Ken Segall. A must-read for any product or organization architect.
11. Blaise Pascal, 1657: "I have only made this letter longer because I have not had the time to make it shorter."
12. Wikipedia: A kludge or kluge is a workaround or quick-and-dirty solution that is clumsy, inelegant, inefficient, difficult to extend, and hard to maintain.

Part VII

Healthcare Case Study

The journey is the reward.

Steve Jobs

This section will provide an actual example of how some of the things we talked about up to this point came together in my role as a healthcare Chief Digital Information Officer (CDIO).

Healthcare Digital Context

Can you tell us about your joining healthcare in the middle of a pandemic, choosing to leave Disney behind?

(Translation: What in the world were you thinking???)

Common question I repeatedly get in various speaking engagements.

I have always tried to be where the transformation and significant change happened,[1] whether in technology, digital, or business or all of the above.

However, big and potentially disruptive transformations don't perpetually happen in organizations, and that is a good thing. Healthy organizations should evolve and improve constantly and organically in ways that help them not find themselves in do-or-die moments.

Unfortunately, too many organizations don't do that and instead stay stagnant in one area or another or in one way or another for extended periods of time. Organizational or individual comfort with status quo,[2] fear of failure during or after the change,[3] or plain fear of endangering today's cash cow[4] are the most common reasons for inaction and lack of change. Just look at companies having to suddenly rush to do a digital transformation when the pandemic hit, and their old business model was not working well anymore, and you'll know who preferred the status quo for too long. Sudden crises always reveal long-known but ignored weaknesses.

For healthcare, I would add two more reasons for inaction, both meaningful in the context of this book. The first is having been impervious to whatever happened outside healthcare in terms of technology[5] or consumer experiences.[6] The second simply manifested as a minimal focus on the consumer part of the healthcare experience – accessing care services and meaningful medical records – as opposed to the medical care that happens in a consult, hospital, or operating room.[7]

That last point, as uncomfortable as it may be, is mostly driven by the healthcare business and incentive model, where between medical providers, insurers/payers (including the government), and Pharma, the patient is *not* the customer as in most other industries, but rather the product *onto* which things happen. For insurers, the customer is usually employer plans, for medical providers it's mostly the payers (who pay for services performed onto patients),[8] etc.

What this boils down to is healthcare technology and digital experiences lagging far behind most other industries.[9] And we can all see this any time we try to access care – confusing, baffling, and disjointed digital experiences – that is, when a digital experience is available at all.

As such, after satisfying roles in previous industries doing technology and digital, it seemed natural to me that I should apply all that I knew and could do toward healthcare, given all the incredible challenges and opportunities existing there to make digital experiences great. Besides, at some point in our lives, we all become increasingly dependent on healthcare, so any change to make that better by even an inch was also a good investment for my own future patient-centric needs.

I did not expect it to be easy, otherwise it would have been done by now at scale by someone – but that was part of the allure.[10] Adrenaline rush alert.

Fortunately for us all, there are some healthcare operators who truly understand the imperative need for digital experiences and digital transformation, beyond empty declarations. My move into healthcare, which usually promotes internally, was probably something that raised a lot of eyebrows everywhere.[11]

Starting from Scratch

Most overnight successes took a long time.

Steve Jobs

Starting something from scratch is never easy, but at times it's less so than having to demolish first and then rebuild. When you have to do both, then things are really difficult. Unfortunately, that is what most, if not all, CDIOs face.

When I arrived in the healthcare organization, there was no meaningful digital to speak of, beyond some digitization, so everything had to be built from the ground up. There was plenty of technology, but not capable of supporting digital, so that also had to be rebuilt. And little talent to do either[12] (talent only supporting existing systems).

So, the starting approach was four-pronged.

First, since digital transformation is sometimes a confusing and vague concept (ballooned to ridiculous sizes by consultants) to most companies and their boards, I needed to define what digital and digital transformation (starting on the consumer side, followed by in-patient, provider, and then operations) had to be – and not be. This required some months of discussions and evangelizing at all levels, from the system's executive committee down to operational leaders, culminating with the (first of many) presentation to the board.

That first presentation to the board had a couple of very well-defined goals, starting with explaining what digital is (and what it's not). The articulation was 99% experiential (not technology or roadmap or projects), comparing what consumers could do (or rather not do) at that moment and what they'll experience in two to three years.[13]

Establishing the parameters for a successful evolution was the other important goal: the role of the digital team in driving digital products and features through design thinking, the board and executive committee's support, dedicated funding, and special administrative processes.

Second, and parallel to the first, was to define the vision and articulate the strategy and principles for digital products. This was defined in a first consumer digital document and infused into everything I wrote and said in crystal-clear ways over that first year. I brought all that together in a formal Consumer Digital Product Vision and Strategy document to explicitly guide the team and the organization, roughly about a year into the effort.[14]

At the same time, I also defined at a high level the products, features, and prioritization on what we needed to do. This list was purely directional and indicative of the ambitious nature of the effort and never intended in any way to be precise and ultimate – and indeed, it changed many times.

Third, and the most important,[15] was (the start of[16]) building a digital team and selecting team members – product management, digital engineering, and creative design – as well as the structure and team processes. This was a from-scratch effort, as nothing really existed before.

Fourth was defining an overall vision and strategy for *the technology organization* and scope (with my CIO hat on, which was beyond just digital technology) – focus areas, changes and transformations, migrations, uplifts, and upgrades (including for Enterprise Medical Record (EMR) and Enterprise Resource Planning (ERP) systems), internal processes, technologies and tools, teams and leadership structure, talent acquisition, tech currency efforts, etc. Agile processes, integration with transactional systems (aka digital enterprise services), and cloud deployments were three fundamental pillars supporting, first and foremost, digital.

Vision or What We Want to Enable Consumers and Patients to Do

Obviously, the principles I talked about earlier in the book for this four-pronged approach were what we used, with a strong focus on the state of digital in healthcare – consumers frustrated and confused by incoherent and overly complex experiences in their need of accessing care and information to the point that they feel powerless. And while that may be tolerable (it's not) for a freely chosen experience – say, entertainment – the worst time for incoherent and cumbersome experiences is when people are sick.

The vision was about providing self-service access to care and information[17] for the target consumers for all the materially important experiences (big positive impact to the largest number of target consumers). Of course, the ultimate goal of that was consumer satisfaction and thus long-term loyalty to the system through consistent qualitative differentiation.

> *Consumers will have simple, meaningful, comprehensive, and empowering digital access to care and information.*[18]

The main thrust of the digital efforts thus focused primarily on solving problems *most* consumers and patients experienced *often*. The primary goal was *not* staff productivity gains, although that is a great secondary benefit that is usually implicit when putting self-service capabilities in the hands of consumers. That was an extraordinarily important but controversial decision to make, given healthcare's traditional inward-looking and narrow focus on operators and providers and their experiences[19] and not on consumers' digital experiences. We chose the consumer first because choosing operators first would have pretty much assured that we would never get to focus on consumers and patients.

The following would be the next generation of consumer digital for healthcare:

> *Provide quality of health and wellbeing through continuous digital journeys and engagement.*

This vision example doesn't talk about care access anymore – assuming that was addressed in the previous iteration, but about health and well-being. Patients' goals are really to get their life back and be well – the end goal – not really to get care, which is just a means.

The two generations of visions are intrinsically related as they form a **virtuous cycle of health**. Great care today, through great results, builds engagement in the future, toward constant consumer involvement in maintaining their health to avoid serious health situations. If those are, unfortunately, encountered, then the digital product will assist timely with detection and access to acute interventions, followed by supportive recovery assistance and back to active health maintenance mode.

Healthcare, mostly due to the inherent dysfunction of the funding and the fee-for-service model, is beholden to a transaction-based model, not a relationship model. Even the EMRs are architected mostly around transactions, not long-term care and condition management. I wanted our digital capabilities, instead, to focus on building long-term relationships and loyalty through high-quality digital experiences – and not merely enabling transactions.

Target Consumers and Patients

What about consumers? We chose to focus (as in first and foremost) our digital efforts on those consumers and patients who tend to visit us on a regular basis. Why those first? Because those are the ones who can consistently get value from digital capabilities that justify *their* investment of time in digital – by creating digital profiles that can be constantly used for future interactions. That meant focusing on the top, say, 60% of consumers – not everyone for the first two years.

Of course, healthcare is built on the premise of providing care to everyone who needs it. But it wouldn't be realistic for us in digital to attempt everything (it never is), so we had to decide whom we focused on.

Strategy: What to Do and What Not to Do and How

The focus was on delivering a high percentage of known consumer needs and capabilities in three years, but not 100%,[20] with a preference for providing less-than-complete (but still valuable) experiences as soon as possible versus waiting for completeness for an extended period. This was a significant deviation in an industry thinking in terms of nothing else but 100%

of everything. 100% when providing lifesaving care should be the ultimate goal for healthcare – yet to be achieved anywhere – but that doesn't realistically apply in non-life-threatening experiences (like check-in/registration for a Primary Care Physician (PCP) visit, especially given the questions asked "just in case" have answers already known). It's pointless to debate 100% vs 80% when you currently have barely over 20%.

Digital efforts were put into designing and implementing user-friendly[21] but fully integrated and coherent experiences. And the only way to achieve that is by controlling the end-to-end user experience. This is another big deal in healthcare: provider systems too often fall prey to niche digital health vendors providing siloed and disjointed experiences, as well as being constrained by their own digital technology limitations (few choose to build and own their own user experiences, leaving that to either EMR or other vendors).

It's easy to get sucked up into unrelated process reengineering efforts, given how much it's needed, and halt the digital progress. It's a fine balance that must be maintained. I chose to create a separate group focusing on reengineering and RPA and had that group work in parallel, but with touchpoints back into the digital stream.

We preferred action (followed by learning and adjusting) in the short term over extended theoretical discussions. This was yet another major departure in an operations culture focused on discussions extending over many months or years[22] as well as expanded participation driven solely by FOMO rather than providing value.

In the End, the Product Is What Users Experience

We had a mobile-first strategy. This was controversial, once again, in healthcare, because of the (mis)perception that most patients prefer desktop or even mobile web. Some of that's true, based on certain demographics preferring larger screens. But we had strong indications that consumers would use the mobile more than the desktop version, as the technology to use on the go in a physical business such as healthcare, *if and only if* the mobile experience was of high quality (which in the industry it usually isn't[23]).

We were right: we started with desktop web – mostly used to check medical records, specifically lab results – being dominant by a factor of 4×–5×, which moved over time into an intermediary relative equal split of 50–50 between desktop web and mobile apps, and then a 2× in favor of apps for some features.

With enough perseverance, we moved the conversation from "who prefers what all the time and everywhere" to "who prefers what, where and when" – at a minimum, desktop at home, mobile on the go – as expected. But increasingly, the experience split: booking at home on desktop but finishing check-in on site through the app.

We decided not to design features just for niche categories of users. An interesting need became evident for employees who were also consumers and patients. If the experience was designed just for them as employees in the consumer app, it would become unusable and/or at least confusing for the other 99.9% of consumers. What we planned to do, instead, was to design the feature in a way that would be usable for both categories, with some neat but transparent processing in the back end.

More on Flows and Journeys, Not Tasks and Transactions

We talked earlier in the book about the importance of modeling consumer journeys through digital experiences and not simply providing them with transactional capabilities. The latter being the ability to book a medical appointment, the former the ability to follow the flow from finding a doctor, booking an appointment, checking-in/registering, paying (or providing insurance), accessing appointment results and summaries, etc.

For the business operators, activities are designed as tasks and processes. They operate them and thus understand these flows and processes well. They're trained in them, and they repeat them a thousand times. But the consumers that are supposed to navigate semi-blindly on the other side of those same flows have no such training or practice, and they are understandably overwhelmed, confused, and frustrated. It's like being blindfolded in a labyrinth where unseen arbiters judge how well the user finds the exit – or not. So, most of the time those customers are only shown the *next task* to be executed, with no visibility or understanding of the entire flow or journey. For each next step, they're surprised and unprepared.

Figure 7.1   User journey flow.

This flow/journey equally applies to a hotel or resort stay or hospital appointment (replace Account with Medical Record). If you view it through this lens, you'll ask why you can do these operations for a hotel but not for a hospital appointment.[24]

However, if instead digital externalizes and represents the full journey as a user flow, showing the steps in the process and the status, including what is required, what has been provided, and what not been provided at each step, then the picture is a lot clearer.

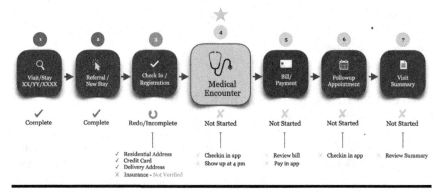

Figure 7.2   Digital user journey flow with step by step status.

In the absence of an explicit and visible flow in digital, consumers need to develop their own mental models of what will likely (need to) happen.[25] That is usually incomplete and thus full of unpleasant surprises ("I booked the appointment. Now you tell me that my insurance doesn't cover it? Why couldn't you have told me that when I made the appointment??? ").

Providing guided journeys is the ultimate goal. However, when you start from very little or nothing, it's difficult to offer digital journeys. We had to start with transactions first (still providing significant value versus paper forms) and then gradually start to build the journeys to include those point transactions.

Marketing

Consumers must become aware of the value the products offer for their specific access and care needs. This value must be expressed in clear and meaningful ways. A big part of making consumers and patients aware, in an intensely physical environment such as healthcare, is for staff interacting face to face with them to recommend the product to their customers, close friends, and family.

This is a blessing – if you have an in-person advocate at the point of need that consumers can trust – and a curse – when you don't. It's taking a while to get staff on board with the value of digital experiences to the point they become evangelists[26] – simply because digital has never been important before or worth mentioning.

A big part of the problem was non-digital demands on the staff's time and effort – the pandemic, burnout, etc. – that made promoting digital less urgent than other demands. But some of it was an insufficient marketing effort on our part.

It turns out, quite predictably, that when you start a digital product effort from scratch, most likely adjacent services like product marketing are not as robust and mature as they need to be. Messaging is usually highly unfocused and untargeted, not to mention being late, happening *after* product and features launches.

I have never experienced a digital product team launching features faster than the marketing can catch up, despite the digital team designing the positioning and the messaging. This is very counter-productive when you want to put your product in the hands of as many consumers as you can so that they can benefit from it. But here we were.

Growing Pains Are Always to Be Expected: or You're Not Evolving

Even when you have done something similar before, you'll make mistakes. That is OK, if you timely and correctly assess the new situation and adjust fast.

When you grow a team and practice from virtually nothing, or even when you have to right a big ship that is not navigating properly, you'll need to start with a structure, team, and team members and then continually adjust as you go, tweaking for the team's optimal functioning[27] and when the need for change becomes evident.[28]

For the first year and a half, I had to continually adjust the structure: teams, people, relationships, and roles. One of the main actions I had to take on the engineering side, as we were growing, was to clearly separate the consumer front-end responsibilities – UI/UX development and experience services – from the backend, shared enterprise services engineering. The move was eased by the need to build capabilities that were shared with non-consumer-facing capabilities.

While I started building the product management and creative design team from the beginning and continued to strengthen both, we also had to start building up and elevate the consumer feedback and insights team,[29] as well as start building the system's feedback mechanism tracking and reporting user behavior – who was using what flows and capabilities, how many were abandoning what flows and when.

Systems feedback tracking is one of the most valuable sources of insights[30] on what is working and what is not in your product. For example, it became obvious that some consumers were abandoning the self-schedule flows when reaching the page with the available slots to choose from. And the immediate reason was that the slots were too far in the future (who wants to wait for five weeks to book a primary care physician's visit?). But an additional reason was that, as they were used to calling the support center, they thought they would get better (sooner) slots that way. But that was not accurate, as the digital capability offered *more* slots than the call center could. So, we clarified to consumers that, in a scarcity of slots, what they see now on the app or web may be gone by the time they call the call center. We also introduced a feature allowing selection not by provider, but by first available slot.

The other major adjustment was to separate the product delivery by channel – mobile vs app. While the underlying technology and the product were identical, there were enough technical and logistical differences between channels to make the change. The new leaders of each engineering team had special affinities to their chosen channel and that was a nice added bonus. Some people just are better at certain computing or experience paradigms.[31]

I probably waited too long to make these changes – breaking my own rule of decisiveness – by adjusting each team's leadership for skill and personality, but in the end it wasn't catastrophic. But it could have been.

The Extended Team Can Make a Big Positive Difference

> *We need teams of missionaries, not teams of mercenaries.*
>
> **Marty Cagan**

I talked about the importance of "other" teams earlier in the book and I want to reemphasize that. What I did when I started, as I always do, was to search the organization for those folks who exist in any organization but are maybe marginalized and hidden, who want to drive change and transformation for the betterment of the firm and its customers. Those whose spirit is closest to how I described the digital team core members – missionaries. They are thought leaders, people with thought influence rather than power influence (although, if present, it helps).

So, I brought into the sausage-making process – all those digital team discussions where most of what is discussed here happens – people from finance, operations, revenue cycle (billing and payments), physical patient experience, customer satisfaction folks, etc. The people who got invited and didn't get uninvited weren't passive participants. They all started contributing in some way, while also learning how we operated. Maybe we didn't explicitly talk about design thinking to those folks, but that is exactly what we were practicing.

But among all those folks, head over shoulders were a few executives who called themselves *Consumer Access*. With a role somewhat misunderstood by the rest of the organization (and often confused with the customer call center), they were change makers. They were everywhere with the digital product team, pulling, pushing, cajoling, and gently shaming people into supporting and changing. While technically not part of my team, their mindset, spirit, and efforts put them squarely in that group – in the inner core. They're wonderful people, and I would have them with me anywhere else.[32] Having those folks on board was the best thing I could have hoped for.

Find those folks in your organization and get them onto your digital product bus.

Mistakes or What I Would Do Differently

Mistakes are those things that you did and wish you could do over again. Some mistakes are deep, others not. But if your intent was pure, they are almost always enriching in some way.

Steve Jobs

My consumer digital product team deserves an immense amount of credit for what they have accomplished and still do, but I must accept some strategic mistakes that I have made.

Overestimating the ability of the overall organization – with all their other priorities and constraints – to adjust to the speed of progress made by the digital team was a big one, despite alignments, executive, and board support. I talked about marketing readiness earlier in the chapter. Others are procurement, financial, and budgeting, as well as HR processes.[33] I tried to shield digital (and the rest of the Technology transformation) as much as possible from that speed mismatch, with some moderate success through priority processes (as described earlier in this book), but not sufficiently. Digital efforts and the firm do not exist on different planets, but they do have different revolution cycles.

Another big miss was underestimating the technical, solution, and support readiness of various healthcare technology vendors. Or I should more correctly say the lack of readiness. It's stunning to me, in this day and age, how many vendor solutions are incomplete, non-interoperable (web pages are not Application Programming Interfaces (APIs) or lack of APIs as a lock-in strategy), insecure, not properly tested, with unreliable architectures (single points of failures abundant), not scalable, and not properly supported. Often, instead of simply being able to use and rely on vendors, we had to either work around their limitations, work with vendors to technically build them up (yes, we even offered to build the APIs for them if they exposed their database schemas!) or just do it ourselves without them.

Sure, that happens in other industries, but not to this widespread extent. And I think there are two reasons: **first**, most of the healthcare startups we dealt with drowned in VC funding in 2020–2022 and had just put stuff out there hoping it would stick but with little strategy or urgency for success; **second**, because healthcare, without internal strong technology teams, has not been demanding enough of high-quality technical implementations – including and especially in security!

Finally, we had a completely surprising problem: the more we delivered – beyond digital, into data, automation, EMR, infrastructure, etc. – past what everyone else was doing, the more the organization asked of us to deliver – beyond what could be realistically expected – and the more it felt like we were falling behind, even when both the quantity and quality were miles ahead of what was previously delivered (think in places 2×). The only explanation for that, outside of internal factors, is that all this demand was bottled up for years and was never met; when folks saw that we were delivering, they started competing with each other by asking for more. And more.

While digital stayed focused on the consumer, all these other demands – that the organization had a hard time prioritizing – stretched the rest of the technology team, ultimately impacting digital to some extent. While on the face of it, this is great news – people battling for what you provide – it created a lot of tension with the entire team. So, I did the only thing I could do, other than constantly enhancing bandwidth and internal efficiency – I put it in front of the executive committee to prioritize.

I take responsibility for underestimating all of these. Painful lessons have been learned. Now that you're forewarned, learn them yourself and do better than I did.

But while I would do some things differently, I never regretted driving the transformation, however, difficult and intensely frustrating as it was. Not even once.

What Is the Future of Healthcare: Aka Is It Getting Any Better?

I get asked this question quite often in interviews, podcasts, or panels. Maybe every speaker gets that nervous question or maybe folks look at me to bring some magic pixie dust from my past to apply in healthcare. I don't have any, but there is no doubt that healthcare needs to get a lot better and fast. So here are my technology-focused predictions, driven by three major trends.

First, the US healthcare system – with its three pillars of providers, insurance companies, and Pharma (and other medical technology vendors) – as it has evolved in the last 40 years or so since the expansion of employer-based insurance, suffers from a plethora of structural and systemic efficiency and cost-effective challenges. Maybe understandably with the increase in demand for medical care, these three pillars have focused on growth and not on operational efficiency (supported by new distributed care technologies), new forms of care, and certainly not on patient experience. This creates massive access, affordability, and care quality problems for everyone. That is how the US got to be something like 39th in medical care in the world yet is spending $4TN in 2023, double per capita than the next expensive country.

Second, that astronomical number, coupled with the belief they can operate more efficiently (probably correctly) by employing better technologies – mostly in the administrative areas – constantly attracts like a magnet new entrants such as Amazon, Walmart, Best Buy, etc., into the healthcare marketplace. They have the technology, the lack of poor legacy practices and systems, and certainly the financial resources to do so. But nothing is easy or straightforward in healthcare, which to be clear is a new area for them (the smaller healthcare providers they acquired aside), so all these firms have their work cut out for them. They'll need fortitude, perseverance, patience, and money to succeed. But they'll need even more another key ingredient, one that is in short supply, unless there is another way.

Third, the key ingredient is qualified medical personnel. That is obvious but that's a problem, as we cannot scale that fast enough to compensate for the increased demand for medical services by an aging population with more chronic afflictions, on the one hand, and reduction in the supply of providers, themselves also aging fast, on the other hand. So, putting it simply, all healthcare provider systems will fight to employ the same doctors and nurses, which doesn't solve either the cost problem nor the increased supply of services. This means everybody will compete for the same diminished healthcare providers' pool. While tech, retail, and other companies introduce operational efficiencies, there are only so many physicians and they can only work safely for so many hours a day and still provide quality care for everyone to compete for.

So, is all this hopeless? Not if we start to employ technology on a significant scale to compensate – after all, as Albert Einstein once quipped "We can't solve problems by using the same kind of thinking we used when we created them". The true disruption will come when a lot more of the monitoring and even care move to at home or with the patient using a variety of consumer-grade sensors controlled by AI filtering for a signal from noise. Clearly, providing high acuity care is not changing, but lower acuity remote monitoring, diagnosis, and even some treatment (aka hospital-at-home, which is a lot cheaper than patient-in-hospital-bed) are all increasingly possible. This opens up opportunities for more and better (i.e., more immediate and less transactional) care.

I think, on balance, competition and more efficiency will benefit consumers and patients, whoever can provide it with quality, that is, better health and more focused and adequate care when and only when needed, to the right amount and no more.

How are traditional healthcare organizations going to respond and stay in business? **First**, by doing consumer digital right – as hopefully described in this book. **Second**, by transforming their operations into increased levels of efficiency, with the help of technology. That could level out the playing field, so the competition is not only about digital experience or efficiency – where traditional healthcare players sorely lack – but in the realm of quality medical care – where traditional healthcare entities (should, in theory) have an advantage. But that is harder to do than it sounds: established players have an *innovators' dilemma* problem.[34] They're structured to benefit from the old models that made them very successful without realistically innovative competition. That mindset is not easy to change.

I was recently asked to share my opinions on where healthcare will be in 100 years.[35] That far ahead is unfathomably long to predict when technology and medical science evolution is gaining steam so fast. I offered something for a much shorter interval, maybe 20–30 years: a highly personalized care, driven by genomics and real-time sensors monitoring, with conditions diagnosed by devices in a variety of locations – with hospitals being the exception, not the rule – continuously managed and treated by AI homes and other locations.

Will people get to trust AI equally or more than human doctors, at least for low-acuity services? It depends on how we do it – privacy and accuracy are top concerns – but we should not underestimate how much better AI will get and that, with the imbalance between demand for medical services and the supply of practitioners, we may have no other choice to get care.

And so, this is my prediction: technology will make for better health (care). Let's all hope, for our own sakes as healthy persons or patients, that I'm (just about) right.

Notes

1. Either to provide meaning to what I was doing or for the adrenaline rush. Or both. There's something to be said about either/both as a driver to push for change and transformation.

2. I once got a question from company lawyers when reviewing a change to an existing but very cumbersome consumer-facing process: "It's been working well [translation: nobody sued us] for us for a very long time, why change now and take risks?" The answer of "Because it's terrible for consumers!" did not seem to sway their *opinions*. But the argument still carried the day after vibrant argumentation.

3. Better ask for forgiveness than permission, which is, fear more being said no to when asking for permission than being punished for doing.

4. Again, see Clayton Christiansen's *Innovators' Dilemma*.

5. I was once told that cloud doesn't work in healthcare and its use shouldn't be even attempted. The real reason: nobody knew how to do it, and nobody wanted to work hard to learn.

6. Supposedly, consumers live rich and sophisticated lives outside their healthcare experiences, but then they somehow are more than happy to fill in paper forms, *over and over again with the same information*.

7. As I was doing a review of this book, I encountered this article: "ViVE 2023: Cash-strapped health systems demanding clear financial returns from their digital investments" (https://www.fiercehealthcare.com/digital-health/vive-2023 -cash-strapped-health-systems-demanding-clear-financial-returns-their). In it, a number of CDIOs for healthcare are quoted as supporting the concept that *any* investment in digital in healthcare must have a positive return on investment (ROI) (that is, to make more money than invested) to the tune of 50%, as one of the leaders is quoted, *in one year* or else it should not be made.

   I can only shake my head in disbelief. First, I have never seen that happening that fast in any industry, and healthcare is not exactly the poster child for effective digital. Second, it absolutely puts money and the system's financials above consumer experience – and consumer experiences, remember, also mean better access to care, even if, from a healthcare institution, it doesn't mean more care being *charged for*. Third, nowhere in this discussion is there a reference to long-term relationships with consumers (at least not the type driven by choice, rather than forced lack of options). Do we still wonder why consumer digital experiences are so incredibly bad in healthcare? Do these people not feel any empathy for patients? Are they not patients themselves, but only healthcare executives? Do all investments hospitals make – buildings, equipment, training, etc. - have a one-year 50% ROI? While I attended VIVE, I missed that one talk; otherwise, it would have been a lively Q&A session.

8. This is by no means to say that medical providers don't care about the patients' *medical* outcomes. They absolutely do. But they're too overworked to think of the rest of the patient experience.

9. By some estimates as big of a lag as 15–20 years, according to a 2023 Advisory Board (healthcare think tank part of Optum/United Healthcare) paper by Eric Larsen.

10. As President Kennedy once famously said: "We choose to [...] do the other things, not because they're easy, but because they're hard".

11. And someone told me, "bets on how long I will want to continue in healthcare given the many frustrating realities of that industry".

12. This is why in this section I use "I" and not "we". During this time, before assembling the start of the team, it was mainly me, myself, and I. Fortunately for the success of the effort, as we built up talent, it became intensely about "we" and no longer about "I".

13. In case you're wondering about the other 1%, it was half a slide at the very end of my presentation quickly listing all the tools buzzwords – like agile, cloud, and AI/ML. Why just list them there without much discussion? Because they're how the sausage is made, not what it will taste like to customers – which is the goal of all consumer-focused digital efforts. Why put them there at all if that is the case? So, executives/board members have those boxes checked when they invariably hear chatter from vendors peddling those technologies later on.

14. When I published a draft for comments and debate to the team, a senior executive, who very kindly took the time to review and provide edits (she has a background in newspapers, and once an editor, always an editor), exclaimed: "This document has your voice in it". Presumably a nice way of saying that I write as I speak, with strong opinions, which is true but with the caveat that I hold strong opinions weakly – that is, I am willing to be *proven* I'm wrong.

15. Third from a timing perspective, not relative importance. You need the board and the executive leadership team's support to start building teams, processes, and ultimately products.

16. We talked before that this is an ongoing process, starting from storming and forming and leading to gradual tweaks driven by either team members maturing or gaps in the operational processes or the nature of the product capabilities at hand. For example, we did not have a team interviewing/observing consumers until about a year or more into the journey – simply because we did not have people to operate that team. During that time, we had to rely on our informed instincts and watch for feedback. Not ideal.

17. This was for both consumers – not yet patients and not in care already – as well as in-patients and acute (in hospital). Providing capabilities for patients in a hospital enabling them to understand what is happening, what they need to do, what is the care plan and schedule, ordering food as if in a restaurant and not a what-we-have-is-what-you-get cantina, who visits them, and why is *priceless*. For the in-room digital experience, we got emotional feedback such as "This system restored some of my dignity of being able to do things for myself". That is the kind of emotional stuff fueling your drive to make things better for patients, whatever other frustrations you may have.

18. We talked about simple – aka *usable* – meaningful – aka *valuable* – and empowering – aka *self-service and self-managed* – earlier in the *Strategy* and *Product* chapters.

19. It's always important to try to keep employees' experiences and their satisfaction with them roughly in line with the customers. Employees lacking proper (digital) tools can't effectively help customers. Plus, dissatisfied and frustrated employees are always bad for both customers and the business. With that being said, my philosophy is about the consumer first followed by a *balance* with employees, and not employees above customers. The idea that what is good for employees' satisfaction – in this case providers – is necessarily good for customers is *not* immediately true.

20. A goal of 100% should trigger alarms by itself. You can't do it all, plus customer needs and other circumstances change, so how can you declare completeness as a goal in three years when you don't know what that will be? And indeed, as we built more, we understood more of what consumers needed and thus it became clear that we had a lot more to provide than we originally thought.

21. That is, how closely they match what the user expects. User-friendliness is more than very good usability – it's about how users *feel* when using the product and achieving the desired outcome (see IDFMads, *The Basics of User Design:* "You can add all the features and functionality to a site or application, but the success of the project rides on a single factor: how the users feel about it"). A great user-friendly experience must feel *satisfying*, not merely functional. When you can book a medical appointment in an app in just over two minutes, that is very good, but if the process/flow is also easy, intuitive, and natural, then that *feels* wonderful.

22. A few months after my arrival in healthcare, I was instructed to provide a solution for referrals. I simply asked for a definition of the problem and expected outcomes (in non-technology terms). As I write this, two years later, I am still waiting for that definition, and the discussions are still ongoing.

23. A lot of firms choose to deploy a mobile app presence. Unfortunately, most are just links to a mobile web experience, and they do not integrate well with sensors, location, or other native platform services. I guess it's intended to stake out the mobile space. With that being said, sometimes it is OK, while building a proper native mobile app experience, to include a mobile web (usually in a web frame) experience – but only until you have something much better to offer.

24. Of course, hospitals will tell you that their operations are a lot more complex than a hotel, and that is indeed accurate. But that doesn't change the consumer experience and perception.

25. As we discussed before, mental models are important. But they develop after experiencing something repeatedly, not trying to figure out something that is unfamiliar.

26. "People would be more likely to adopt digital technologies if a provider recommended them (33%)". Accenture study: https://www.accenture.com/us-en/insights/health/digital-adoption-healthcare-reaction-or-revolution

27. How do you know it's functioning right? When you push harder than anyone else and the team is still delivering better than everyone else.

28. How do you know it's time for a change? When parts of the team and process work well, while others don't, and they impact the activities of the former.

29. As you start, you'll have to rely on your best but limited analysis and consumer insights and then see what consumers make of it. At some point, sooner rather than later, you must get a lot more systematic about talking to and observing customers "in the act".

30. Be prepared for some of the insights to be baffling, raising questions like "why?" and "how can this be possible?". The answers to those questions may reveal yet more interesting insights. Follow the insights into their ultimate cause. Sometimes that means devising more metrics that generate more insights. The process must

be disciplined and well structured; otherwise, you're like the proverbial drunk who's looking for his wallet under a lamppost just because that is where there's light to enable the search.

31. I live my digital life in mobile apps. My wife, on the other hand, lives in desktop and mobile web.

32. Whether I would hire someone in a new job (if there was a suitable spot) is usually my criterion to rate people the highest. It's the equivalent of "If you found yourself on a deserted island, who and what would you want to have with you?"

33. I don't want to come across as critical of these enterprise functions. They each have been optimized for a certain status quo of doing things a certain way and at a certain speed. It's just that those ways and speeds are not what digital transformation needs.

34. For example, not wanting to promote telehealth or ambulatory procedures that may be reimbursed less than in-person visits or hospital-based procedures. But that is exactly the strategy of new entrants.

35. Read more here from Becker's Hospital Review: https://www.beckershospital review.com/hospital-physician-relationships/hospitals-be-will-rare-exception -what-healthcare-will-look-like-in-100-years.html

Conclusion

First and foremost, consumers reign supreme in digital experiences. They want to be in control of the experience and at the center of it. But understanding and meeting correctly what their true needs really are is not easy and requires patience and often, multiple try-fail-learn cycles.

Don't debate if you need to do digital. You do. The sooner you start, the sooner you'll be doing it.

You must start with a crisp vision. Definitely have a robust strategy but don't overspend time on details. Things will change or you'll learn new things.

Have the right people on the team, based on professional competence and mindset. People who have convictions are optimistic and ready to learn. Missionaries.

Have the right stakeholders and thought leaders with you on the bus. Thought leaders and influencers may not have fancy titles, but they're priceless, nevertheless.

Digital, if done well, must be rigorous and experiences must be very well thought through. Don't abandon your consumers. For that to be successful, you must build robust technology, design, and digital product management capabilities.

To create truly great experiences, drive changes in business processes.

Experience your (digital) experience yourself. Instrument to measure and tune. Don't rely on those who don't experience it themselves as users.

Mistakes will be made. That in itself is neither unexpected nor unique. But the secret to recovery from mistakes is by learning from them and being able to quickly turn around, pivot, and fix.

And finally, this is a hard but exhilarating journey, so enjoy yourself *Doing Digital*.

Tony Ambrozie, Orlando, 2023

Epilogue: Digital in the Age of AI

We tend to overestimate the effect of a technology in the short run and underestimate the effect in the long run.

Ron Amara

To ChatGPT or Not to ChatGPT

As I was writing this book (Q4/2022-Q2/2023), ChatGPT, a generative AI from the OpenAI foundation (or is it a commercial corporation?) burst onto society, with all the (yet) unforeseen consequences. It arrived a few years earlier than most of us thought it would, but I guess, had we paid enough attention, the signs were there for all to see. And it reached one million users in only five days.

What to make of it and what will it mean to society, our industries, and lives?

ChatGPT and similar models are large language-generative models (LLM), not knowledge models. In other words, they generate text, pixels, and equivalents in human-usable format based on previously ingested human-generated text and images. Beyond aggregating text with sometimes surprising insights, they don't generate new knowledge. They'll not find a cure for cancer, unless that cure is already spread in a variety of ingested texts that nobody put together somehow. There are other Machine Learning (ML) models that analyze and can generate knowledge. They're not necessarily built to fact-check the data they're ingesting or producing – although filters to correct them are appearing. They do have problems with "hallucination", that is, inventing facts to sustain their predictions, which is a major problem when accuracy is needed.

They are foundational models – that is, not domain-specific, as they were trained on a vast amount of Internet data – and thus can be used for a dizzying array of purposes. And with the access offered by APIs and associated composability, beyond the current chat paradigm implementation, we will see a profound and pervasive infusion of this technology in a variety of tools and applications at all levels, all of them digital. From the trivial – like suggesting email phrases or even full text bodies – to the more involved processes of creating presentations or code or even suggesting simple medical diagnostics, to the much more involved continuously running and context-aware smart assistants (possibly running smaller but good enough models on edge and consumer devices) that are actively co-collaborators with humans in a variety of activities.

But what about job losses to AI? Sure, there will be some, but most people losing their jobs will be replaced by other people using AI effectively. At least for now.

Clearly, OpenAI started the open AI arms race, with Microsoft at its side and Google responding. With many others on their heels, running maybe smaller but still good-enough models, the competition for fast evolution is only getting more intense. It is by no means clear that these companies, in the quest for commercial dominance, are taking the right steps to implement adequate controls and safeguards for AI, from an alignment and emergence viewpoint.[1] And the models and the data sets are only getting better, thus self-constrained responsible and ethical implementations (despite being driven by commercial or military competition) is becoming stringently critical, especially in the absence of a regulatory framework.

We can go into endless debates on consciousness, emergence, or how intelligent ChatGPT and others like it are, but they're neither sentient nor GAI (Generalized Artificial Intelligence). Though I am not sure that matters very much, from an impact to society viewpoint.

If we, as the collective humanity, manage to develop AI responsibly, it is undeniable that opportunities for these technologies and their applications *could* be endlessly valuable. But we will require an immense amount of adaptation at a societal level to the reality of these tools being widely available.

AI for Doing Digital

Human wants and needs are endless.

Milton Friedman

The interesting question is probably on everybody's mind: will GPT-like models, which already can take a text specification for a mobile app or a website, replace everything that we're talking about in this book and thus make readying them superfluous, with no need for product management, designers, and engineers? After all, there are already some examples of very basic Swift-based iOS applications or JavaScript web sites, where both the code and basic UI/UX designs were generated by GPT (or LLMs in general).

Long-term, I think AI will be doing a lot of the things that humans do *today*, both mundane activities and grunt work, as well as (some of) the creative work. The findings and contents of many books (this one included), articles, blogs, podcasts, webinars, consumer reviews and feedback, etc., will make their way into the training data and predictor models to make AI continuously getting better into some future *AI Digital Designer*. After the seemingly sudden jump of publicly available capabilities of AI through ChatGPT at the end of 2022, any prediction of what long-term means (3 years? 5? 10?) would be perilous and foolish. We may be surprised if it happens sooner than we think unless previous IP (that LLMs need to consume) considerations or effective constraining regulations slow the advancement in a considerable way.[2]

But I think that the critical word here, which I discreetly italicized in the previous paragraph, *today*, is key to imagining what could happen, from two different perspectives.

First, today's digital products and the experience they provide are very far from the qualities we describe as necessary, from a consumer viewpoint. In addition, building products is still very complex and lengthy. So, there is a lot of work to do and we're not doing it fast enough, even against *today's* expectations. The number 1 complaint about digital products is that they are not able to support a feature that consumers need to solve their problems fast enough. The number 2 complaint is that the experience is not good enough for consumers to solve their problems effectively. AI will help build more and faster, hopefully better, of what we need *today*. From that perspective, AI will help us scale faster, in ways that today's technologies would never allow us.

Second, the world has not stopped evolving in what we wanted and needed the day ChatGPT was announced. We always want and need more technical and human-based sciences to help us evolve our products and experiences in ways we can only imagine from SCI-FI movies (have you noticed the sophistication of UI/UX in Marvel or Pandora movies, some years old?[3]). If indeed that is what will be beneficial for us to manage our experiences and interactions with the world, then we need a lot more complex technology than what we have today, that we can only *scale up*[4] to with better tools, like AI. Unless we are willing to wait for a very long time, which we humans never do if we can help it.

Very likely we will see AI becoming that intelligent smart assistant that will extend the capabilities in all digital team's activities – product management, design, engineering – but allowing them to do more, faster, and better.

Doing user research and talking to customers will always be a very human endeavor with marginal opportunities for machines – with only about 5%–10% of users responding to automated customer surveys, imagine the reaction to an intelligent bot asking them a lot of intrusive questions. But the insights obtained may be analyzed, categorized, summarized, and maybe even suggested by AI, making it possible for the researchers to ask customers even better questions next time. Similarly for system logs describing users' actions. And with more complex products and experiences, the insights to be obtained are even more complex. AI computer vision observing consumers using digital may sound creepy, but it is not impossible.

Engineers will use intelligent code-generating tools – some actually do that already – to write code faster – and hopefully more securely and more resiliently. Adjacent technologies like APIs (at some point, systems will be intelligent enough to negotiate the contracts of their interactions by themselves, all described by humans through expected outcomes) and cloud, not to mention the personalization and contextualization smarts I mentioned in previous sections, will hopefully dominate.

Designers will use AI to start their designs and then hone them. Between that and easier code creation, prototypes will only be easier to put in the hands of consumers for faster feedback.

Will all this be a lot more complex for everyone to operate? Of course, despite the tools being smarter. For one, everyone must do a lot more. But it will also be a lot more rewarding as the results of this work, the customer experience, and satisfaction will be a lot better.

Notes

1. See https://www.nytimes.com/2023/04/07/technology/ai-chatbots-google-microsoft.html
2. See *"Generative AI Has an Intellectual Property Problem"*, by Gil Appel, Juliana Neelbauer, and David A. Schweidel at https://hbr.org/2023/04/generative-ai-has-an-intellectual-property-problem
3. What's up with the 1970s-like semi-mechanical UI/UX of Star Wars? Even SpaceX modules have more sophisticated UI today.
4. Humans can only scale up what they do with the help of tools. True for stone axes, true for AI.

An Old Story: How the Journey Started

The reasonable person adapts themselves to the world; the unreasonable one persists in trying to adapt the world to themselves. Therefore, all progress depends on the unreasonable people.

George Bernard Shaw

I have spent most of my career in corporate environments, most of it in great and legendary companies like American Express and Disney. Great companies with great leaders. It has been a privilege to have been hired and retained and to have helped to grow. What more can one ask for than that? Seriously.

I hold a special debt of gratitude to American Express. Amex has been an incubator of great leaders at all levels, some of whom went on to lead great companies like Mastercard, PayPal, and others. That is where I learned to put together all the pieces: engineering, product, business, and leadership.

That being said, many folks don't know I started my career in a startup.

My first money-earning job – notice I did not say salary-earning – was actually my own startup, which I started while still in graduate school. Believe it or not, the company was carrying my first name and "International" in its name. Guts – or hubris – galore.

I wanted to build great software simply because we were good at it, and it was fun to build. And this being very early 1990s, in my unbound optimism and naiveté, I thought I could take on Microsoft.[1]

I borrowed some money from parents and their friends – later I found out they're called *investors and shareholders*. And I decided we're going to build this software package and sell it to someone for lots of money. Only later did I discover that there were a couple of (better funded and infinitely better marketed) similar packages out there.

I decided what features the software would have and proceeded to build it all, to the very last feature and screen. When it was done – and it was a neat piece of software – after some nine months of work, I then looked for some folks to get it commercialized.

On the day of the grand launch, I showed it to those folks. And the reaction was "…Yeah … Nice … What about it?" So that didn't go anywhere.

Now, by this time we (by now joined by a good friend) had used up a lot of our money – later we learned to call it *capital* – and we had to figure out how to recover by changing direction and using whatever we could out of the code already written – later I learned Silicon Valley calls that a "*pivot*" (isn't that a cool term for failing and changing directions out of dire need?).

So, we talked to other folks and discovered a heavily underserved market that needed a certain type of product. The need had been there all along, had we bothered to look. We then proceeded to build something for that need. But because by then we had used up a lot of our capital, we just built enough to show folks how it would work and get input. Later, I learned that is called *MVP* – minimum viable product.[2]

Once we validated the MVP with potential customers, we started to add features as they were asking for them and only those features *someone* was asking for – by meeting with them during the day and coding during nights and weekends. Later we learned that was *Agile* methodology. And since we only had one PC, we were apparently doing *pair programming*.

Long story short, we were modestly successful although we couldn't scale. Microsoft was safe.

Beyond the experience having been exhilarating, although gruesome, and earning some decent money for our investors, ahem, friends, and family, I learned a number of lessons the hard way, some that we formalized in our minds, others at a gut level that I formalized many years later when we re-encountered them in the real world. You could say we were re-inventing the wheel, but at that time nobody talked about a better way.

Most of those basic learnings are at the core of this book on how to build products.

Notes

1. No, I did not know the full extent of Microsoft's offerings. I just wanted to be better than Bill Gates.
2. Read a lot more about this in Eric Ries' book, *The Lean Startup*.

Recommended Reading

The following is a list of books that are instructing and inspiring on digital and product topics, innovation, leadership, and design thinking. I strongly recommend anyone interested in these topics to read them, as these authors do much better justice to their topics than I could ever do.

1. *Build* – Tony Fadell
2. *The Design of Everyday Things* – Don Norman
3. *Emotional Design* – Don Norman
4. *Innovators Dilemma* – Clayton Christensen
5. *Competing Against Luck* – Clayton Christensen
6. *Empowered* – Marty Cagan and Chris Jones
7. *Inspired* – Marty Cagan
8. *User-friendly* – Cliff Kuang
9. *Pirates in the Navy* – Tendayi Wiki
10. *Juggaad Innovation* – Navi Radjou
11. *Ten Types of Innovation* – Larry Keeley
12. *Sprint* – Jake Knapp
13. *Loonshots* – Safi Bahcall
14. *The Ride of a Lifetime* – Robert Iger
15. *Doing Agile Right* – Darrell Rigby
16. *The Digital transformation Playbook* – David Rogers
17. *Loved* – Martina Lauchengco
18. *Think Simple* – Ken Segall
19. *Simplify* – Richard Koch and Greg Lockwood
20. *The Convenience Revolution* – Shep Hyken
21. *The Basics of User Experience Design by Interaction Design Foundation* – IDFMads
22. *A New Way to Think* – Roger L. Martin
23. *Change by Design, Revised and Updated* – Tim Brown
24. *Creative Confidence* – Tom and David Kelley

25. *The Design of Business* – Roger Martin
26. *Crossing the Chasm* – Geoffrey A Moore
27. *Thinking Fast and Slow* – Daniel Kahleman
28. *Continuous Discovery Habits* – Teresa Torres
29. *The Art of Innovation: Lessons in Creativity from IDEO* – Tom Kelley
30. *The Ten Faces of Innovation* – Tom Kelley

For more, go to my regularly updated list of books at:
https://www.librarything.com/catalog/tambrozie/yourlibrary

More from the Author

Speaking Engagements

- Air Force Symposium – Keynote: *"Innovation in Large Organizations" – Mar 2019.*
- IDG Korea CXO Summit – *Leadership in a Time of Unprecedented Challenges – Oct 2020.*
- American CIO and IT Summit – *Innovation and Emerging Technologies – Oct 2020.*
- Healthsystemcio.com – *Future State: Envisioning 2021 & Beyond.*
- ExecutiveRoundtable.org – CXO Virtual Roundtable Panel – *Leading in Innovation, Digital Transformation, and Change-Management – Mar 2021.*
- American CIO and IT Summit 2021 – *The future of mobility: Steps for Innovation and Disruption.*
- NG Healthcare Digital Summit North America – *Jun 2021.*
- HIMSS – 2021 – *Scale Care Anywhere With a Comprehensive Digital Engagement Strategy.*
- Martech.com/BackStage Pass 2021 – *Unlocking New Opportunities to Engage Consumers and Convert Their Demand Online.*
- *Greystoke/Kyruus Digital Health Panel – Jul 2021.*
- *Becker's 6th Annual Health IT and RC Conference – Sep 2021.*
- *Witkieffer Healthcare CIO Playbook for 2022 – Sep 2021.*
- *Mindtree Technology Symposium – Oct 2021.*
- *DSC Digital Transformation of Healthcare Delivery – Oct 2021.*
- *Damo Consulting Webinar – Digital Transformation in 2022: Getting your Priorities Right – Jan 2022.*
- *TBJ/Accenture Webinar – Feb/Mar 2022.*
- *McDermott's Digital Health Forum – May 2022.*
- *AWS – Transforming Public Sector Mission and Citizen Experience – May 2022.*
- *Becker's Data and Innovation – How to Build q Best in Class Data Team – May 2022.*

- *HIMMS Data Justice: Ethical Practices for Equitable Health Webinar – Jun 2022.*
- *Oracle Cerner Symposium – Jun 2022.*
- *CTN – CIO Talk Network – The Chief Digital Officer 2.0 – Jul 2022.*
- HeallthsystemCIO.com – *Keys to Developing a Hybrid Cloud Strategy – Sep 2022.*
- *Becker's 7th Annual Health IT and RC Conference – Keynote – Oct 2022.*
- *TechXChange – The Strategic Imperative – Shift from Doing Digital to Being Digital – Oct 2022.*
- *CHIME – The Future CIO, Enabling the Evolution of Healthcare – Nov 2022.*
- *healthsystemCIO.com Webinar: Patient Matching to Fuel Interoperability – Dec 2022.*

Podcasts

- Executive Corner Podcast – 2020 – *The 7 Most Important Characteristics of Leaders.*
- Becker's Healthcare Podcast – Feb 2021.
- Becker's Healthcare Podcast – Aug 2021.
- Healthsystemcio.com Podcast – Parts 1 and 2.
- *The Ivy Podcast – 2021 – How to Build a Winning Culture of Innovation.*
- *The Big Unlock Podcast – Aug 2021.*
- *Executive Podcast – Jan 2022.*
- *MyBasePay – Building a Culture of Innovation and High Performing Hybrid Teams – May 2022.*
- *Prophet Podcast – Jun 2022.*
- *The Digital Patient Podcast – Jul 2022.*
- *Becker's Podcast – Aug 2022.*
- *Bill Russell Podcast – Advancing the Healthcare Experience – Sep 2022.*
- *Cloud Realities Podcast – Dec 2022.*

Articles

- healthtechmagazines.com – Positioning Healthcare Providers for the Digital Age – Feb 2021.
- healthtechmagazines.com – Taking AI and Machine Learning to the Next Level in Healthcare – Nov 2021.

- InformationWeek – Lessons Learned, Tips and Tricks for Digital Transformation Strategies – Apr 2022.
- Authority Magazine – How to Use Digital Transformation to Take Your Company to the Next Level – Jul 2022.
- CIO.com – Why Digital Initiatives Fail – Oct 2022.

Index

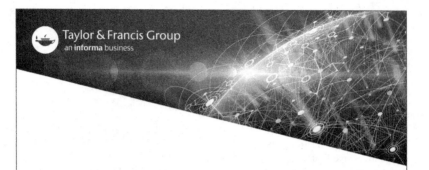

Printed in the United States
by Baker & Taylor Publisher Services